PRENTICE HALL

# SCIENCE EXPLORER

# *From Bacteria to Plants*

**PRENTICE HALL**
Needham, Massachusetts
Upper Saddle River, New Jersey

PRENTICE HALL
SCIENCE EXPLORER

# From Bacteria to Plants

## Program Resources

Student Edition
Annotated Teacher's Edition
Teaching Resources Book with Color Transparencies
*From Bacteria to Plants* Materials Kits

## Program Components

Integrated Science Laboratory Manual
Integrated Science Laboratory Manual, Teacher's Edition
Inquiry Skills Activity Book
Student-Centered Science Activity Books
Program Planning Guide
Guided Reading English Audiotapes
Guided Reading Spanish Audiotapes and Summaries
*Product Testing Activities* by Consumer Reports™
*Event-Based Science* Series (NSF funded)
Prentice Hall Interdisciplinary Explorations
*Cobblestone, Odyssey, Calliope,* and *Faces* Magazines

## Media/Technology

*Science Explorer* Interactive Student Tutorial CD-ROMs
*Odyssey of Discovery* CD-ROMs
Resource Pro® (Teaching Resources on CD-ROM)
Assessment Resources CD-ROM with Dial-A-Test®
Internet site at www.science-explorer.phschool.com
Life, Earth, and Physical Science Videodiscs
Life, Earth, and Physical Science Videotapes

## Science Explorer Student Editions

*From Bacteria to Plants*

*Animals*

*Cells and Heredity*

*Human Biology and Health*

*Environmental Science*

*Inside Earth*

*Earth's Changing Surface*

*Earth's Waters*

*Weather and Climate*

*Astronomy*

*Chemical Building Blocks*

*Chemical Interactions*

*Motion, Forces, and Energy*

*Electricity and Magnetism*

*Sound and Light*

## Staff Credits

The people who made up the *Science Explorer* team—representing editorial, editorial services, design services, field marketing, market research, marketing services, on-line services/multimedia development, product marketing, production services, and publishing processes—are listed below. Bold type denotes core team members.

Kristen E. Ball, **Barbara A. Bertell,** Peter W. Brooks, **Christopher R. Brown, Greg Cantone,** Jonathan Cheney, **Patrick Finbarr Connolly,** Loree Franz, Donald P. Gagnon, Jr., **Paul J. Gagnon, Joel Gendler,** Elizabeth Good, Kerri Hoar, **Linda D. Johnson,** Katherine M. Kotik, Russ Lappa, Marilyn Leitao, David Lippman, **Eve Melnechuk, Natania Mlawer,** Paul W. Murphy, **Cindy A. Noftle,** Julia F. Osborne, Caroline M. Power, Suzanne J. Schineller, **Susan W. Tafler,** Kira Thaler-Marbit, Robin L. Santel, Ronald Schachter, **Mark Tricca,** Diane Walsh, Pearl B. Weinstein, Beth Norman Winickoff

Copyright ©2000 by Prentice-Hall, Inc., Upper Saddle River, New Jersey 07458. All rights reserved. No part of this book may be reproduced or transmitted in any form or by any means, electronic or mechanical, including photocopying, recording, or by any information storage and retrieval system, without permission in writing from the publisher. Printed in the United States of America.

ISBN 0-13-434490-1
3 4 5 6 7 8 9 10   05 04 03 02 01 00 99

Cover: A Panama Pacific water lily blooms in a Florida lake.

## Program Authors

**Michael J. Padilla, Ph.D.**
Professor
Department of Science Education
University of Georgia
Athens, Georgia

Michael Padilla is a leader in middle school science education. He has served as an editor and elected officer for the National Science Teachers Association. He has been principal investigator of several National Science Foundation and Eisenhower grants and served as a writer of the National Science Education Standards.

As lead author of *Science Explorer,* Mike has inspired the team in developing a program that meets the needs of middle grades students, promotes science inquiry, and is aligned with the National Science Education Standards.

**Ioannis Miaoulis, Ph.D.**
Dean of Engineering
College of Engineering
Tufts University
Medford, Massachusetts

**Martha Cyr, Ph.D.**
Director, Engineering
    Educational Outreach
College of Engineering
Tufts University
Medford, Massachusetts

*Science Explorer* was created in collaboration with the College of Engineering at Tufts University. Tufts has an extensive engineering outreach program that uses engineering design and construction to excite and motivate students and teachers in science and technology education.

Faculty from Tufts University participated in the development of *Science Explorer* chapter projects, reviewed the student books for content accuracy, and helped coordinate field testing.

CHAPTER PROJECT

## Book Author

**Jan Jenner, Ph.D.**
Science Writer
Talladega, Alabama

## Contributing Writers

**James Robert Kaczynski, Jr.**
Science Teacher
Barrington Middle School
Barrington, Rhode Island

**Evan P. Silberstein**
Science Teacher
Spring Valley High School
Spring Valley, New York

**Joseph Stukey, Ph.D.**
Department of Biology
Hope College
Holland, Michigan

## Reading Consultant

**Bonnie B. Armbruster, Ph.D.**
Department of Curriculum
    and Instruction
University of Illinois
Champaign, Illinois

## Interdisciplinary Consultant

**Heidi Hayes Jacobs, Ed.D.**
Teacher's College
Columbia University
New York, New York

## Safety Consultants

**W. H. Breazeale, Ph.D.**
Department of Chemistry
College of Charleston
Charleston, South Carolina

**Ruth Hathaway, Ph.D.**
Hathaway Consulting
Cape Girardeau, Missouri

# Teacher Reviewers

**Stephanie Anderson**
Sierra Vista Junior
    High School
Canyon Country, California

**John W. Anson**
Mesa Intermediate School
Palmdale, California

**Pamela Arline**
Lake Taylor Middle School
Norfolk, Virginia

**Lynn Beason**
College Station Jr. High School
College Station, Texas

**Richard Bothmer**
Hollis School District
Hollis, New Hampshire

**Jeffrey C. Callister**
Newburgh Free Academy
Newburgh, New York

**Judy D'Albert**
Harvard Day School
Corona Del Mar, California

**Betty Scott Dean**
Guilford County Schools
McLeansville, North Carolina

**Sarah C. Duff**
Baltimore City Public Schools
Baltimore, Maryland

**Melody Law Ewey**
Holmes Junior High School
Davis, California

**Sherry L. Fisher**
Lake Zurich Middle
    School North
Lake Zurich, Illinois

**Melissa Gibbons**
Fort Worth ISD
Fort Worth, Texas

**Debra J. Goodding**
Kraemer Middle School
Placentia, California

**Jack Grande**
Weber Middle School
Port Washington, New York

**Steve Hills**
Riverside Middle School
Grand Rapids, Michigan

**Carol Ann Lionello**
Kraemer Middle School
Placentia, California

**Jaime A. Morales**
Henry T. Gage Middle School
Huntington Park, California

**Patsy Partin**
Cameron Middle School
Nashville, Tennessee

**Deedra H. Robinson**
Newport News Public Schools
Newport News, Virginia

**Bonnie Scott**
Clack Middle School
Abilene, Texas

**Charles M. Sears**
Belzer Middle School
Indianapolis, Indiana

**Barbara M. Strange**
Ferndale Middle School
High Point, North Carolina

**Jackie Louise Ulfig**
Ford Middle School
Allen, Texas

**Kathy Usina**
Belzer Middle School
Indianapolis, Indiana

**Heidi M. von Oetinger**
L'Anse Creuse Public School
Harrison Township, Michigan

**Pam Watson**
Hill Country Middle School
Austin, Texas

# Activity Field Testers

**Nicki Bibbo**
Russell Street School
Littleton, Massachusetts

**Connie Boone**
Fletcher Middle School
Jacksonville Beach, Florida

**Rose-Marie Botting**
Broward County
    School District
Fort Lauderdale, Florida

**Colleen Campos**
Laredo Middle School
Aurora, Colorado

**Elizabeth Chait**
W. L. Chenery Middle School
Belmont, Massachusetts

**Holly Estes**
Hale Middle School
Stow, Massachusetts

**Laura Hapgood**
Plymouth Community
    Intermediate School
Plymouth, Massachusetts

**Sandra M. Harris**
Winman Junior High School
Warwick, Rhode Island

**Jason Ho**
Walter Reed Middle School
Los Angeles, California

**Joanne Jackson**
Winman Junior High School
Warwick, Rhode Island

**Mary F. Lavin**
Plymouth Community
    Intermediate School
Plymouth, Massachusetts

**James MacNeil, Ph.D.**
Concord Public Schools
Concord, Massachusetts

**Lauren Magruder**
St. Michael's Country
    Day School
Newport, Rhode Island

**Jeanne Maurand**
Glen Urquhart School
Beverly Farms, Massachusetts

**Warren Phillips**
Plymouth Community
    Intermediate School
Plymouth, Massachusetts

**Carol Pirtle**
Hale Middle School
Stow, Massachusetts

**Kathleen M. Poe**
Kirby-Smith Middle School
Jacksonville, Florida

**Cynthia B. Pope**
Ruffner Middle School
Norfolk, Virginia

**Anne Scammell**
Geneva Middle School
Geneva, New York

**Karen Riley Sievers**
Callanan Middle School
Des Moines, Iowa

**David M. Smith**
Howard A. Eyer Middle School
Macungie, Pennsylvania

**Derek Strohschneider**
Plymouth Community
    Intermediate School
Plymouth, Massachusetts

**Sallie Teames**
Rosemont Middle School
Fort Worth, Texas

**Gene Vitale**
Parkland Middle School
McHenry, Illinois

**Zenovia Young**
Meyer Levin Junior
    High School (IS 285)
Brooklyn, New York

# Contents

# From Bacteria to Plants

**Nature of Science: Disease Detective Solves Mystery** .......**10**

**Chapter 1 Living Things** ......................................**14**
    **1** What Is Life? ............................................16
    **2** Integrating Earth Science: The Origin of Life ............25
    **3** Classifying Organisms .................................28
    **4** The Six Kingdoms ....................................40

**Chapter 2 Viruses and Bacteria** .............................**46**
    **1** Viruses .................................................48
    **2** Bacteria ................................................56
    **3** Integrating Health: Viruses, Bacteria, and Your Health ......68

**Chapter 3 Protists and Fungi** ...............................**78**
    **1** Protists .................................................80
    **2** Integrating Environmental Science: Algal Blooms .......90
    **3** Fungi ..................................................95

***Chapter 4*** **Introduction to Plants** . . . . . . . . . . . . . . . . . . . . . .**108**
    **1** The Plant Kingdom . . . . . . . . . . . . . . . . . . . . . . . . . . . .110
    **2** Integrating Physics: Photosynthesis and Light . . . . . . . . . . .120
    **3** Mosses, Liverworts, and Hornworts . . . . . . . . . . . . . . . . .125
    **4** Ferns and Their Relatives . . . . . . . . . . . . . . . . . . . . . . . .130

***Chapter 5*** **Seed Plants** . . . . . . . . . . . . . . . . . . . . . . . . . . . . . .**138**
    **1** The Characteristics of Seed Plants . . . . . . . . . . . . . . . . . . .140
    **2** Gymnosperms . . . . . . . . . . . . . . . . . . . . . . . . . . . . . . .150
    **3** Angiosperms . . . . . . . . . . . . . . . . . . . . . . . . . . . . . . . .156
    **4** Plant Responses and Growth . . . . . . . . . . . . . . . . . . . . . .164
    **5** Integrating Technology: Feeding the World . . . . . . . . . . . .168

**Interdisciplinary Exploration:**
   **Corn—The Amazing Grain** . . . . . . . . . . . . . . . . . . . .**174**

**Reference Section**
    **Skills Handbook** . . . . . . . . . . . . . . . . . . . . . . . . . . . . .**182**
       Think Like a Scientist . . . . . . . . . . . . . . . . . . . . . . . . . .182
       Making Measurements . . . . . . . . . . . . . . . . . . . . . . . . .184
       Conducting a Scientific Investigation . . . . . . . . . . . . . . . .186
       Thinking Critically . . . . . . . . . . . . . . . . . . . . . . . . . . .188
       Organizing Information . . . . . . . . . . . . . . . . . . . . . . . .190
       Creating Data Tables and Graphs . . . . . . . . . . . . . . . . . .192
    Appendix A: Laboratory Safety . . . . . . . . . . . . . . . . . . . . .195
    Appendix B: Using the Microscope . . . . . . . . . . . . . . . . . .198
    Glossary . . . . . . . . . . . . . . . . . . . . . . . . . . . . . . . . . . .200
    Index . . . . . . . . . . . . . . . . . . . . . . . . . . . . . . . . . . . . .203
    Acknowledgments . . . . . . . . . . . . . . . . . . . . . . . . . . . . .208

# Activities

## Inquiry Activities

### CHAPTER PROJECT
**Opportunities for long-term inquiry**

Chapter 1: Mystery Object . . . . . . . . . . . . . . .15
Chapter 2: Be a Disease Detective . . . . . . . .47
Chapter 3: A Mushroom Farm . . . . . . . . . . .79
Chapter 4: Become a Moss Expert . . . . . . .109
Chapter 5: Cycle of a Lifetime . . . . . . . . . .139

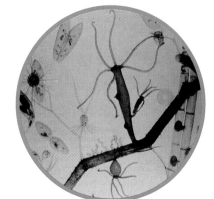

### DISCOVER
**Exploration and inquiry before reading**

Is It Living or Nonliving? . . . . . . . . . . . . . . . .16
How Can the Composition of Air Change? . . .25
Can You Organize a Junk Drawer? . . . . . . . . .28
Which Organism Goes Where? . . . . . . . . . . . .40
Can You Cure a Cold? . . . . . . . . . . . . . . . . . .48
How Quickly Can Bacteria Multiply? . . . . . . .56
How Do Infectious Diseases Spread? . . . . . . .68
What Lives in a Drop of Pond Water? . . . . . . .80
How Can Algal Growth Affect Pond Life? . . . .90
Do All Molds Look Alike? . . . . . . . . . . . . . . .95
What Do Leaves Reveal About Plants? . . . . .110
What Colors Make Up Sunlight? . . . . . . . . . .120
Will Mosses Absorb Water? . . . . . . . . . . . . .125
How Quickly Can Water Move Upward? . . . .130
Which Plant Part Is It? . . . . . . . . . . . . . . . . .140
Are All Leaves Alike? . . . . . . . . . . . . . . . . . .150
What Is a Fruit? . . . . . . . . . . . . . . . . . . . . . .156
Can a Plant Respond to Touch? . . . . . . . . . .164
Will There Be Enough to Eat? . . . . . . . . . . .168

## Sharpen your Skills
**Practice of specific science inquiry skills**

Designing an Experiment . . . . . . . . . . . . . . .22
Observing . . . . . . . . . . . . . . . . . . . . . . . . . . .32
Graphing . . . . . . . . . . . . . . . . . . . . . . . . . . . .59
Predicting . . . . . . . . . . . . . . . . . . . . . . . . . . .87
Interpreting Data . . . . . . . . . . . . . . . . . . . . .113
Calculating . . . . . . . . . . . . . . . . . . . . . . . . . .146

## TRY THIS
**Reinforcement of key concepts**

React! . . . . . . . . . . . . . . . . . . . . . . . . . . . . . .18
Modeling a Virus . . . . . . . . . . . . . . . . . . . . . .51
Bacteria for Breakfast . . . . . . . . . . . . . . . . . .61
Feeding Paramecia . . . . . . . . . . . . . . . . . . . . .84
Making Spore Prints . . . . . . . . . . . . . . . . . . .97
Spreading Spores . . . . . . . . . . . . . . . . . . . . . .98
Examining a Fern . . . . . . . . . . . . . . . . . . . . .132
The In-Seed Story . . . . . . . . . . . . . . . . . . . .142
The Scoop on Cones . . . . . . . . . . . . . . . . . .153

## Skills Lab

**In-depth practice of inquiry skills**

Please Pass the Bread! ....................24
How Many Viruses Fit on a Pin? ..........55
What's for Lunch? .....................100
Eye on Photosynthesis ..................118
Masses of Mosses ......................129
Which Way Is Up? .....................167

## Real-World Lab

**Everyday application of science concepts**

Living Mysteries .......................38
Do Disinfectants Work? ..................66
An Explosion of Life ....................93
A Close Look at Flowers ...............162

# Interdisciplinary Activities

## Science and History

Bacteria and Foods of the World ..........62
Unraveling the Mysteries of Photosynthesis .122

## Science and Society

Antibiotic Resistance—An Alarming Trend ..74
Eutrophication—The Threat to Clear,
    Clean Water ........................94

## Connection

Language Arts ........................30
Social Studies .........................70
Language Arts ........................103
Social Studies ........................127
Visual Arts ..........................158

## EXPLORING

**Visual exploration of concepts**

The Experiments of Redi and Pasteur .......20
How Viruses Multiply ..................52
Protozoans ...........................82
Plant Adaptations .....................114
A Leaf ...............................145
The Life Cycle of a Gymnosperm .........154
The Life Cycle of an Angiosperm .........159

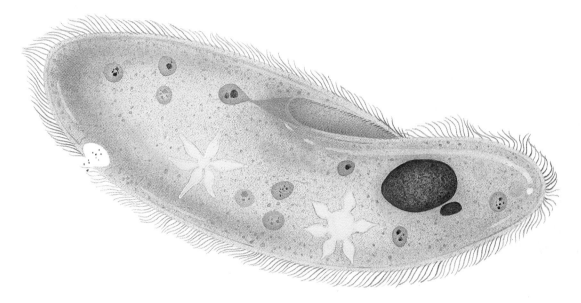

# DISEASE DETECTIVE SOLVES
# MYSTERY

**The Colorado Health Department had a problem.**

**Seven children had become sick with diarrhea, stomach cramps, fever, and vomiting.**

**Within days, another 43 people had the same symptoms.**

Tests indicated that they all had become infected with salmonella. Salmonella are bacteria that are usually transmitted through foods such as contaminated meat or eggs.

How did these children become infected with salmonella? To find the answer, Colorado health officials called in Dr. Cindy Friedman. Dr. Friedman works at the Centers for Disease Control and Prevention (CDC), a United States government agency that tracks down and studies the transmission of diseases throughout the world.

Cindy Friedman studies outbreaks of diseases in groups of people rather than in individuals. Her specialty is infectious diseases, illnesses that spread from person to person. She has investigated outbreaks of disease in such places as rural Bolivia in South America, Cape Verde Islands off the coast of Africa, and a Vermont farm.

**Dr. Cindy Friedman** is a physician and investigator in the Foodborne and Diarrheal Diseases Branch of the Centers for Disease Control and Prevention (CDC). The youngest of three sisters, Dr. Friedman is originally from Brooklyn, New York. In her spare time she enjoys horseback riding.

## An Interview With Dr. Cindy Friedman

**Q** *How did you get started in science?*

**A** When I was young, we always had pets around the house and a lot of books about medicine and science. I wanted to be a veterinarian. In college I decided that I loved animals but didn't want to practice medicine on them. I'd rather keep them as a hobby and devote my career to human medicine.

**Q** *How did you come to specialize in infectious diseases?*

**A** Out of all the subjects I studied in medical school, I liked microbiology the best—learning about different viruses and bacteria. Then, when I did my medical training in New Jersey, we had a lot of patients from Latin America. So I saw quite a few tropical and exotic diseases, which further heightened my interest.

**Q** *What do you enjoy about your job?*

**A** I really like being able to help more than one patient at a time. We do this by figuring out the risk factors for a disease and how to prevent people from getting it. Sometimes the answer is complicated, like adding chlorine to the water. Sometimes it's simple measures, like washing your hands or cooking your food thoroughly.

**Q** *What clues did you have in the Colorado case?*

**A** At first, state investigators thought the bacteria came from some contaminated food. But when they questioned the children, they couldn't identify one place where they had all eaten.

**Q** *How did you find out what experiences the children had in common?*

**A** The investigators did a second set of interviews and learned that the children had all visited the zoo the week before they got sick. They didn't eat the same food at the zoo. But they all went to a special exhibit at the reptile house.

> **How did the children get infected?**

> **Did the salmonella come from infected food?**

> **What common place had the children visited?**

**Q** *Did you think the exhibit might be a new clue?*

**A** Yes. It was a clue because reptiles frequently carry the salmonella bacteria without becoming ill. In the special exhibit, there were four baby Komodo dragons, meat-eating lizards from the island of Komodo in Indonesia. They were displayed in a pen filled with mulch, surrounded by a wooden barrier about two feet high. We tested the Komodo dragons and found that one of them had salmonella bacteria. But it wasn't a petting exhibit, so I couldn't understand how the children got infected.

**Q** *How did you gather new data?*

**A** I questioned the children who became ill and compared their answers with those of children who didn't become ill. I asked about their behavior at the exhibit—where they stood, what they touched, and whether they had anything to eat or drink there. I also asked all the children if they washed their hands after visiting the exhibit. Those who did destroyed the bacteria. It was only the children who didn't wash their hands who became ill.

**Could reptiles provide the clue?**

**Q** *How did you figure out the source of contamination?*

**A** I found that anyone who touched the wooden barrier was much more likely to have gotten sick. Children would go up to the barrier and put their hands on it. Then some of them would put their hands in their mouth or would eat without washing their hands first. Those were the children who became infected with salmonella.

**Why did some children get infected and not others?**

The Komodo dragon is the largest lizard species in existence. Found on Komodo Island in Indonesia, it is nearly extinct.

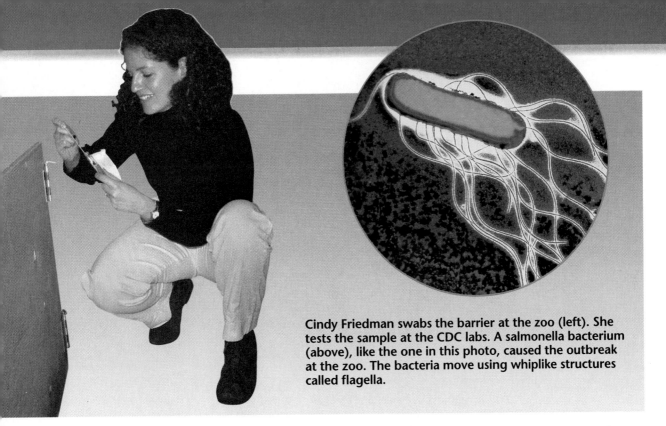

Cindy Friedman swabs the barrier at the zoo (left). She tests the sample at the CDC labs. A salmonella bacterium (above), like the one in this photo, caused the outbreak at the zoo. The bacteria move using whiplike structures called flagella.

**Q** *How did you test your hypothesis?*

**A** We took cultures—swabs from the top of the barrier where the children put their hands. When we tested those cultures in the lab, we found salmonella bacteria.

**Q** *What did you conclude about the bacteria on the barrier?*

**A** The infected Komodo dragon left its droppings in the mulch and the animals walked in it. Then they would stand on their hind legs, bracing themselves by putting their front paws on top of the barrier.

**Q** *What recommendations did you make?*

**A** We didn't want to tell zoos not to have reptile exhibits, because they're a good thing. And children should be able to get close to the animals. But at this particular exhibit, the outbreak could have been prevented with a double barrier system, so that the reptiles and the children couldn't

touch the same barrier. And hand-washing is really important. Zoos should have signs instructing people to wash their hands after going to that kind of exhibit. In homes and schools with pet reptiles, hand-washing is important, too.

**Q** *What's it like being a disease detective?*

**A** It's more the old-fashioned idea of medicine. What I do is examine the patients and listen to the stories they tell—where they've traveled, what they ate, and what they were exposed to. Then I try to figure out what caused their illness.

**How can the zoo prevent future infections?**

*In Your Journal*

Review the scientific process that Dr. Friedman used to solve the case of salmonella infections. What makes her a disease detective? Write a paragraph or two about the skills and character traits that Cindy Friedman needs to track down the source of an infectious disease.

# CHAPTER
# 1 Living Things

### WHAT'S AHEAD

**SECTION 1** **What Is Life?**

**Discover** Is It Living or Nonliving?
**Try This** React!
**Sharpen Your Skills** Designing an Experiment
**Skills Lab** Please Pass the Bread!

*Integrating Earth Science*
**SECTION 2** **The Origin of Life**

**Discover** How Can the Composition of Air Change?

**SECTION 3** **Classifying Organisms**

**Discover** Can You Organize a Junk Drawer?
**Sharpen Your Skills** Observing
**Real-World Lab** Living Mysteries

# Mystery Object

**S**uppose that you visited a location like the one in this scene. Imagine yourself standing perfectly still, all your senses alert to the things around you. You wonder which of the things around you are alive. The newt clearly is, but what about the rest? Is the pink thing alive? Are the other things living or nonliving?

In this chapter, you will learn that it is not always easy to determine whether something is alive. This is because living things share some characteristics with nonliving things. To explore this idea firsthand, you will be given a mystery object to observe. How can you determine if your object is a living thing? What signs of life will you look for?

**Your Goal** To study an object for several days to determine whether or not it is alive.

To complete this project successfully, you must

◆ care for your object following your teacher's instructions
◆ observe your object each day, and record your data
◆ determine whether your object is alive, and if so, which kingdom it belongs in
◆ follow the safety guidelines in Appendix A

**Get Started** With a few classmates, brainstorm a list of characteristics that living things share. Can you think of any nonliving things that share some of these characteristics? Which characteristics on your list can help you conclude whether or not your mystery object is alive?

**Check Your Progress** You'll be working on this project as you study this chapter. To keep your project on track, look for Check Your Progress boxes at the following points.
Section 1 Review, page 23: Carry out your tests.
Section 2 Review, page 27: Record your observations daily.
Section 4 Review, page 42: Classify the object as living or nonliving.

**Wrap Up** At the end of the chapter (page 45), you will display your object and present evidence for whether or not it is alive. Be prepared to answer questions from your classmates.

Both the beautiful pink coral fungus and the newt sitting beside it are alive.

SECTION

4  The Six Kingdoms

Discover **Which Organism Goes Where?**

# SECTION
## ① What Is Life?

## DISCOVER •••••••••••••••••••••••••••••••••••••••••• ACTIVITY ••••

### Is It Living or Nonliving?

1. Your teacher will give you and a partner a wind-up toy.

2. With your partner, decide who will find evidence that the toy is alive and who will find evidence that the toy is not alive.

3. Observe the wind-up toy. Record the characteristics of the toy that support your position about whether or not the toy is alive.

4. Share your lists of living and nonliving characteristics with your classmates.

**Think It Over**

**Forming Operational Definitions** Based on what you learned from the activity, create a list of characteristics that living things share.

---

### GUIDE FOR READING

◆ What characteristics do all living things share?

◆ What do living things need to survive?

*Reading Tip* As you read, use the headings to make an outline of the characteristics and needs of living things.

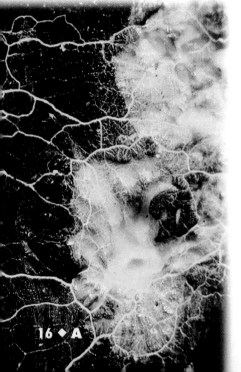

Looking like the slimy creatures that star in horror movies, the "blobs" appeared in towns near Dallas, Texas, in the summer of 1973. Jellylike masses, like the ones in Figure 1, overran yards and porches all over the towns. The glistening blobs oozed slowly along the ground. Terrified homeowners didn't know what the blobs were. Some people thought that they were life forms from another planet. People around Dallas were worried until biologists, scientists who study living things, put their minds at ease. The blobs were slime molds—living things usually found on damp, decaying material on a forest floor. The unusually wet weather around Dallas that year provided ideal conditions for the slime molds to grow in people's yards.

## The Characteristics of Living Things

If you were asked to name some living things, or **organisms,** you might name yourself, a pet, and maybe some insects or plants. But you would probably not mention a moss growing in a shady spot, the mildew on bathroom tiles, or the slime molds that oozed across the lawns in towns near Dallas. But all of these things are also organisms that share six important characteristics

**Figure 1** Slime molds similar to these grew in yards and porches in towns near Dallas, Texas, one summer.

◄ **Animal cells**

◄ **Plant cells**

**Figure 2** Like all living things, the butterfly and the leaf are made of cells. Although the cells of different organisms are not identical, they share important characteristics. *Making Generalizations In what ways are cells similar?*

with all other living things. **All living things have a cellular organization, contain similar chemicals, use energy, grow and develop, respond to their surroundings, and reproduce.**

**Cellular Organization** All organisms are made of small building blocks called cells. A **cell** is the basic unit of structure and function in an organism. The smallest cells are so tiny that you could fit over a million of them on the period at the end of this sentence. To see most cells, you need a microscope—a tool that uses lenses, like those in eyeglasses, to magnify small objects.

Organisms may be composed of only one cell or of many cells. **Unicellular,** or single-celled organisms, include bacteria (bak TEER ee uh), the most numerous organisms on Earth. A bacterial cell carries out all of the functions necessary for the organism to stay alive. **Multicellular** organisms are composed of many cells. The cells of many multicellular organisms are specialized to do certain tasks. For example, you are made of trillions of cells. Specialized cells in your body, such as muscle and nerve cells, work together to keep you alive. Nerve cells carry messages from your surroundings to your brain. Other nerve cells then carry messages to your muscle cells, making your body move.

**The Chemicals of Life** The cells of all living things are composed of chemicals. The most abundant chemical in cells is water. Other chemicals called carbohydrates (kahr boh HY drayt) are a cell's energy source. Two other chemicals, proteins (PROH teenz) and lipids (LIP idz), are the building materials of cells, much like wood and bricks are the building materials of houses. Finally, nucleic (noo KLEE ik) acids are the genetic material—the chemical instructions that direct the cell's activities.

**Figure 3** Over time, a tiny acorn develops into a giant oak tree. A great deal of energy is needed to produce the trillions of cells that make up the body of an oak tree.
*Comparing and Contrasting  In what way does the seedling resemble the oak tree? In what ways is it different?*

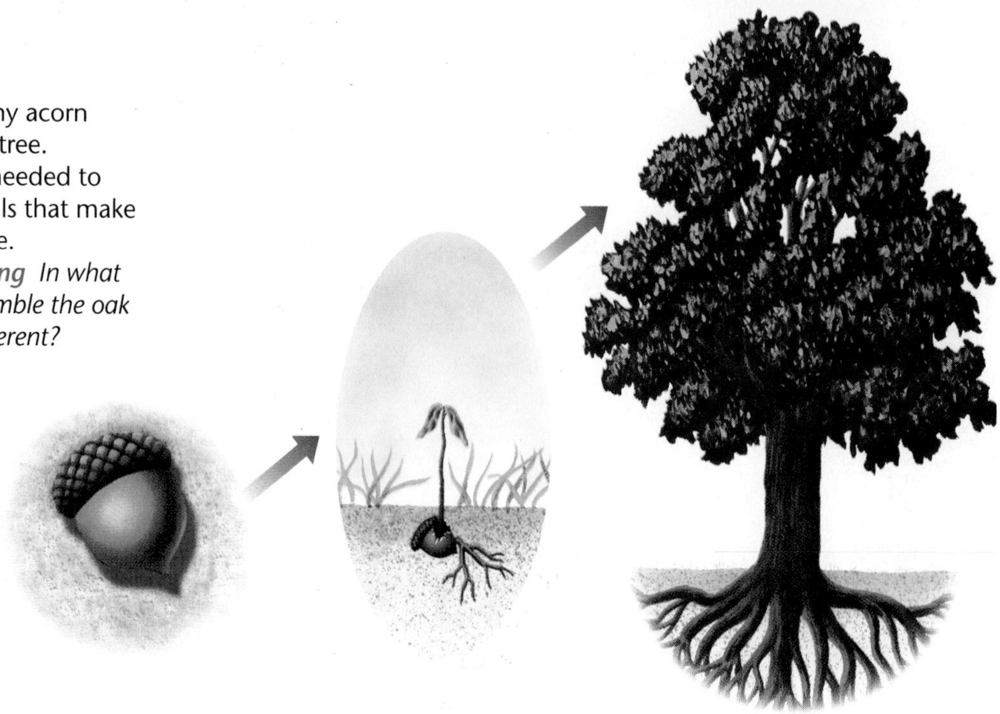

Acorn                Seedling                Oak tree

**Energy Use** The cells of organisms use energy to do what living things must do, such as grow and repair injured parts. An organism's cells are always hard at work. For example, as you read this paragraph, not only are your eye and brain cells busy, but most of your other cells are working, too. The cells of your stomach and intestine are digesting food. Your blood cells are moving chemicals around your body. If you've hurt yourself, some of your cells are repairing the damage.

**Growth and Development** Another characteristic of living things is that they grow and develop. Growth is the process of becoming larger. **Development** is the process of change that occurs during an organism's life to produce a more complex organism. To grow and develop, organisms use energy to create new cells. Look at Figure 3 to see how an acorn develops as it grows into an oak tree.

You may argue that some nonliving things grow and change as they age. For example, a pickup truck rusts as it ages. Icicles grow longer as more water freezes on their tips. But pickup trucks and icicles do not use energy to change and grow. They also don't become more complex over time.

**Response to Surroundings** If you've ever seen a plant in a sunny window, you may have observed that the plant's stems have bent so that the leaves face the sun. Like a plant bending toward the light, all organisms react to changes in their environment. A change in an organism's surroundings that causes the organism to react is called a **stimulus** (plural *stimuli*). Stimuli include changes in temperature, light, sound, and other factors.

An organism reacts to a stimulus with a **response**—an action or change in behavior. For example, has someone ever leapt out at you from behind a door? If so, it's likely that you jumped or screamed. Your friend's sudden motion was the stimulus that caused your startled response. Nonliving things, such as rocks, do not react to stimuli as living things do.

**Reproduction** Another characteristic of organisms is the ability to **reproduce,** or produce offspring that are similar to the parents. Robins lay eggs that develop into young robins that closely resemble their parents. Sunflowers produce seeds that develop into sunflower plants, which in turn make more seeds. Bacteria produce other bacteria exactly like themselves.

✓ *Checkpoint* *How do growth and development differ?*

## Life Comes From Life

Today, when people observe young plants in a garden or see a litter of puppies, they know that these new organisms are the result of reproduction. Four hundred years ago, however, people believed that life could appear suddenly from nonliving material. For example, when people saw flies swarming around decaying meat, they concluded that flies could arise from rotting meat. When frogs appeared in muddy puddles after heavy rains, people concluded that frogs could sprout from the mud in ponds. The mistaken idea that living things arise from nonliving sources is called **spontaneous generation.**

It took hundreds of years of experiments to convince people that spontaneous generation does not occur. One scientist who did some of these experiments was an Italian doctor, Francesco Redi. In the mid-1600s, Redi designed a controlled experiment to show that flies do not spontaneously arise from decaying meat. In a **controlled experiment**, a scientist carries out two tests that are identical in every respect except for one factor. The one factor that the scientist changes is called the **variable.** The scientist can conclude that any differences in the results of the two tests must be due to the variable.

Even after Redi's work, many people continued to believe that spontaneous generation occurred in bacteria. In the mid-1800s,

**Figure 4** All organisms respond to changes in their surroundings. This willow ptarmigan's feathers have turned white in response to its snowy surroundings. This Alaskan bird's plumage will remain white until spring.

the French chemist Louis Pasteur designed some controlled experiments that finally disproved spontaneous generation. The controlled experiments of Francesco Redi and Louis Pasteur helped to convince people that living things do not arise from nonliving material. Look at *Exploring the Experiments of Redi and Pasteur* to learn more about the experiments they performed.

☑ *Checkpoint* *What is a controlled experiment?*

## The Needs of Living Things

Imagine yourself biking through a park on a warm spring day. As you ride by a tree, you see a squirrel running up the tree trunk. Although it may seem that squirrels and trees do not have the

---

# EXPLORING the Experiments of Redi and Pasteur

**R**edi designed one of the first controlled experiments. By Pasteur's time, controlled experiments were standard procedure. As you explore, identify the variable in each experiment.

**FRANCESCO REDI**

## REDI'S EXPERIMENT

1. Redi placed meat in two identical jars. He left one jar uncovered. He covered the other jar with a cloth that let in air.

2. After a few days, Redi saw maggots (young flies) on the decaying meat in the open jar. There were no maggots on the meat in the covered jar.

3. Redi reasoned that flies had laid eggs on the meat in the open jar. The eggs hatched into maggots. Because flies could not lay eggs on the meat in the covered jar, there were no maggots there. Therefore, Redi concluded that the decaying meat did not produce maggots.

same basic needs as you, they do. All organisms need four things to stay alive. **Living things must satisfy their basic needs for energy, water, living space, and stable internal conditions.**

**Energy**   You read earlier that organisms need a source of energy to live. They use food as their energy source. Organisms differ in the ways they obtain their energy. Some organisms, such as plants, capture the sun's energy and use it along with carbon dioxide, a gas found in Earth's atmosphere, and water to make their own food. Organisms that make their own food are called **autotrophs** (AW tuh trawfs). *Auto-* means "self" and *-troph* means "feeder." Autotrophs use the food they make as an energy source to carry out their life functions.

## PASTEUR'S EXPERIMENT

**LOUIS PASTEUR**

1 In one experiment, Pasteur put clear broth into two flasks with curved necks. The necks would let in oxygen but keep out bacteria from the air. Pasteur boiled the broth in one flask to kill any bacteria in the broth. He did not boil the broth in the other flask.

2 In a few days, the unboiled broth became cloudy, showing that new bacteria were growing. The boiled broth remained clear. Pasteur concluded that bacteria do not spontaneously arise from the broth. New bacteria appeared only when living bacteria were already present.

Later, Pasteur took the curve-necked flask containing the broth that had remained clear and broke its long neck. Bacteria from the air could now enter the flask. In a few days, the broth became cloudy. This evidence confirmed Pasteur's conclusion that new bacteria appear only when they are produced by existing bacteria.

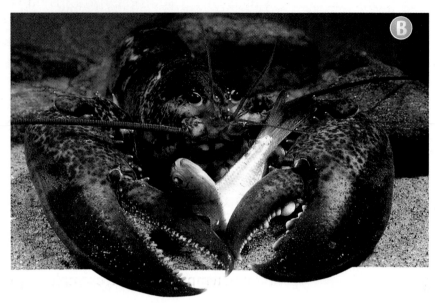

**Figure 5** All organisms need a source of energy to live. **A.** *Volvox* is an autotroph that lives in fresh water, where it uses the sun's energy to make its own food. **B.** This American lobster, a heterotroph, is feeding on a herring it has caught. *Applying Concepts* How do heterotrophs depend on autotrophs for energy?

Organisms that cannot make their own food are called **heterotrophs** (HET uh roh trawfs). *Hetero-* means "other." A heterotroph's energy source is also the sun—but in an indirect way. Heterotrophs either eat autotrophs and obtain the energy in the autotroph's stored food, or they consume other heterotrophs that eat autotrophs. Animals, mushrooms, and slime molds are examples of heterotrophs.

**Water** All living things need water to survive—in fact, most organisms can live for only a few days without water. Organisms need water to do things such as obtain chemicals from their surroundings, break down food, grow, move substances within their bodies, and reproduce.

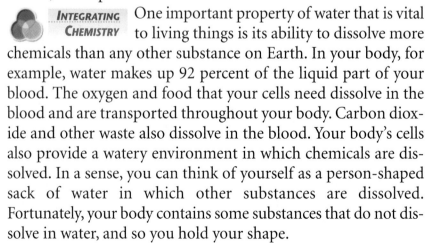

**INTEGRATING CHEMISTRY** One important property of water that is vital to living things is its ability to dissolve more chemicals than any other substance on Earth. In your body, for example, water makes up 92 percent of the liquid part of your blood. The oxygen and food that your cells need dissolve in the blood and are transported throughout your body. Carbon dioxide and other waste also dissolve in the blood. Your body's cells also provide a watery environment in which chemicals are dissolved. In a sense, you can think of yourself as a person-shaped sack of water in which other substances are dissolved. Fortunately, your body contains some substances that do not dissolve in water, and so you hold your shape.

**Sharpen your Skills**

**Designing an Experiment**

**ACTIVITY**

Your teacher will give you a slice of potato. Predict what percentage of the potato's mass is water. Then come up with a plan to test your prediction. For materials, you will be given a hairdryer and a balance. Obtain your teacher's approval before carrying out your plan. How does your result compare with your prediction?

**Living Space** All organisms need a place to live—a place to get food and water and find shelter. Because there is a limited amount of living space on Earth, some organisms may compete for space. Plants, for example, occupy a fixed living space. Above the ground, their branches and leaves compete for living space with those of other plants. Below ground, their roots compete for water and minerals. Unlike plants, organisms such as animals move around. They may either share living space with others or compete for living space.

**Stable Internal Conditions** Because conditions in their surroundings can change significantly, organisms must be able to keep the conditions inside their bodies constant. The maintenance of stable internal conditions despite changes in the surroundings is called **homeostasis** (hoh mee oh STAY sis). You know that when you are healthy your body temperature stays constant despite temperature changes in your surroundings. Your body's regulation of temperature is an example of homeostasis.

Other organisms have different mechanisms for maintaining homeostasis. For example, imagine that you are a barnacle attached to a rock at the edge of the ocean. At high tide, the ocean water covers you. At low tide, however, your watery surroundings disappear, and you are exposed to hours of sun and wind. Without a way to keep water in your cells, you'd die. Fortunately, a barnacle can close up its hard outer plates, trapping a bubble of water inside. In this way, the barnacle can keep its body moist until the next high tide.

**Figure 6** A tree trunk provides these mushrooms with food, water, and shelter.

## Section 1 Review

1. Name six characteristics that you have in common with a tree.
2. List the four things that all organisms need to stay alive.
3. How did Pasteur's experiment show that bacteria do not arise spontaneously in broth?
4. **Thinking Critically Applying Concepts** You see a crowd of gulls fighting over an object on the wet sand at the ocean's edge. You investigate. The object is a vase-shaped, pink blob about as round as a dinner plate. How will you decide if it is a living thing?

**Check Your Progress** CHAPTER PROJECT 1
At this point, you should be ready to carry out your tests for signs of life following your teacher's directions. Before you start, examine your mystery object carefully, and record your observations. Also, decide whether you need to revise the list of life characteristics you prepared earlier. *(Hint:* Do not be fooled by the object's appearance—some organisms appear dead during a certain stage of their life.)

# Please Pass the Bread!

**I**n this lab, you will control variables in an investigation into the needs of living things.

## Problem

What factors are necessary for bread molds to grow?

## Materials

paper plates                     tap water
plastic dropper                  packing tape
bread without preservatives
sealable plastic bags

## Procedure

1. Brainstorm with others to predict which factors might affect the growth of bread mold. Record your ideas.
2. To test the effect of moisture on bread mold growth, place two slices of bread of the same size and thickness on separate, clean plates.
3. Add drops of tap water to one bread slice until the whole slice is moist. Keep the other slice dry. Expose both slices to the air for 1 hour.
4. Put each slice into its own sealable bag. Press the outside of each bag to remove the air. Seal the bags. Then use packing tape to seal the bags again. Store the bags in a warm, dark place.
5. Copy the data table into your notebook.

6. Every day for at least 5 days, briefly remove the sealed bags from their storage place. Record whether any mold has grown. Estimate the area of the bread where mold is present. **CAUTION:** *Do not unseal the bags. At the end of the experiment, give the sealed bags to your teacher.*
7. Choose another factor that may affect mold growth, such as temperature or the amount of light. Set up an experiment to test the factor you choose. Remember to keep all conditions the same except for the one you are testing.

## Analyze and Conclude

1. What conclusions can you draw from each of your experiments?
2. What was the variable in the first experiment? In the second experiment?
3. What basic needs of living things were demonstrated in this lab? Explain.
4. **Think About It** What is meant by "controlling variables"? Why is it necessary to control variables in an experiment?

## Design an Experiment

Suppose that you lived in Redi's time. A friend tells you that living things such as molds just suddenly appear on bread. Design an experiment that might convince your friend that the new mold comes from existing mold.

### DATA TABLE

|  | Moistened Bread Slice | | Unmoistened Bread Slice | |
|---|---|---|---|---|
|  | Mold Present? | Area with Mold | Mold Present? | Area with Mold |
| Day 1 |  |  |  |  |
| Day 2 |  |  |  |  |

# SECTION 2 The Origin of Life

## DISCOVER •••••••••••••••••••••••••••••••••••• ACTIVITY

### How Can the Composition of Air Change?

1. 🐭 🌱 Your teacher will give you two covered, plastic jars. One contains a plant and one contains an animal.

2. Observe the organisms in each jar. Talk with a partner about how you think each organism affects the composition of the air in its jar.

3. Write a prediction about how the amount of oxygen in each jar would change over time if left undisturbed.

4. Return the jars to your teacher.

### Think It Over

***Inferring*** Scientists hypothesize that Earth's early atmosphere was different from today's atmosphere. What role might early organisms have played in bringing about those changes?

You stare out the window of your time machine. You have traveled back to Earth as it was 3.6 billion years ago. The landscape is rugged, with bare, jagged rocks and little soil. You search for a hint of green, but there is none. You see only blacks, browns, and grays. Lightning flashes all around you. You hear the rumble of thunder, howling winds, and waves pounding the shore.

You neither see nor hear any living things. However, you know that this is the time period when scientists think that early life forms arose on Earth. You decide to explore. To be safe, you put on your oxygen mask. Stepping outside, you wonder what kinds of organisms could ever live in such a place.

## Earth's Early Atmosphere

You were smart to put on your oxygen mask before exploring early Earth. Scientists think that early Earth had a different atmosphere than it has today. **Nitrogen, water vapor, carbon dioxide, and methane were probably the most abundant gases in Earth's atmosphere 3.6 billion years ago. Although all these gases are still found in the atmosphere today, the major gases are nitrogen and oxygen.** You, like most of today's organisms, could not have lived on Earth 3.6 billion years ago, because there was no oxygen in the air. However, scientists think that life forms appeared on Earth at that time.

### GUIDE FOR READING

◆ How was the atmosphere of early Earth different from today's atmosphere?

◆ How do scientists hypothesize that life arose on early Earth?

***Reading Tip*** Before you read, preview Figure 7. List some ways that you think early Earth differed from today's Earth.

**Figure 7** The atmosphere of early Earth had little oxygen. There were frequent volcanic eruptions, earthquakes, and violent weather. *Inferring What conditions on early Earth would have made it impossible for modern organisms to survive?*

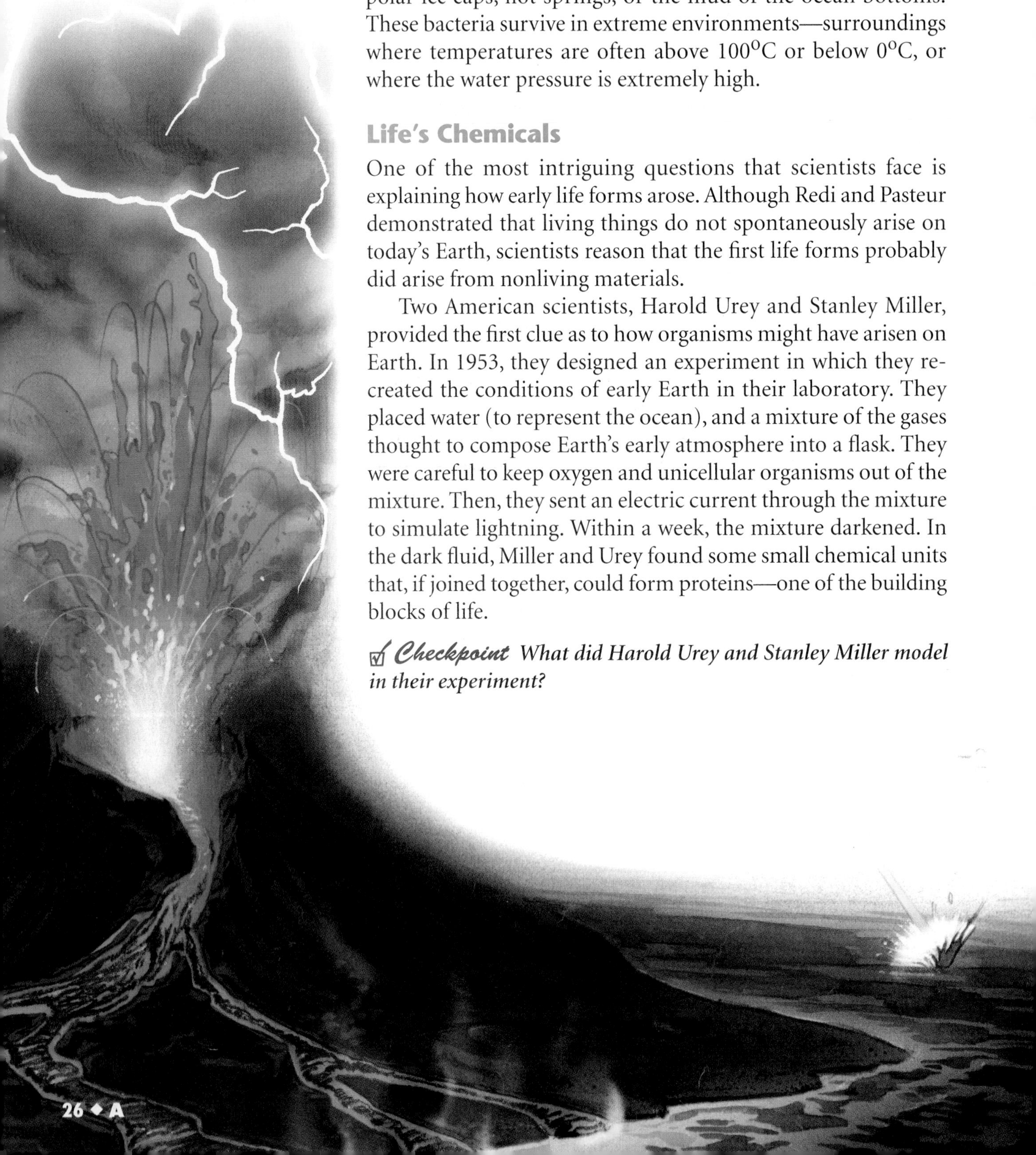

No one can ever be sure what the first life forms were like, but scientists have formed hypotheses about them. First, early life forms did not need oxygen to survive. Second, they were probably unicellular organisms. Third, they probably lived in the oceans. Many scientists think that the first organisms resembled the bacteria that live today in places without oxygen, such as the polar ice caps, hot springs, or the mud of the ocean bottoms. These bacteria survive in extreme environments—surroundings where temperatures are often above 100°C or below 0°C, or where the water pressure is extremely high.

## Life's Chemicals

One of the most intriguing questions that scientists face is explaining how early life forms arose. Although Redi and Pasteur demonstrated that living things do not spontaneously arise on today's Earth, scientists reason that the first life forms probably did arise from nonliving materials.

Two American scientists, Harold Urey and Stanley Miller, provided the first clue as to how organisms might have arisen on Earth. In 1953, they designed an experiment in which they re-created the conditions of early Earth in their laboratory. They placed water (to represent the ocean), and a mixture of the gases thought to compose Earth's early atmosphere into a flask. They were careful to keep oxygen and unicellular organisms out of the mixture. Then, they sent an electric current through the mixture to simulate lightning. Within a week, the mixture darkened. In the dark fluid, Miller and Urey found some small chemical units that, if joined together, could form proteins—one of the building blocks of life.

*Checkpoint* *What did Harold Urey and Stanley Miller model in their experiment?*

## The First Cells

In experiments similar to Miller and Urey's, other scientists succeeded in producing chemical units that make up carbohydrates and nucleic acids. **From the results of these experiments, scientists hypothesized that the small chemical units of life formed gradually over millions of years in Earth's waters.** Some of these units joined to form the large chemical building blocks that are found in cells. Eventually, some of these large chemicals accumulated and became the forerunners of the first cells.

These hypotheses are consistent with evidence from fossils. **Fossils** are traces of ancient organisms that have been preserved in rock or other substances. The fossils in Figure 8 are of bacteria-like organisms that were determined to be between 3.4 and 3.5 billion years old. Scientists think that these ancient cells may be evidence of Earth's earliest life forms.

The first cells could not have needed oxygen to survive. They probably were heterotrophs that used the chemicals in their surroundings for energy. As they grew and reproduced, their numbers increased. In turn, the amount of chemicals available to them decreased. At some point, some of the cells may have developed the ability to make their own food. These early ancestors of today's autotrophs had an important effect on the atmosphere. As they made their own food, they produced oxygen as a waste product. As the autotrophs thrived, oxygen accumulated in Earth's atmosphere. Over millions of years, the amount of oxygen increased to its current level.

No one will ever know for certain how life first appeared on Earth. However, scientists will continue to ask questions, construct models, and look for both experimental and fossil evidence about the origin of life on Earth.

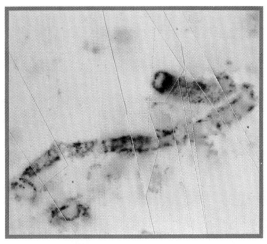

**Figure 8** This fossil of bacteria-like cells was found in western Australia. It is the oldest fossil known—about 3.5 billion years old.

---

## Section 2 Review

1. Explain why you could not have survived in the atmosphere of early Earth.
2. Describe how scientists think that life could have arisen on Earth.
3. Describe Urey and Miller's experiment.
4. **Thinking Critically Inferring** How is the existence of organisms in hot springs today consistent with the scientific hypothesis of how life forms arose on Earth?

**Check Your Progress** CHAPTER PROJECT 1

Observe your object at least once a day. Record your observations in a data table. Draw accurate diagrams. (*Hint:* Measuring provides important information. Take measurements of your object regularly. If you cannot measure it directly, make estimates.)

# SECTION 3 Classifying Organisms

### Can You Organize a Junk Drawer?

1. Your teacher will give you some items that you might find in the junk drawer of a desk. Your job is to organize the items.

2. Examine the objects and decide on three groups into which you can sort them.

3. Place each object into one of the groups based on how the item's features match the characteristics of the group.

4. Compare your grouping system with those of your classmates.

**Think It Over**
*Classifying* Explain which grouping system seemed most useful.

---

### GUIDE FOR READING

◆ Why do scientists organize living things into groups?

◆ What is the relationship between classification and evolution?

*Reading Tip* Before you read, make a list of the boldfaced vocabulary terms. As you read, write the meaning of each term in your own words.

Suppose you had only ten minutes to run into a supermarket to get what you need—milk and tomatoes. Could you do it? In most supermarkets this would be an easy task. First, you might go to the dairy aisle and find the milk. Then you'd go to the produce aisle and find the tomatoes. Finally, you'd pay for the items and leave the store.

Now imagine shopping for these same items in a market where the shelves were organized in a random manner. To find what you need, you'd have to search through boxes of cereal, cans of tuna, bins of apples, and much more. You could be there for a long time!

## Why Do Scientists Classify?

Just as shopping can be a problem in a disorganized store, finding information about one of the millions of kinds of organisms can also be a problem. Today, scientists have identified at least 2.5 million kinds of organisms on Earth. This number includes all forms of life, from plants and animals to bacteria. It is important for biologists to have all these living things organized.

People organize a lot of things into groups. For example, if a friend asks you what kind of music you like, you might say that you like country or rap music. Although you may not know it, you have grouped the music you like. **Classification** is the process of grouping things based on their similarities.

Biologists use classification to organize living things into groups so that the organisms are easier to study. The scientific study of how living things are classified is called **taxonomy** (tak SAHN uh mee). Taxonomy is useful because once an organism is classified, a scientist knows a lot about that organism. For example, if you know that crows are classified as birds, you know that crows have wings, feathers, and a beak.

**INTEGRATING EARTH SCIENCE** Biologists aren't the only scientists who classify things. For example, geologists—scientists who study the structure and history of Earth—classify rocks. Geologists separate rocks into three groups according to how they formed. By classifying rocks in this way, geologists can make sense of the variety of rocks on Earth.

## Early Classification Systems

The first scientist to develop a classification system for organisms was the Greek scholar Aristotle. In the fourth century B.C., Aristotle observed many animals. He recorded each animal's appearance, behavior, and movement. Then he divided animals into three groups: those that fly, those that swim, and those that walk, crawl, or run.

Aristotle could see that even though organisms in a group moved in a similar way, they were different in many other ways. So he used their differences to divide each group into subgroups— smaller groups of organisms that shared other similarities.

Aristotle's method of using careful observations as the basis for classification and his idea of creating subgroups are still used today. However, organisms are no longer classified into large groups on the basis of how they move or where they live.

*Checkpoint* *What were the three major groups of animals in Aristotle's system of classification?*

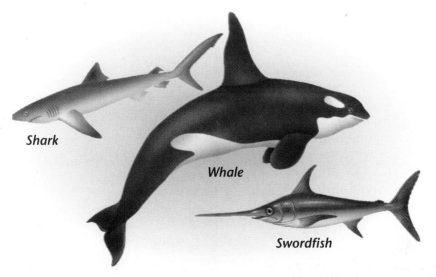

Shark

Whale

Swordfish

**Figure 9** Aristotle would have classified this shark, whale, and swordfish together. However, he would have separated them into subgroups because they differ from each other in many ways. *Classifying List two differences that would place these animals into separate subgroups.*

## What's In a Name?

You don't have to know Latin to understand the meaning of a scientific name. Just hearing the name *Ursus horribilis* should tell you that you don't want to meet that organism up close. *Ursus horribilis* is commonly known as a grizzly bear. The Latin word *ursus* means "bear" and *horribilis* means "horrible or feared."

A species name describes an organism like an adjective describes the noun it modifies. Some names describe a specific trait; others tell who discovered the organism. For example, *Pheidole fullerae* is the name of a species of ants discovered by an office worker named Fuller. Other names tell you where the organism was discovered or where it lives. Guess where you'd find the plant *Viola missouriensis*.

### In Your Journal

Look in dictionaries or other reference books to find the meaning of these species names: *Musca domestica*, *Hirudo medicinalis*, and *Cornus florida*. Then try to identify English words that are derived from the Latin terms.

## The Classification System of Linnaeus

In the 1750s, a Swedish scientist named Carolus Linnaeus expanded on Aristotle's ideas of classification. Like Aristotle, Linnaeus used observations as the basis of his system. He wrote descriptions of organisms from his observations, and placed organisms in groups based on their observable features.

Linnaeus also used his observations to devise a naming system for organisms. In Linnaeus's naming system, called **binomial nomenclature** (by NOH mee ul   NOH men klay chur), each organism is given a two-part name.

The first part of an organism's scientific name is its genus. A **genus** (JEE nus) (plural *genera*) is a classification grouping that contains similar, closely related organisms. For example, pumas, ocelots, and house cats are all classified in the genus *Felis*. Organisms that are classified in the genus *Felis* share characteristics such as sharp, retractable claws and behaviors such as hunting other animals.

The second part of an organism's scientific name is its species name. A **species** (SPEE sheez) is a group of similar organisms that can mate and produce fertile offspring in nature. A species name sets one species in a genus apart from another. The species name often describes a distinctive feature of an organism, such as where it lives or its color. For example, the scientific name for many pumas, or mountain lions, is *Felis concolor*. *Concolor* means "the same color" in Latin. The scientific name for some ocelots is *Felis pardalis*. The word *pardalis* means "spotted like a panther" in Latin. The scientific name for house cats is *Felis domesticus*. The species name *domesticus* means "of the house" in Latin.

**Figure 10** These animals belong to the genus *Felis*. The species names of the animals distinguish them from each other. **A.** This puma's coat is one color, which is indicated by its species name *concolor*. **B.** This ocelot has a spotted coat, which is described by its species name *pardalis*. **C.** The species name of this kitten is *domesticus*, which indicates that it is a house cat.

Linnaeus's system might remind you of the way you are named because you, also, have a two-part name made up of your first name and your family name. Your two-part name distinguishes you from others. In a similar way, binomial nomenclature ensures that a combination of two names distinguishes one kind of organism from another. Together, a genus and a species name identify one kind of organism.

Notice that both the genus and species names are Latin words. Linnaeus used Latin words in his naming system because Latin was the language that scientists communicated in during that time. Notice also that a complete scientific name is written in italics. The genus is capitalized while the species name begins with a small letter.

Binomial nomenclature makes it easy for scientists to communicate about an organism because everyone uses the same name for the same organism. Look at the organism in Figure 11. This photograph shows one type of pine tree that grows in the southern United States. People call this tree by any one of a number of common names: loblolly pine, longstraw pine, or Indian pine. Fortunately, this tree has only one scientific name, *Pinus taeda*.

☑ *Checkpoint* *Which part of a scientific name is like your first name? Your family name?*

**Figure 11** Although there are many common names for this tree, it has only one scientific name.
*Making Generalizations What is the advantage of having scientific names for organisms?*

## Observing  ACTIVITY

Test your observational skills using Figure 12. Look carefully at the organisms pictured together at the kingdom level. Make a list of the characteristics that the organisms share. Then make two more lists of shared characteristics—one for the organisms at the class level and the other for those at the genus level. How does the number of characteristics on your lists change at each level?

## Levels of Classification

The classification system that scientists use today is based on the contributions of Aristotle and Linnaeus. But today's classification system uses a series of seven levels to classify organisms. To help you understand the levels in classification, imagine a room filled with everybody who lives in your state. First, all of the people who live in your *town* raise their hands. Then, those who live in your *neighborhood* raise their hands. Then, those who live on your *street* raise their hands. Finally, those who live in your *house* raise their hands. Each time, fewer people raise their hands. But you'd be in all of the groups. The most general group you belong to is the state. The most specific group is the house. The more levels you share with others, the more you have in common with them.

**The Seven Levels of Classification** Modern biologists classify organisms into the seven levels shown in Figure 12. Of course, organisms are not grouped by where they live but rather by their shared characteristics. First an organism is placed in a broad group, which in turn is divided into more specific groups.

A kingdom is the broadest level of organization. Within a kingdom, there are phyla (FY luh) (singular *phylum*). Within each phylum are classes. Each class is divided into orders. Each order contains families, and each family contains at least one genus. Finally, within a genus, there are species. The more classification levels that two organisms share, the more characteristics they have in common.

**Classifying an Owl** Take a closer look at Figure 12 to see how the levels of classification apply to the great horned owl, a member of the animal kingdom. Look at the top row of the figure. As you can see, a wide variety of organisms also belong to the animal kingdom. Now, look at the phylum, class, and order levels. Notice that as you move down the levels in the figure, there are fewer kinds of organisms in each group. More importantly, the organisms in each group have more in common with each other. For example, the class Aves includes all birds, while the order Strigiformes only includes owls. Different owls have more in common with each other than they do with other birds.

☑ *Checkpoint* List the seven levels of classification from the broadest to the most specific.

# Kingdom Animalia

# Phylum Chordata

# Class Aves

# Order Strigiformes

# Family Strygidae

## Genus *Bubo*

## Species *Bubo virginianus*

**Figure 12** Scientists use seven levels to classify organisms such as the great horned owl. Notice that, as you move down the levels, the number of organisms decreases. The organisms at lower levels share more characteristics with each other. *Interpreting Diagrams How many levels do a robin and the great horned owl share?*

**Figure 13** These three species of finches that live on the Galapagos Islands may have arisen from a single species. Notice the differences in these birds' appearances, especially their beaks. **A.** This cactus finch uses its pointed beak to pierce the outer covering of cactus plants. **B.** The warbler finch uses its needlelike beak to trap insects. **C.** The large-billed ground finch cracks open large seeds with its strong, wide beak.

## Evolution and Classification

At the time that Linnaeus developed his classification system, people thought that species never change. They could see that some organisms were similar. They thought that these organisms had always been similar, yet distinct from each other. In 1859, a British naturalist named Charles Darwin published a theory about how species can change over time. Darwin's theory has had a major impact on how species are classified.

Darwin collected much of the data for his theory on the Galapagos Islands off the western coast of South America. As he studied the islands' finches, he observed that some species of finches were similar to each other but different from finches living in South America. Darwin hypothesized that some members of a single species of finch flew from South America to the islands. Once on the islands, the species changed little by little over a long time until it was very different from the species remaining in South America. In this way, two groups of a single species can accumulate enough differences over a long time to become two separate species. This process by which species gradually change over time is called **evolution**.

☑ *Checkpoint* Who first proposed the theory of evolution?

## Classification Today

The theory of evolution changed the way biologists think about classification. Today, scientists understand that certain organisms are similar because they share a common ancestor. For example, Darwin hypothesized that the finches that lived on the Galapagos Islands shared a common ancestor with the finches that live in South America. When organisms share a common ancestor, they share an evolutionary history. Today's system of classification considers the history of a species when classifying the species. **Species with similar evolutionary histories are classified more closely together.**

How do scientists get information about the evolutionary history of a species? One way is by studying fossils. Scientists compare the body structures as well as the chemical makeup of fossils to each other and to modern organisms. This information adds to their knowledge of evolutionary relationships among organisms.

Scientists also obtain clues about the evolutionary history of a species by comparing the body structures of living organisms. For example, look at the organisms in Figure 14. Notice that the bones in the flipper of a whale are similar to the bones in the wing of a bat and in the arm of a human. This similarity indicates that whales, bats, and humans have a similar evolutionary history.

Additional information about evolutionary history can be learned by comparing the early development of different organisms. Humans and rabbits, for example, go through similar stages in their early development before birth. The similarity provides evidence that humans and rabbits may share some evolutionary history.

**Figure 14** Compare the bones in the limbs of the bat, whale, and human. Although a bone may differ in size and shape, it is in a similar location in each of the limbs. *Inferring What do the bones in the limbs suggest about the animals' evolutionary history?*

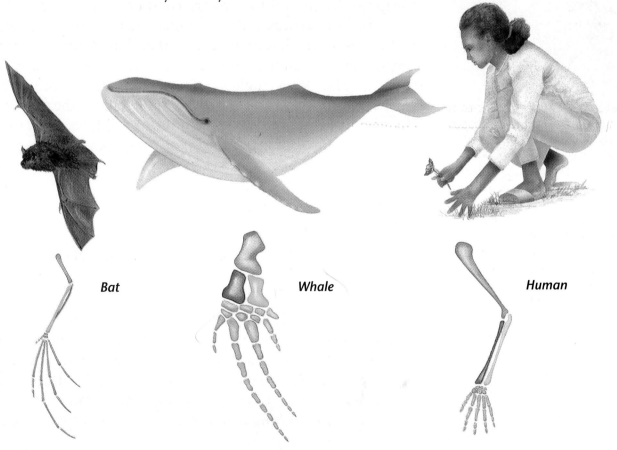

Bat          Whale          Human

**Figure 15** Scientists analyze the chemical makeup of an organism's cells to learn about its evolutionary history. By comparing the chemicals in the cells of weasels, top, and skunks, bottom, scientists learned that these organisms are not as closely related as once thought.

Today, scientists rely primarily on information about the chemical makeup of cells to determine evolutionary history. The more closely two species are related, the more similar the chemicals that make up their cells. The skunk and weasel had been classified in the same family for 150 years. Recently, however, scientists compared some nucleic acids from the cells of skunks and weasels. Surprisingly, they found many differences, suggesting that these organisms are not as closely related as they had thought. Some scientists propose changing the classification of skunks. They suggest removing skunks from the family Mustelidae, which contains members of the weasel family. They want to reclassify skunks into a family called Mephitidae, which means "noxious gas" in Latin.

☑ *Checkpoint* *How do scientists use fossils to learn about the evolutionary history of organisms?*

## Using the Classification System

You may be wondering why you should care about taxonomy. Suppose you wake up and feel something tickling your ankle. You fling back the covers and stare at a tiny creature crouching in the sheets by your right foot. Although it's only the size of a small melon seed, you don't like the looks of its two claws waving at you. Then, in a flash, it's gone—darting off under the safety of your covers.

How could you learn the identity of the organism that tickled you awake? One way to identify the organism would be to use a field guide. Field guides are books with illustrations that highlight differences between similar-looking organisms.

Another tool you could use to identify the organism is called a taxonomic key. A **taxonomic key** is a series of paired statements that describe the physical characteristics of different organisms.

## Taxonomic Key

**Step 1**

| | | |
|---|---|---|
| **1a.** | Has 8 legs | Go to Step 2. |
| **1b.** | Has more than 8 legs | Go to Step 3. |

**Step 2**

| | | |
|---|---|---|
| **2a.** | Has one oval-shaped body region | Go to Step 4. |
| **2b.** | Has two body regions | Go to Step 5. |

**Step 3**

| | | |
|---|---|---|
| **3a.** | Has one pair of legs on each body segment | Centipede |
| **3b.** | Has two pairs of legs on each body segment | Millipede |

**Step 4**

| | | |
|---|---|---|
| **4a.** | Is less than 1 millimeter long | Mite |
| **4b.** | Is more than 1 millimeter long | Tick |

**Step 5**

| | | |
|---|---|---|
| **5a.** | Has clawlike pincers | Go to Step 6. |
| **5b.** | Has no clawlike pincers | Spider |

**Step 6**

| | | |
|---|---|---|
| **6a.** | Has a long tail with a stinger | Scorpion |
| **6b.** | Has no tail or stinger | Pseudoscorpion |

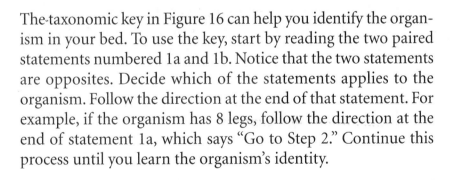

**Figure 16** A taxonomic key is a series of paired statements that describe the physical characteristics of different organisms. There are six pairs of statements in this key. *Drawing Conclusions What is the identity of the organism shown in the picture?*

The taxonomic key in Figure 16 can help you identify the organism in your bed. To use the key, start by reading the two paired statements numbered 1a and 1b. Notice that the two statements are opposites. Decide which of the statements applies to the organism. Follow the direction at the end of that statement. For example, if the organism has 8 legs, follow the direction at the end of statement 1a, which says "Go to Step 2." Continue this process until you learn the organism's identity.

## Section 3 Review

1. Why is it important for biologists to classify organisms into groups?
2. How is an organism's evolutionary history related to the way in which it is classified?
3. Explain Linnaeus's contribution to modern taxonomy.
4. **Thinking Critically** **Applying Concepts** Create a taxonomic key that could help identify a piece of fruit as either an apple, an orange, a strawberry, or a banana.

### Science at Home

With a family member, go on a "classification hunt" in the kitchen. Look in your cabinets, refrigerator, and drawers to discover what classification systems your family uses to organize items. Discuss the advantages of organizing items in your kitchen in the way that you do. Then explain to your family member the importance of classification in biology.

# Living Mysteries

In this lab, you will discover how some familiar mammals are classified.

## Problem

How does a taxonomic key help you classify living things?

## Skills Focus

observing, inferring, classifying

## Materials

pencil          paper

## Procedure

1. Observe the five organisms labeled A through E. All of these organisms belong to the class known as mammals, a group that includes you and many of the animals that are most familiar to you. Each of these mammals belongs to a different order of mammals.

2. Examine the paired statements in the taxonomic key for mammals. Begin at Step 1 to identify the order to which the mammal in photograph A belongs. Because the animal in photograph A does not have five digits or hands with flexible thumbs, go to Step 2. Keep following the key until you identify this mammal's order.

3. Use the key to identify the order to which the mammals in photographs B through E belong.

## Taxonomic Key for Mammals

| Step 1 | | |
|---|---|---|
| 1a. | Have five digits on all limbs, and hands with flexible thumbs | Primates (includes monkeys, chimpanzees, and humans) |
| 1b. | Do not have five digits on all limbs, and hands with flexible thumbs | Go to Step 2. |
| **Step 2** | | |
| 2a. | Have limbs with claws or nails, not hooves | Go to Step 3. |
| 2b. | Have limbs with hooves, not claws or nails | Go to Step 4. |
| **Step 3** | | |
| 3a. | Have long muscular trunks | Proboscidea (includes all types of elephants) |
| 3b. | Have sharp teeth for biting and tearing flesh | Carnivora (includes lions, bears, and raccoons) |
| **Step 4** | | |
| 4a. | Have limbs with an even number of hooved toes | Artiodactyla (includes antelopes, sheep and cows) |
| 4b. | Have limbs with an odd number of hooved toes | Perissodactyla (includes horses and rhinoceroses) |

## Analyze and Conclude

1. For each organism in the photographs, name the order of mammals to which it belongs.
2. Why is it important that the pair of statements at Step 1 be opposites?
3. Could you use this taxonomic key to classify animals that are not mammals? Explain.
4. Could you use this key to classify different types of carnivores, such as foxes, skunks, and walruses? Explain.

5. **Think About It** Based on your answers to questions 3 and 4, what can you infer about the limits of specific taxonomic keys?

## More to Explore

Try making a taxonomic key to sort four or five everyday objects such as writing implements or shoes. Try out your key on a partner to test it. Make any necessary changes. Then, exchange keys with a classmate. Use the keys to sort the selected objects.

# SECTION
# ④ The Six Kingdoms

## DISCOVER

### Which Organism Goes Where?

1.  Your teacher will give you some organisms to observe. Two of the organisms are classified in the same kingdom.

2. Observe the organisms. Decide which organisms might belong in the same kingdom. Write the reasons for your decision. Wash your hands after handling the organisms.

3. Discuss your decision and reasoning with your classmates.

### Think It Over

*Forming Operational Definitions* What characteristics do you think define the kingdom into which you placed the two organisms?

### GUIDE FOR READING

◆ What are the six kingdoms into which all organisms are grouped?

*Reading Tip* Before you read the section, make a list of the headings. As you read, list the characteristics of organisms in each kingdom.

When Linnaeus developed his system of classification, there were two kingdoms: plant and animal. But, the use of the microscope led to the discovery of new organisms and the identification of differences among cells. A two-kingdom system was no longer useful. **Today, the system of classification includes six kingdoms: archaebacteria, eubacteria, protists, fungi, plants, and animals.** Organisms are placed into kingdoms based on their type of cells, their ability to make food, and the number of cells in their bodies.

## Archaebacteria

In 1983, scientists took a water sample from a spot deep in the Pacific Ocean where hot gases and molten rock boiled into the ocean from Earth's interior. To their surprise, they discovered unicellular organisms in the sample. Today, scientists classify these organisms in a kingdom called Archaebacteria (ahr kee bak TEER ee uh), which means "ancient bacteria."

Archaebacteria can be either autotrophic or heterotrophic. Some live on the ocean floor, some in salty water, and some in hot springs. Don't be alarmed, but some even live in your intestines.

**Figure 17** Heat-loving archaebacteria thrive in this hot spring in Yellowstone National Park.

Archaebacteria are **prokaryotes** (proh KAR ee ohtz), organisms whose cells lack a nucleus. A **nucleus** (NOO klee us) (plural *nuclei*) is a dense area in a cell that contains nucleic acids—the chemical instructions that direct the cell's activities. In prokaryotes, nucleic acids are not contained within a nucleus.

## Eubacteria

What do the bacteria that produce yogurt have in common with the bacteria that give you strep throat? They both belong to the kingdom known as Eubacteria (yoo bak TEER ee uh). Like archaebacteria, eubacteria are unicellular prokaryotes. And like archaebacteria, some eubacteria are autotrophs while others are heterotrophs. Eubacteria are classified in their own kingdom, however, because their chemical makeup is different from that of archaebacteria.

Unlike some eubacteria, such as those that cause strep throat, most eubacteria are helpful. Some produce vitamins, some produce foods like yogurt, and some recycle essential chemicals, such as nitrogen.

☑ *Checkpoint* *How are eubacteria similar to archaebacteria? How do they differ?*

## Protists

Slime molds, like the ones that frightened people near Dallas, are protists (PROH tists). The protist kingdom is sometimes called the "odds and ends" kingdom because its members are so different from one another. For example, some protists are autotrophs, while others are heterotrophs. Also, although most protists are unicellular, some, such as the organisms that are commonly called seaweeds, are multicellular.

You may be wondering why those protists that are unicellular are not classified in one of the kingdoms of bacteria. It is because, unlike bacteria, protists are **eukaryotes** (yoo KAR ee ohtz)—organisms with cells that contain nuclei.

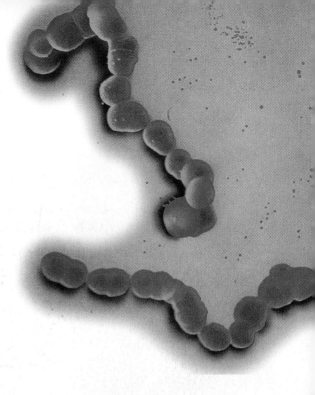

**Figure 18** Most eubacteria are helpful. However, these eubacteria are *Streptococci,* which can give you strep throat! *Classifying What characteristics do eubacteria share?*

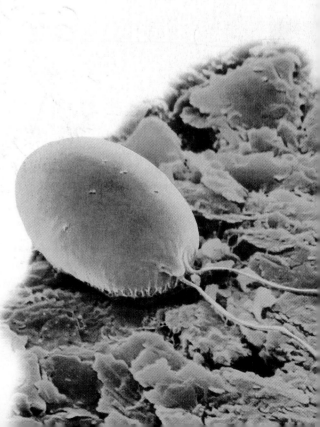

**Figure 19** The protist kingdom contains diverse organisms. This unicellular green protist, which lives in fresh water, is called *Chlamydomonas.*

## Fungi

If you have ever seen mushrooms, you have seen fungi (FUN jy). Mushrooms, molds, and mildew are all fungi. Most fungi are multicellular eukaryotes. A few, such as yeast, are unicellular eukaryotes. Fungi are found almost everywhere on land, but only a few live in fresh water. All fungi are heterotrophs. Most fungi feed on dead or decaying organisms. The cuplike fungus you see in Figure 20 obtains its food from the parts of plants that are decaying in the soil.

## Plants

Dandelions on a lawn, mosses in a forest, and tomatoes in a garden are familiar kinds of plants. Plants are all multicellular eukaryotes. In addition, plants are autotrophs that make their own food. Without plants, life on Earth would not exist. Plants feed almost all of the heterotrophs on Earth. The plant kingdom includes a variety of organisms. Some plants produce flowers, while others do not. Some plants, such as a giant sequoia tree, can grow very tall. Others, like mosses, never grow taller than a few centimeters.

## Animals

A dog, a flea on the dog's ear, and a rabbit the dog chases have much in common because all are animals. All animals are multicellular eukaryotes. In addition, all animals are heterotrophs. Animals have different adaptations that allow them to locate food, capture it, eat it, and digest it. Members of the animal kingdom are found in diverse environments on Earth.

**Figure 20** The animal you see peeking out of this cuplike fungus is a poison arrow frog. These organisms live in the forests of Central America. *Interpreting Photographs Which organisms in the photograph are heterotrophs?*

## Section 4 Review

1. List the six kingdoms into which all organisms are classified.
2. Which two kingdoms include only prokaryotes?
3. Which kingdoms include only heterotrophic organisms?
4. **Thinking Critically Classifying** In a rain forest, you see an unfamiliar green organism. As you watch, an ant walks onto one of its cuplike leaves. The leaf closes and traps the ant. Do you have enough information to classify this organism? Why or why not?

**Check Your Progress**

CHAPTER PROJECT
1

Now that you have completed your observations, analyze your data. Conclude whether your object is alive. Then review what you learned about the six kingdoms. Which kingdom does your object belong in or most resemble? (*Hint: Recall that an organism's nutrition is an important distinction among some of the kingdoms. How did your mystery object obtain its food?*)

## SECTION 1 — What Is Life?

**Key Ideas**

◆ All living things have a cellular organization, contain similar chemicals, use energy, grow and develop, respond to their surroundings, and reproduce.

◆ Organisms arise from other organisms similar to themselves.

◆ All living things must satisfy their basic needs for energy, water, living space, and stable internal conditions.

**Key Terms**

organism                variable
cell                    autotroph
unicellular             heterotroph
multicellular           homeostasis
development
stimulus
response
reproduce
spontaneous generation
controlled experiment

## SECTION 2 — The Origin of Life

INTEGRATING EARTH SCIENCE

**Key Ideas**

◆ Nitrogen, water vapor, carbon dioxide, and methane were probably the most abundant gases in Earth's atmosphere 3.6 billion years ago. Today the major gases are nitrogen and oxygen.

◆ Scientists hypothesize that over millions of years, the small chemical units of life formed in Earth's oceans. Some joined to form the large chemical building blocks found in cells.

**Key Term**

fossil

## SECTION 3 — Classifying Organisms

**Key Ideas**

◆ Biologists use classification to organize living things into groups so that the organisms are easy to study.

◆ Carolus Linnaeus devised a system of naming organisms called binomial nomenclature.

◆ Today, organisms are classified into seven levels: kingdom, phylum, class, order, family, genus, and species.

◆ Species with similar evolutionary histories are classified more closely together.

**Key Terms**

classification
taxonomy
binomial
  nomenclature
genus
species
evolution
taxonomic key

## SECTION 4 — The Six Kingdoms

**Key Ideas**

◆ All organisms are grouped into six kingdoms: archaebacteria, eubacteria, protists, fungi, plants, and animals.

◆ Some characteristics used to classify organisms into kingdoms are cell structure, the way organisms obtain food, and the number of cells in organisms.

**Key Terms**

prokaryote          nucleus          eukaryote

USING THE INTERNET

www.science-explorer.phschool.com

ACTIVITY

## Reviewing Content

 *For more review of key concepts, see the Interactive Student Tutorial CD-ROM.*

### Multiple Choice

*Choose the letter of the answer that best completes each statement.*

1. The idea that life could spring from nonliving matter is called
   a. development.
   b. spontaneous generation.
   c. homeostasis.
   d. evolution.

2. Which gas was not part of Earth's atmosphere 3.6 billion years ago?
   a. methane          b. nitrogen
   c. oxygen           d. water vapor

3. The science of placing organisms into groups based on shared characteristics is called
   a. development.     b. biology.
   c. taxonomy.        d. evolution.

4. A genus is divided into
   a. species.         b. phyla.
   c. families.        d. classes.

5. Which organisms have cells that do not contain nuclei?
   a. protists         b. archaebacteria
   c. plants           d. fungi

### True or False

*If the statement is true, write true. If it is false, change the underlined word or words to make the statement true.*

6. Your first teeth fall out and are replaced by permanent teeth. This is an example of <u>development</u>.

7. When you eat salad, you are acting like an <u>autotroph</u>.

8. The first organisms on Earth were probably <u>heterotrophs</u>.

9. <u>Aristotle</u> devised a system of naming organisms that is called binomial nomenclature.

10. The process by which organisms gradually change over a long period of time is called <u>evolution</u>.

## Checking Concepts

11. Your friend thinks that plants are not alive because they do not move. How would you respond to your friend?

12. Describe where Earth's early organisms lived, and how they obtained food.

13. What are the advantages of identifying an organism by its scientific name?

14. What evidence do scientists use to learn about the evolutionary history of a species?

15. What is the major difference between fungi and plants?

16. **Writing to Learn** Write a paragraph that describes how your pet, or a friend's pet, meets its needs as a living thing.

## Thinking Visually

17. **Concept Map** Copy the concept map about the needs of organisms onto a separate sheet of paper. Then complete it and add a title. (For more on concept maps, see the Skills Handbook.)

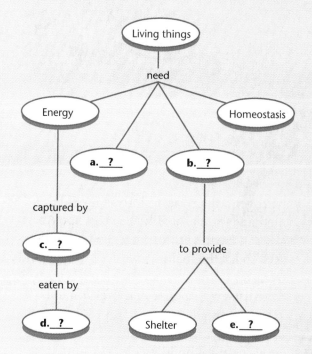

## Applying Skills

*A student designed an experiment to test how light affects the growth of plants. Refer to the illustrations below to answer Questions 18–21.*

**18. Controlling Variables** Is this a controlled experiment? If not, why not? If so, identify the variable.

**19. Developing Hypotheses** What hypothesis might this experiment be testing?

**20. Predicting** Based on what you know about plants, predict how each plant will have changed after two weeks.

**21. Designing Experiments** Design a controlled experiment to determine whether the amount of water that a plant receives affects its growth.

## Thinking Critically

**22. Applying Concepts** How do you know that a robot is not alive?

**23. Classifying** Which two of the following organisms are most closely related: *Entamoeba histolytica, Escherichia coli, Entamoeba coli*? Explain your answer.

**24. Relating Cause and Effect** When people believed that spontaneous generation occurred, there was a recipe for making mice: Place a dirty shirt and a few wheat grains in an open pot; wait three weeks. List the reasons why this recipe might have worked. How could you demonstrate that spontaneous generation was not responsible for the appearance of mice?

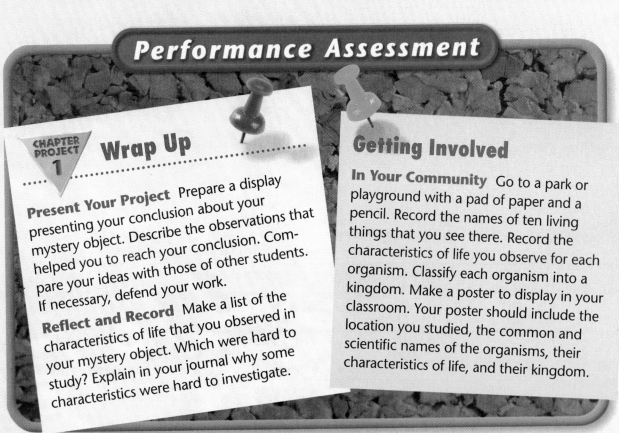

# Performance Assessment

**CHAPTER PROJECT 1** **Wrap Up**

**Present Your Project** Prepare a display presenting your conclusion about your mystery object. Describe the observations that helped you to reach your conclusion. Compare your ideas with those of other students. If necessary, defend your work.

**Reflect and Record** Make a list of the characteristics of life that you observed in your mystery object. Which were hard to study? Explain in your journal why some characteristics were hard to investigate.

**Getting Involved**

**In Your Community** Go to a park or playground with a pad of paper and a pencil. Record the names of ten living things that you see there. Record the characteristics of life you observe for each organism. Classify each organism into a kingdom. Make a poster to display in your classroom. Your poster should include the location you studied, the common and scientific names of the organisms, their characteristics of life, and their kingdom.

# CHAPTER 2 Viruses and Bacteria

If you've ever had chicken pox, this virus was responsible for your illness.

## WHAT'S AHEAD

### SECTION 1 Viruses

Discover **Can You Cure a Cold?**
Try This **Modeling a Virus**
Skills Lab **How Many Viruses Fit on a Pin?**

### SECTION 2 Bacteria

Discover **How Quickly Can Bacteria Multiply?**
Sharpen Your Skills **Graphing**
Try This **Bacteria for Breakfast**
Real-World Lab **Do Disinfectants Work?**

*Integrating Health*

### SECTION 3 Viruses, Bacteria, and Your Health

Discover **How Do Infectious Diseases Spread?**

46 ◆ A

# Be a
# Disease Detective

The virus pictured on this page may look harmless, but it's not. If you've ever had chicken pox, you've experienced it firsthand. Soon after the virus enters your body, red blotches appear on your skin, and you begin to itch. The chicken pox virus as well as many other viruses and bacteria cause diseases that pass from person to person. In this chapter, you will learn about viruses and bacteria, and how they affect other living things.

Not too long ago, catching certain viral and bacterial "childhood diseases" was a routine part of growing up. Those diseases included chicken pox, mumps, and pertussis (whooping cough), as well as others. In this project, you will select one childhood disease to investigate. You'll then survey people of all ages to learn who has had the disease. You'll also find out what people of different generations know about the disease.

**Your Goal**  To survey people of different ages to find out what they know about a childhood disease.

To complete this project successfully, you must
- ◆ select and research one disease to learn more about it
- ◆ prepare a questionnaire to survey people about their knowledge and experience with the disease
- ◆ question a total of 30 people in different age groups, and report any patterns that you find

**Get Started**  With several classmates, make a list of childhood diseases. Choose one disease for your survey. Do some research to find out more about the disease. Also write down the steps involved in carrying out a survey. What questions will you need to ask? How will you select the people for your survey? Draft your questionnaire.

**Check Your Progress**  You'll be working on this project as you study this chapter. To keep your project on track, look for Check Your Progress boxes at the following points.

**Section 1 Review**, page 54: Write your questionnaire, and identify the people to survey.

**Section 3 Review**, page 73: Analyze your survey results and look for patterns.

**Wrap Up**  At the end of the chapter (page 77), you will present your survey results to your classmates.

DISCOVER

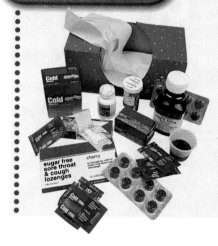

## Can You Cure a Cold?

1. Look at the cold medications that your teacher displays. You may have used some of these products when you had a cold.

2. Read the ingredient labels on the products. Read the product claims.

3. Decide which medication you would use if you had a cold. Record the reasons for your choice of product.

**Think It Over**

*Inferring* Do medications cure colds? Explain your answer.

### GUIDE FOR READING

◆ Why are viruses considered to be nonliving?

◆ What is the basic structure of a virus?

◆ How do viruses multiply?

*Reading Tip* As you read, use the headings to outline information about the characteristics of viruses.

It is a dark and quiet night. An enemy spy slips silently across the border. Invisible to the guards, the spy creeps cautiously along the edge of the road, heading toward the command center. Undetected, the spy sneaks by the center's security system and reaches the door. Breaking into the control room, the spy takes command of the central computer. The enemy is in control.

Moments later the command center's defenses finally activate. Depending on the enemy's strength and cunning, the defenses may squash the invasion before much damage is done. Otherwise the enemy will win and take over the territory.

## What Is a Virus?

Although this spy story may read like a movie script, it describes events that can occur in your body. The spy acts very much like a virus invading an organism. A **virus** is a small, nonliving particle that invades and then reproduces inside a living cell.

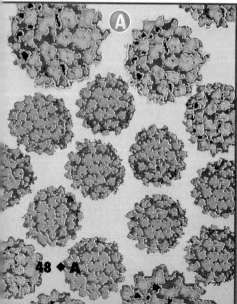

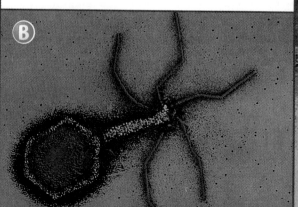

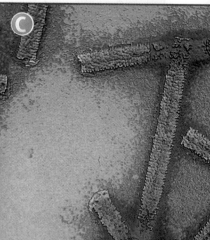

Biologists consider viruses to be nonliving because viruses are not cells. Viruses do not use energy to grow or to respond to their surroundings. Viruses also cannot make food, take in food, or produce wastes.

The only way in which viruses are like organisms is in their ability to multiply. But, although viruses can multiply, they do so differently than organisms. Viruses can only multiply when they are inside a living cell. The organism that a virus enters and multiplies inside is called a host. A **host** is a living thing that provides a source of energy for a virus or an organism. Organisms that live on or in a host and cause harm to the host are called **parasites** (PA ruh syts). Almost all viruses act like parasites because they destroy the cells in which they multiply.

No organisms are safe from viruses. Viruses can infect the organisms of all six kingdoms—archaebacteria, eubacteria, protists, fungi, plants, and animals. Each virus, however, can enter, or infect, only a few types of cells in a few specific species. For example, most cold viruses only infect cells in the nose and throat of humans. The tobacco mosaic virus only infects the leaf cells of tobacco plants.

✓ *Checkpoint* *When you have a cold, are you the host or the parasite?*

## Naming Viruses

Because viruses are not alive, scientists do not use binomial nomenclature to name them. Instead, scientists may name a virus, such as the polio virus, after the disease it causes. Other viruses are named for the organisms they infect, as is the case with the tomato mosaic virus, which infects tomato plants. Scientists named the Ebola virus after the place in Africa where it was first found. And scientists sometimes name viruses after people. The Epstein-Barr virus, for example, was named for the two scientists who first identified the virus that causes the disease known as infectious mononucleosis.

**Figure 1** Viruses are tiny nonliving particles that invade and reproduce inside living cells. Viruses can infect the organisms of all six kingdoms. **A.** Papilloma viruses cause warts to form on human skin. **B.** This virus, called a bacteriophage, infects bacteria. **C.** Tobacco mosaic viruses infect tobacco plants. **D.** The rabies virus infects nerve cells in certain animals. **E.** The blue circles in this photo are viruses that cause German measles in humans.

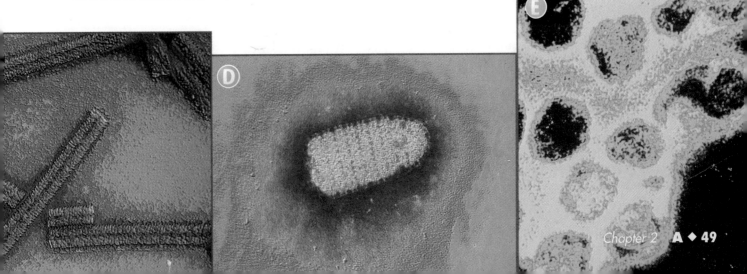

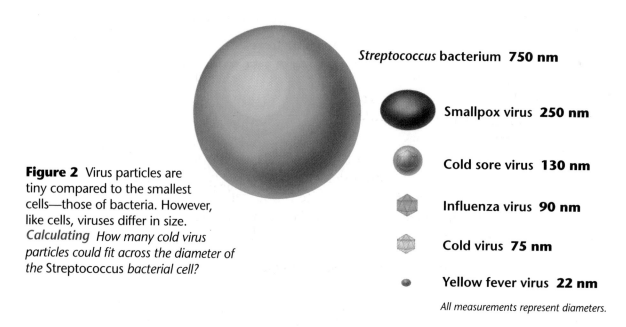

*Streptococcus* bacterium **750 nm**

Smallpox virus **250 nm**

Cold sore virus **130 nm**

Influenza virus **90 nm**

Cold virus **75 nm**

Yellow fever virus **22 nm**

*All measurements represent diameters.*

**Figure 2** Virus particles are tiny compared to the smallest cells—those of bacteria. However, like cells, viruses differ in size. *Calculating* How many cold virus particles could fit across the diameter of the *Streptococcus* bacterial cell?

## The Shapes and Sizes of Viruses

As you can see from the photographs in Figure 1, viruses vary widely in shape. Some viruses are round, while some others are rod-shaped. Other viruses have bricklike, threadlike, or bulletlike shapes. There are even some viruses, such as the bacteriophage in Figure 1B, that have complex, robotlike shapes. A **bacteriophage** (bak TEER ee oh fayj) is a virus that infects bacteria. In fact, its name means "bacteria eater."

Just as viruses vary in shape, they also vary in size. Viruses are smaller than cells and cannot be seen with the microscopes you use in school. Viruses are so small that they are measured in units called nanometers (nm). One nanometer is one billionth of a meter (m). The smallest viruses, such as yellow fever viruses, are about 22 nanometers in diameter. The largest viruses, such as smallpox viruses, are about 250 nanometers in diameter. Most viruses measure between 50 and 60 nanometers in diameter. The smallest cells, those of bacteria, are much larger than the average virus, as you can see in Figure 2.

## Structure of Viruses

Although the viruses in Figure 1 may look very different, they all have a similar structure. **All viruses have two basic parts: an outer coat that protects the virus and an inner core made of genetic material.** A virus's genetic material contains the instructions for making new viruses. Figure 3 shows the basic structure of a virus. The structure might remind you of a chocolate-covered candy. The outer coat of a virus is like the chocolate on the outside of a candy. The inner core is like the gooey filling inside the candy.

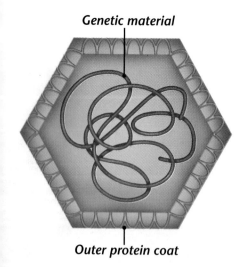

*Genetic material*

*Outer protein coat*

**Figure 3** All viruses have a similar structure. They have an outer coat made of protein and an inner core that contains genetic material.

The coat of a virus plays an important role during the invasion of a host cell. This coat is made of proteins. Each virus contains unique proteins in its coat. The shape of the proteins allows the virus's coat to attach to, or lock onto, certain cells in the host. Like keys, a virus's proteins only fit into certain "locks," or proteins, on the surface of a host's cells. Figure 4 shows how the lock-and-key action works. Because this action is highly specific, a certain virus will attach to only one or a few types of cells. For example, the human immunodeficiency virus, or HIV, can only attach to one kind of human white blood cell. This blood cell is the one with proteins on its surface that complement, or "fit", those on the virus.

☑ *Checkpoint* *Why does a virus only invade a specific kind of cell?*

## How Viruses Multiply

After a virus attaches to a cell, it enters the cell. **Once inside, a virus's genetic material takes over the cell's functions. The genetic material directs the cell to produce the virus's proteins and genetic material. These proteins and genetic material are then assembled into new viruses.** Some viruses take over the cell's functions immediately. Other viruses wait for a while.

**Active Viruses**  After entering a cell, an active virus immediately goes into action. The virus's genetic material takes over the cell's functions, and the cell quickly begins to produce the virus's proteins and genetic material. Then these parts assemble into new viruses. Like a photocopy machine left in the "on" position, the invaded cell makes copy after copy of new viruses. When it

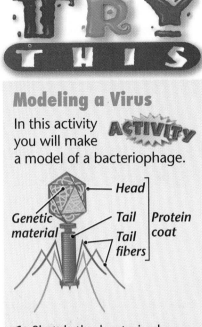

## Modeling a Virus

In this activity **ACTIVITY** you will make a model of a bacteriophage.

Head
Genetic material
Tail
Tail fibers
Protein coat

1. Sketch the bacteriophage above in your notebook.
2. Decide what materials you will use to model the virus.
3. Build your model.

**Making Models**  Label your model. On each label, state the role that the part plays in infecting a host cell.

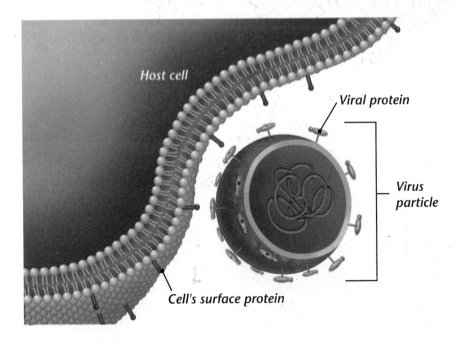

Host cell
Viral protein
Virus particle
Cell's surface protein

**Figure 4** The shape of the proteins in a virus's coat determines what type of cell the virus will infect. The proteins fit together with the cell's proteins in the same way that a key fits a lock. Once attached, the virus can inject its genetic material into the cell.

is full of new viruses, the host cell bursts open and releases the new viruses. In *Exploring How Viruses Multiply*, you can follow how an active virus multiplies.

**Hidden Viruses** Some viruses function differently than active viruses after entering a cell—at least for a while. The genetic material of these viruses enters a host cell. Then, instead of going into action like an active virus does, the virus's genetic material becomes part of the cell's genetic material. The virus does not appear to affect the cell's functions. The virus's genetic material may stay in this inactive state for a long time. Then, for reasons that scientists do not yet fully understand, the virus's genetic material suddenly becomes active. It takes over the cell's

# EXPLORING *How Viruses Multiply*

**A**ctive viruses enter cells and immediately begin to multiply, leading to the quick death of the invaded cells. Other viruses "hide" for a while inside the host cells before they become active.

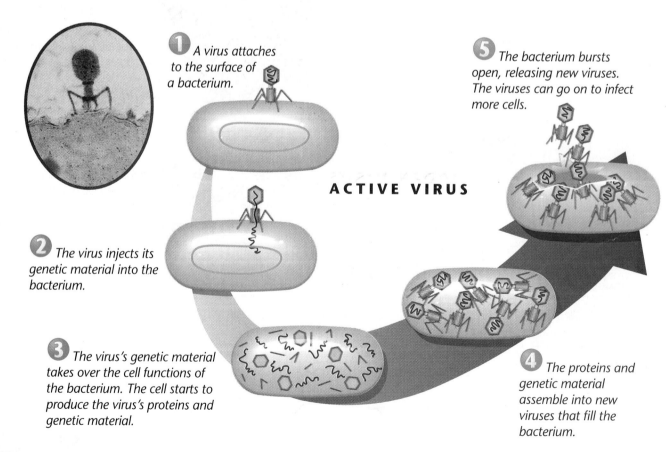

**1** *A virus attaches to the surface of a bacterium.*

**2** *The virus injects its genetic material into the bacterium.*

**3** *The virus's genetic material takes over the cell functions of the bacterium. The cell starts to produce the virus's proteins and genetic material.*

**ACTIVE VIRUS**

**5** *The bacterium bursts open, releasing new viruses. The viruses can go on to infect more cells.*

**4** *The proteins and genetic material assemble into new viruses that fill the bacterium.*

functions in much the same way that active viruses do. In a short time, the cell is full of new viruses, and it bursts open to release them. Look at *Exploring How Viruses Multiply* to see how a hidden virus multiplies.

The virus that causes cold sores in humans is an example of a hidden virus. The virus can remain inactive for months or years inside the nerve cells in the face. While hidden, the virus causes no symptoms. When it becomes active, the virus causes a swollen, painful sore to form near the mouth. Strong sunlight and stress are two factors that scientists believe may activate a cold sore virus. After an active period, the virus once again "hides" in the nerve cells until it becomes active once again.

✓ *Checkpoint* *Give one example of a hidden virus.*

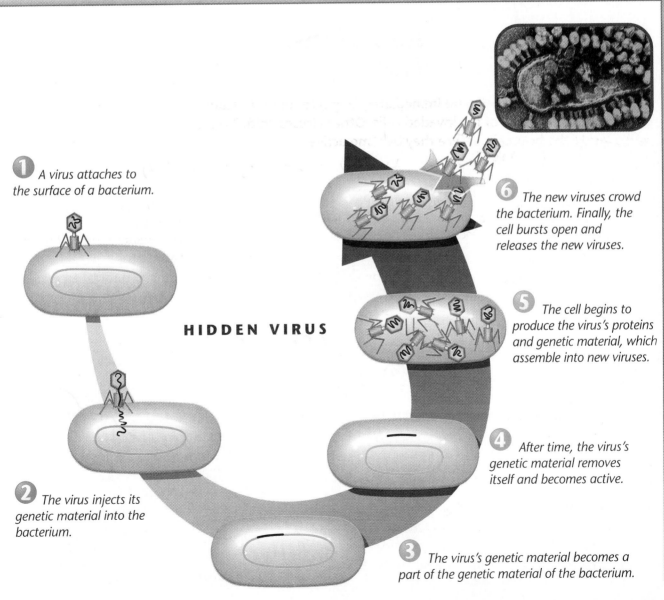

**HIDDEN VIRUS**

**1** *A virus attaches to the surface of a bacterium.*

**2** *The virus injects its genetic material into the bacterium.*

**3** *The virus's genetic material becomes a part of the genetic material of the bacterium.*

**4** *After time, the virus's genetic material removes itself and becomes active.*

**5** *The cell begins to produce the virus's proteins and genetic material, which assemble into new viruses.*

**6** *The new viruses crowd the bacterium. Finally, the cell bursts open and releases the new viruses.*

## Viruses and the Living World

If you've ever had a cold sore or been sick with a cold or flu, you know that viruses can cause disease in organisms. Some diseases, such as colds, are mild—people are sick for a short time but soon recover. Other diseases, such as acquired immunodeficiency syndrome, or AIDS, can cause death.

Viruses also cause diseases in organisms other than humans. For example, the rice dwarf virus stunts the growth of rice plants, resulting in lower yields of this food crop. Alfalfa mosaic disease kills alfalfa plants, an important food source for horses, cattle, and other farm animals. House pets, such as dogs and cats, can get a deadly viral disease called distemper. Dogs, foxes, and raccoons are a few of the animals that rabies viruses can infect. If a rabid animal bites a person, it can transmit rabies to the person.

**Figure 5** The beautiful striped pattern on this Rembrandt tulip was originally caused by the tulip mosaic virus.

**INTEGRATING TECHNOLOGY** By now you might be thinking that viruses do no good. But the news about viruses isn't all bad. Scientists are putting viruses to use in a new technique called gene therapy. In gene therapy, scientists take advantage of a virus's ability to get inside a host cell. They add important genetic material to a virus and then use the virus as a "messenger service" to deliver the genetic material to cells that need it. Scientists have used gene therapy on people with disorders such as cystic fibrosis (SIS tik fy BRO sis). People with cystic fibrosis do not have the genetic material they need to keep their lungs functioning properly. Gene therapy shows some promise to become a medical treatment for cystic fibrosis and other disorders.

## Section 1 Review

1. Explain why biologists consider viruses to be nonliving.
2. Describe the basic structure of a virus.
3. Compare the two ways that viruses can multiply.
4. **Thinking Critically Inferring** Scientists hypothesize that viruses could not have existed on Earth before organisms, such as bacteria, appeared. Use what you know about viruses to support this hypothesis.

### Check Your Progress

CHAPTER PROJECT 2

By now, you should have a draft of the questions you will ask in your survey. Have your teacher review your questions. Then begin your survey. (*Hint*: Design the questionnaire so that you can easily record and tally the responses. Test your survey on a few people you know to make sure the questions are clear.)

# How Many Viruses Fit on a Pin?

**I**n this lab, you will make models to help you investigate the size of viruses.

## Problem

How many viruses could fit on the head of a pin?

## Materials

straight pin
pencil
scissors
calculator (optional)

long strips of paper
meter stick
tape

## Procedure

1. Examine the head of a straight pin. Write a prediction about the number of viruses that could fit on the pinhead. **CAUTION:** *Avoid pushing the pin against anyone's skin.*
2. Assume that the pinhead has a diameter of about 1 mm. If the pinhead were enlarged 10,000 times, its diameter would measure 10 m. Create a model of the pinhead by cutting and taping together narrow strips of paper to make a strip that is 10 m long. The strip of paper represents the diameter of the enlarged pinhead.
3. Lay the 10-m strip of paper on the floor of your classroom or in the hall. Imagine creating a large circle that had the strip as its diameter. The circle would be the pinhead at the enlarged size. Calculate the area of the enlarged pinhead using this formula:

$$\text{Area} = \pi \times \text{radius}^2$$

Remember that you can find the radius by dividing the diameter by 2.

4. A virus particle may measure 200 nm on each side (1 nm equals a billionth of a meter). If the virus were enlarged 10,000 times, each side would measure 0.002 m. Cut out a square 0.002 m by 0.002 m to serve as a model for a virus. *(Hint:* 0.002 m = 2 mm)
5. Next, find the area in meters of one virus particle at the enlarged size. Remember that the area of a square equals side × side.
6. Now divide the area of the pinhead that you calculated in Step 3 by the area of one virus particle to find out how many viruses could fit on the pinhead.
7. Exchange your work with a partner, and check each other's calculations. Make any corrections that are necessary.

## Analyze and Conclude

1. Approximately how many viruses can fit on the head of a pin?
2. How did your calculation compare with your prediction? If the two numbers were very different, explain why they were different.
3. What did you learn about the size of viruses by magnifying both the viruses and pinheads to 10,000 times their actual size?
4. **Think About It** Why do scientists sometimes make and use enlarged models of very small things such as viruses?

## More to Explore

Think of another everyday object that you could use to model some other facts about viruses, such as their shapes or how they infect cells. Describe your model and explain why the object would be a good choice.

# SECTION 2 Bacteria

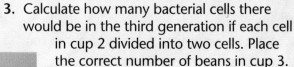

## DISCOVER

### How Quickly Can Bacteria Multiply?

1. Your teacher will give you some beans and paper cups. Number the cups 1 through 8. Each bean will represent a bacterial cell.

2. Put one bean into cup 1 to represent the first generation of bacteria. Approximately every 20 minutes, a bacterial cell reproduces by dividing into two cells. Put two beans into cup 2 to represent the second generation of bacteria.

3. Calculate how many bacterial cells there would be in the third generation if each cell in cup 2 divided into two cells. Place the correct number of beans in cup 3.

4. Repeat Step 3 five more times. All the cups should now contain beans. How many cells are in the eighth generation? How much time has elapsed since the first generation?

#### Think It Over

**Inferring** Based on this activity, explain why the number of bacteria can increase rapidly in a short period of time.

---

### GUIDE FOR READING

◆ How are the cells of bacteria different from those of all other organisms?

◆ What positive roles do bacteria play in people's lives?

*Reading Tip* Before you read, make a list of the boldfaced vocabulary words in the section. Predict the meaning of each word. As you read, check your predictions.

You may not know it, but seconds after you were born, tiny organisms surrounded and invaded your body. Today, millions of these organisms coat your skin. As you read this page, they swarm inside your nose, throat, and mouth. In fact, there are more of these organisms living in your mouth than there are people who are living on Earth. You don't see or feel these organisms because they are very small. But you cannot escape them. They are found nearly everywhere on Earth—in soil, rocks, Arctic ice, volcanoes, and in all living things. These organisms are bacteria.

### The Bacterial Cell

Although there are many bacteria on Earth, they were not discovered until the late 1600s. A Dutch businessman named Anton van Leeuwenhoek (LAY vuhn hook) found them by accident. Leeuwenhoek had a rather unusual hobby—making microscopes. One day, while he was using one of his microscopes to look at scrapings from his teeth, he saw some tiny organisms in the sample. However, because his microscopes were not very powerful, Leeuwenhoek could not see any details inside these tiny organisms.

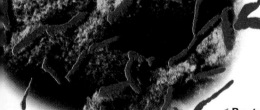

◀ Bacteria on the surface of a human tooth

If Leeuwenhoek had owned one of the high-powered microscopes in use today, he would have seen the single-celled organisms that are known as bacteria in detail. As you learned in Chapter 1, the cells of bacteria differ from the cells of other organisms in many ways. **Bacteria are prokaryotes. The genetic material in their cells is not contained in a nucleus.** In addition to lacking a nucleus, the cells of prokaryotes also lack many other structures that are found in the cells of eukaryotes. However, regardless of the structure of their cells, prokaryotes accomplish all tasks necessary for life. That is, each bacterial cell uses energy, grows and develops, responds to its surroundings, and reproduces.

**Cell Shapes** If you were to look at bacterial cells under a microscope, you would notice that bacterial cells have one of three basic shapes: spherical, rodlike, or spiral shaped. The shape of a bacterial cell helps scientists identify the type of bacteria. For example, bacteria that cause strep throat are spherical. Figure 6 shows the different shapes of bacterial cells.

**Cell Structures** The shape of a bacterial cell is determined by the chemical makeup of its outermost structure—the cell wall. Cell walls surround most bacterial cells. A bacterium's rigid cell wall helps to protect the cell.

Inside the cell wall is the cell membrane, which controls what materials pass into and out of the cell. The region inside the cell membrane, called the **cytoplasm** (SY toh plaz um), contains a gel-like material. Tiny structures called ribosomes are located in the cytoplasm. **Ribosomes** (RY buh sohmz) are chemical factories where proteins are produced. The cell's genetic material, which looks like a thick, tangled string, is also located in the cytoplasm. If you could untangle the genetic material, you would see that it forms a circular shape. The genetic material contains the instructions for all the cell's functions, such as how to produce proteins on the ribosomes.

**Figure 6** Bacteria have three basic shapes. **A.** Like the bacteria that cause strep throat, these *Staphylococcus aureus* bacteria are spherical. They represent over 30 percent of the bacteria that live on your skin. **B.** *Escherichia coli* bacteria have rodlike shapes. These bacteria are found in your intestines. **C.** *Borrelia burgdorferi* bacteria, which cause Lyme disease, are spiral-shaped.

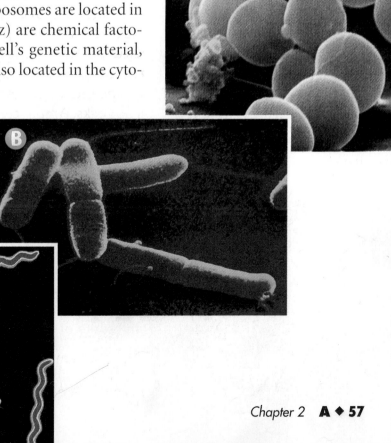

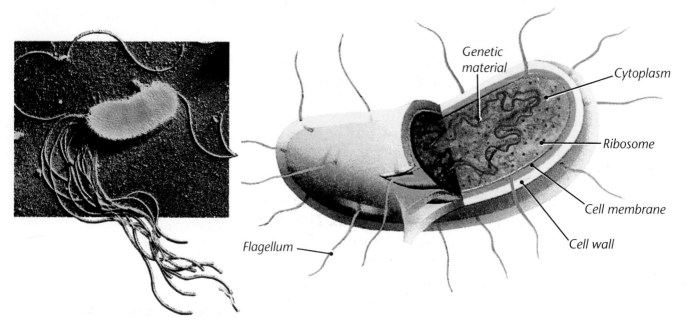

**Figure 7** The diagram shows the structures found in a typical bacterial cell. *Interpreting Photographs Which structures can you locate in the photograph of the bacterium? What roles do these structures play?*

Genetic material

Cytoplasm

Ribosome

Cell membrane

Cell wall

Flagellum

You can see the cell wall, cytoplasm, ribosomes, and genetic material in the bacterial cell in Figure 7. Another structure you see is a flagellum. A **flagellum** (fluh JEL um) (plural *flagella*) is a long, whiplike structure that extends out through the cell membrane and cell wall. Using a back and forth motion, a flagellum helps a cell to move, much as kicking your feet helps you to swim. A bacterial cell can have many flagella, one, or none. Bacteria that do not have flagella cannot move on their own. Instead, they depend on air, water currents, clothing, and other objects to carry them from one place to another.

## Two Kingdoms of Bacteria

Until recently, biologists grouped all bacteria together in a single kingdom on the basis of their similar cellular structure. However, although all bacteria look similar, some differ chemically. After analyzing the chemical differences, scientists have reclassified bacteria into two separate kingdoms—Archaebacteria and Eubacteria.

**Archaebacteria** As you learned in Chapter 1, the word *archaebacteria* means "ancient bacteria." And these bacteria are ancient! Archaebacteria already existed on Earth for billions of years before dinosaurs appeared. Scientists think that today's archaebacteria closely resemble Earth's first life forms.

Many archaebacteria live in extreme environments. They are found in such places as hot springs, where some thrive in water that is as hot as 110°C. Others live in environments that are as acidic as lemon juice. Some archaebacteria live in salty waters, such as Utah's Great Salt Lake. Archaebacteria also live in the intestines of animals, the mud at the bottom of swamps, and in sewage. It is the bacteria that produce the foul odors that you may associate with these places.

**Eubacteria** Unlike archaebacteria, most eubacteria do not live in extreme environments. However, they live everywhere else. For example, millions of eubacteria live on and in your body. Eubacteria coat your skin and swarm in your nose. Don't be alarmed. Most of them are either useful or harmless to you.

**INTEGRATING EARTH SCIENCE** Eubacteria help maintain some of Earth's physical conditions and thus help other organisms to survive. For example, some eubacteria are autotrophs that float near the surfaces of Earth's waters. These bacteria use the sun's energy to produce food and oxygen. Scientists think that billions of years ago autotrophic bacteria were responsible for adding oxygen to Earth's atmosphere. Today, the distant offspring of those bacteria help to keep Earth's current level of oxygen at 20 percent.

*Checkpoint* *Why are archaebacteria and eubacteria placed in separate kingdoms?*

## Reproduction in Bacteria

When bacteria have plenty of food, the right temperature, and other suitable conditions, they thrive and reproduce frequently. Under these ideal conditions, some bacteria can reproduce as often as once every 20 minutes. Fortunately, growing conditions for bacteria are rarely ideal. Otherwise, there would soon be no room on Earth for other organisms!

**Asexual Reproduction** Bacteria reproduce by **binary fission**, a process in which one cell divides to form two identical cells. Binary fission is a form of **asexual reproduction.** Asexual reproduction is a reproductive process that involves only one parent and produces offspring that are identical to the parent. In binary fission, the cell first duplicates its genetic material and then divides into two separate cells. Each new cell gets its own complete copy of the parent cell's genetic material as well as some of the parent's ribosomes and cytoplasm. Figure 8 shows a parent cell forming two new cells by binary fission.

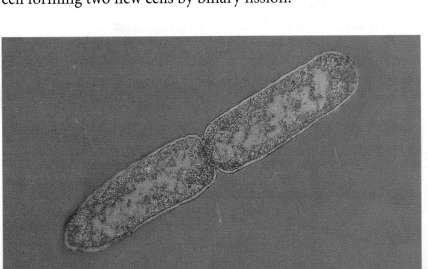

**Figure 8** Bacteria, such as this *Escherichia coli,* reproduce by binary fission. Each new cell is identical to the parent cell.

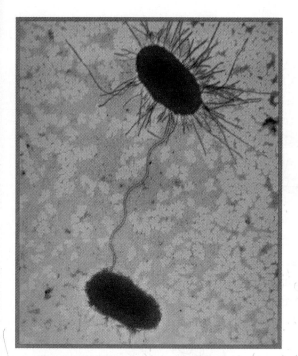

**Figure 9** In conjugation, one bacterium transfers some of its genetic material into another bacterium. *Observing* What structure allows the cells to transfer genetic material?

**Sexual Reproduction** Some bacteria, such as the ones in Figure 9, may at times undergo a simple form of sexual reproduction called conjugation. **Sexual reproduction** involves two parents who combine their genetic material to produce a new organism, which differs from both parents. During **conjugation** (kahn juh GAY shun), one bacterium transfers some of its genetic material into another bacterial cell through a thin, threadlike bridge that joins the two cells. After the transfer, the cells separate.

Conjugation results in bacteria with new combinations of genetic material. When these bacteria divide by binary fission, the new genetic material passes to the new cells. Conjugation does not increase the number of bacteria. However, it does result in the production of new bacteria, which are genetically different than the parent cells.

## Survival Needs

From the bacteria that live inside the craters of active volcanoes to those that live in the pores of your skin, all bacteria need certain things to survive. Bacteria must have a source of food, a way of breaking down the food to release the food's energy, and survival techniques when conditions in their surroundings become unfavorable.

**Obtaining Food** Some bacteria are autotrophs and make their own food. Autotrophic bacteria make food in one of two ways. Some autotrophic bacteria make food by capturing and using the sun's energy as plants do. Other autotrophic bacteria, such as those that live deep in the ocean, do not use the sun's energy. Instead, these bacteria use the energy from chemical substances in their environment to make their food.

Some bacteria are heterotrophs that obtain food by consuming autotrophs or other heterotrophs. Heterotrophic bacteria may consume a variety of foods—from milk and meat, which you might also eat, to the decaying leaves on a forest floor.

**Respiration** Like all organisms, bacteria need a constant supply of energy to carry out their functions. This energy comes from food. The process of breaking down food to release its energy is called **respiration**. Like many other organisms, most bacteria need oxygen to break down their food. But a few kinds of bacteria do not need oxygen for respiration. In fact, those bacteria die if oxygen is present in their surroundings. For them, oxygen is a poison that kills!

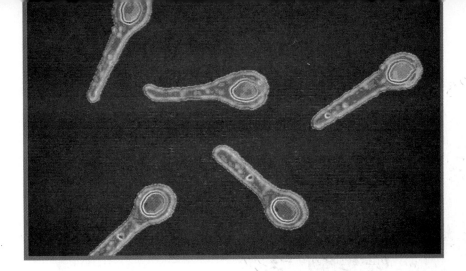

Figure 10 When conditions in the environment become unfavorable for growth, some bacteria form endospores. These endospores of *Clostridium tetani* can survive for years.

**Endospore Formation** Sometimes the conditions in the environment become unfavorable for the growth of bacteria. For example, food sources can disappear or wastes can poison the bacteria. Some bacteria can survive these harsh conditions by forming endospores like the ones you see in Figure 10. An **endospore** is a small, rounded, thick-walled, resting cell that forms inside a bacterial cell. It contains the cell's genetic material and some of its cytoplasm. Because endospores can resist freezing, heating, and drying, they can survive for many years. Endospores are also light—a breeze can lift and carry them to new places. If an endospore lands in a place where conditions are suitable, it opens up. Then the bacterium can begin to grow and multiply.

✓ *Checkpoint* *How do autotrophic bacteria obtain energy to make food?*

## Bacteria and The Living World

When you hear the word *bacteria*, you may think about getting sick. After all, strep throat, many ear infections, and other diseases are caused by bacteria. It is true that some bacteria cause diseases and other harmful effects. However, most bacteria are either harmless or helpful to people. In fact, in many ways, people depend on bacteria. **Bacteria are involved in fuel and food production, environmental recycling and cleanup, and the production of medicines.**

**Fuel** The next time you use natural gas to boil an egg, grill a hamburger, or heat your house, think of archaebacteria. The archaebacteria that live in oxygen-free environments, such as the thick mud at the bottom of lakes and swamps, produce a gas called methane during respiration. The methane produced by archaebacteria that died millions of years ago is the major component in about 20 percent of Earth's deposits of natural gas.

**Bacteria for Breakfast**

In this activity, you will observe helpful bacteria in a common food.

1. Put on your apron. Add water to plain yogurt to make a thin mixture.
2. With a plastic dropper, place a drop of the mixture on a glass slide.
3. Use another plastic dropper to add one drop of methylene blue dye to the slide. **CAUTION:** *This dye can stain your skin.*
4. Put a coverslip on the slide.
5. Observe the slide under both the low and high power lenses of a microscope.

*Observing* Draw a diagram of what you see under high power. Label any cell structures that you see.

**Food** Do you like cheese, yogurt, and apple cider? What about olives and sauerkraut? The activities of helpful bacteria produce all of these foods and more. For example, bacteria that grow in a liquid poured around fresh cucumbers turn the cucumbers into pickles. Bacteria that grow in apple cider change the cider to vinegar. Bacteria that grow in milk produce dairy products such as buttermilk, sour cream, yogurt, and cheeses.

However, some bacteria cause food to spoil when they break down the food's chemicals. Spoiled food usually smells or tastes foul and can make you very sick. Since ancient times, people have

## Bacteria and Foods of the World

Ancient cultures lacked refrigeration and other modern methods of preventing food spoilage. People in these cultures developed ways to use bacteria to preserve foods. You may enjoy some of these foods today.

### 1000 B.C. China

The Chinese salted vegetables and packed them in containers. Naturally-occurring bacteria fed on the vegetables and produced a sour taste. The salt pulled water out of the vegetables and left them crisp. These vegetables were part of the food rations given to workers who built the Great Wall of China.

| 3000 B.C. | 2000 B.C. | 1000 B.C. |
| --- | --- | --- |

### 2300 B.C. Egypt

Ancient Egyptians made cheese from milk. Cheesemaking begins when bacteria feed on the sugars in milk. The milk separates into solid curds and liquid whey. The curds are processed into cheeses, which keep longer than milk.

### 500 B.C. Mediterranean Sea Region

People who lived in the regions around the Mediterranean Sea chopped meat, seasoned it with salt and spices, rolled it, and hung it to dry. Bacteria in the drying meat gave unique flavors to the food. The rolled meat would keep for weeks in cool places.

developed ways to slow down food spoilage. They have used such methods as heating, refrigerating, drying, salting, or smoking foods. These methods help to preserve food by preventing the bacteria that cause spoiling from growing in the food.

**Environmental Recycling**  Do you recycle plastic, glass, and other materials? If you do, you have something in common with some heterotrophic eubacteria. These bacteria, which live in the soil, are **decomposers**—organisms that break down large chemicals in dead organisms into small chemicals. Decomposers are

*In Your Journal*

Find out more about one of these ancient food production methods and the culture that developed it. Write a report about the importance of the food to the culture.

### A.D. 1500
### The West Indies

People in the West Indies mixed beans from the cocoa plant with bacteria and other microorganisms, then dried and roasted them. The roasted beans were then brewed to produce a beverage with a chocolate flavor. The drink was served cold with honey, spices, and vanilla.

A.D. 1      A.D. 1000      A.D.. 2000

### A.D. 500
### China

The Chinese crushed soybeans with wheat, salt, bacteria, and other microorganisms. The microorganisms fed on the proteins in the wheat and soybeans. The salt pulled water out of the mixture. The protein-rich soy paste that remained was used to flavor foods. The soy sauce you may use today is made in a similar manner.

### A.D. 1850
### United States of America

Gold prospectors in California ate a bread called sourdough bread. The bacteria *Lactobacillus san francisco* gave the bread its sour taste. Each day before baking, cooks would set aside some dough that contained the bacteria to use in the next day's bread.

**Figure 11** Bacteria live in the swellings on the roots of this soybean plant. The bacteria convert nitrogen from the air into substances the plant needs. *Applying Concepts Why might farmers plant soybeans in a field that is low in nitrogen?*

"nature's recyclers"—they return basic chemicals to the environment for other living things to reuse. For example, in the fall, the leaves of many trees die and fall to the ground. Decomposing bacteria spend the next months breaking down the chemicals in the dead leaves. The broken-down chemicals mix with the soil, and can then be absorbed by the roots of nearby plants.

Other recycling eubacteria live in swellings on the roots of some plants, such as peanuts, peas, and soybeans. There, they convert nitrogen gas from the air into nitrogen compounds that the plants need to grow. The plants cannot convert nitrogen from the air into the nitrogen compounds they need. Therefore, the bacteria that live in the roots of plants help the plants to survive.

**Environmental Cleanup**  Some bacteria help to clean up Earth's land and water. Can you imagine having a bowl of oil for dinner instead of soup? Well, there are some bacteria that prefer the oil. They convert the dangerous chemicals in oil into harmless substances. Scientists have put these bacteria to work cleaning up oil spills in oceans and gasoline leaks in the soil under gas stations.

**Health and Medicine** You may find it hard to believe that many of the bacteria living in your body actually keep you healthy. In your digestive system, for example, your intestines teem with bacteria. This is a natural and healthy situation. Some of the bacteria help you digest your food. Some make vitamins that your body needs. Others compete for space with disease-

**Figure 12** Scientists use bacteria such as these *Ochrobactrum anthropi* to help clean up oil spills.

causing organisms. They prevent the harmful bacteria from attaching to your intestines and making you sick.

 **INTEGRATING TECHNOLOGY** Scientists have put some bacteria to work making medicines and other substances. People can use these substances to live healthy lives. The first medicine-producing bacteria were made in the 1970s. By manipulating the genetic material of bacteria, scientists engineered bacteria to produce human insulin. Although healthy people can make their own insulin, people with diabetes cannot. Many people with diabetes need to take insulin on a daily basis. Thanks to their fast rate of reproduction, large numbers of insulin-making bacteria can be grown in huge vats. The human insulin they produce is then purified and made into medicine.

## Section 2 Review

1. How is a bacterial cell different from the cells of other kinds of organisms?
2. List four ways in which bacteria are helpful to people.
3. What happens during binary fission?
4. Describe how a bacterium can survive when conditions are unfavorable for growth.
5. **Thinking Critically Applying Concepts** Why are some foods, such as milk, heated to high temperatures before they are bottled?

## Science at Home

With a family member, look around your kitchen for foods that are made using bacteria. Read the labels on the foods to see if the role of bacteria in the food's production is mentioned. Discuss with your family member the helpful roles that bacteria play in the lives of people.

# Do Disinfectants Work?

**W**hen your family goes shopping, you may buy cleaning products called disinfectants. Disinfectants kill microorganisms such as bacteria, which may cause infection or decay. In this lab, you will compare the effects of two different disinfectants.

## Problem

How well do disinfectants control the growth of bacteria?

## Skills Focus

observing, inferring, drawing conclusions

## Materials

clock
2 plastic droppers
2 household disinfectants
3 plastic petri dishes with sterile nutrient agar
wax pencil
transparent tape

## Procedure

1. Copy the data table into your notebook.
2. Work with a partner. Obtain 3 petri dishes containing sterile agar. Without opening them, use a wax pencil to label the bottoms "A," "B," and "C." Write your initials beside each letter.
3. Wash your hands thoroughly with soap, then run a fingertip across the surface of your worktable. Your partner should hold open the cover of petri dish A, while you run that fingertip gently across the agar in a zig-zag motion. Close the dish immediately.
4. Repeat Step 3 for dishes B and C.
5. Use a plastic dropper to transfer 2 drops of one disinfectant to the center of petri dish A. Open the cover just long enough to add the disinfectant to the dish. Close the cover immediately. Record the name of the disinfectant in your data table. **CAUTION:** *Do not inhale vapors from the disinfectant.*
6. Repeat Step 5 for dish B but add 2 drops of the second disinfectant. **CAUTION:** *Do not mix any disinfectants together.*
7. Do not add any disinfectant to dish C.
8. Tape down the covers of all 3 petri dishes so that they will remain tightly closed. Allow the 3 dishes to sit upright on your work surface for at least 5 minutes. **CAUTION:** *Do not open the petri dishes again.* Wash your hands with soap and water.
9. As directed by your teacher, store the petri dishes in a warm, dark place where they can remain for at least 3 days. Remove them only to make a brief examination each day.

## DATA TABLE

| Petri Dish | Disinfectant | Day 1 | Day 2 | Day 3 |
|---|---|---|---|---|
| A | | | | |
| B | | | | |
| C | | | | |

10. After one day, observe the contents of each dish without removing the covers. Estimate the percentage of the agar surface that shows any changes. Record your observations. Return the dishes to their storage place when you have finished making your observations. Wash your hands with soap.

11. Repeat Step 10 after the second day and again after the third day.

12. After you and your partner have made your last observations, return the petri dishes to your teacher unopened.

## Analyze and Conclude

1. How did the appearance of dish C change during the lab?

2. How did the appearance of dishes A and B compare with dish C? Explain any similarities or differences.

3. How did the appearance of dishes A and B compare with each other? How can you account for any differences?

4. Why was it important to set aside one petri dish that did not contain any disinfectant?

5. **Apply** Based on the results of this lab, what recommendation would you make to your family about the use of disinfectants? Where in the house do you think these products would be needed most?

## Design an Experiment

Go to a store and look at soap products that claim to be "antibacterial" soaps. How do their ingredients differ from other soaps? How do their prices compare? Design an experiment to test how well these products control the growth of bacteria.

## SECTION 3 Viruses, Bacteria, and Your Health

### DISCOVER · · · · · · · · · · · · · · · · · · · · · · · · · · · · · · · · · · · · · · · ACTIVITY · · ·

#### How Do Infectious Diseases Spread?

1. Put on goggles and plastic gloves. Your teacher will give you a plastic dropper and a plastic cup half filled with a liquid. Do not taste, smell, or touch the liquid.

2. In this activity, you will model how some diseases spread. Your teacher will signal the start of a "talking" period. Choose a classmate to talk with briefly. As you talk, exchange a dropperful of the liquid in your cup with your classmate.

3. At your teacher's signal, talk to another classmate. Exchange a dropperful of liquid.

4. Repeat Step 3 two more times.

5. Your teacher will add a few drops of a liquid to each student's cup. If your fluid turns pink, it indicates that you have "contracted a disease" from one of your classmates. Wash your hands when you have finished the activity.

**Think It Over**

*Predicting* How many more rounds would it take for everyone in your class to "become infected"? Use your prediction to explain why some diseases can spread quickly through a population.

---

### GUIDE FOR READING

◆ How do infectious diseases spread from person to person?

*Reading Tip* Before you read, rewrite the section's headings as questions. As you read, write answers to the questions.

It started last night with a tickle in the back of your throat. This morning, when you woke up, your nose felt stuffy. By lunchtime, your muscles started to ache. By the time the big game started after school, your mouth felt dry and your throat was scratchy. Now, in the seventh inning of the game, you feel awful. You're sneezing and talking like you have a clothespin on your nose. You can't seem to get warm, and you're shivering on the bench. You've caught a cold—or maybe more accurately, a cold has caught you!

### How Infectious Diseases Spread

Have you ever wondered how you catch a cold, a strep throat, or even the chicken pox? These and many other diseases are called **infectious diseases**—illnesses that pass from one organism to another. **Infectious diseases can spread in one of four ways: through contact with either an infected person, a contaminated object, an infected animal, or an environmental source.** Once contact occurs, some disease-causing agents may enter a person through breaks in the skin, or they may be inhaled or swallowed. Others may enter the body through the moist linings of the eyes, ears, nose, mouth, or other body openings.

**Contact With an Infected Person**  Direct contact such as touching, hugging, or kissing an infected person can spread some infectious diseases. For example, kissing an infected person can transmit cold sores. Many other infectious diseases can be spread by indirect contact with an infected person. A common form of indirect contact is inhaling the tiny drops of moisture that an infected person sneezes or coughs into the air. This is because the drops of moisture contain disease-causing organisms. For example, the flu can be spread by inhaling drops of moisture that contain the flu virus.

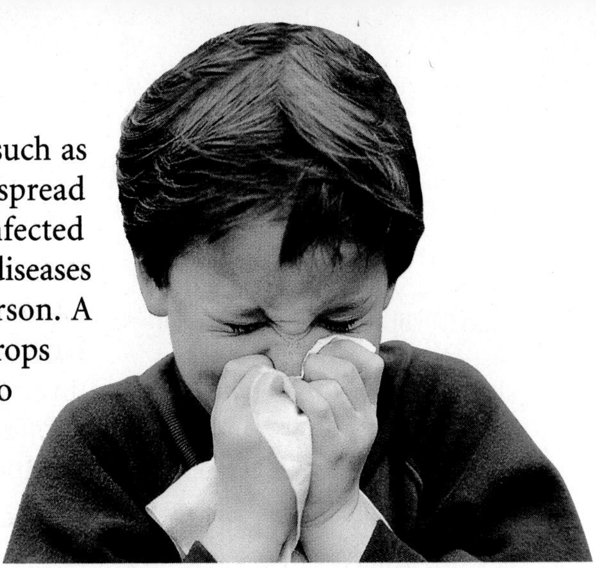

**Figure 14** When you sneeze, tiny drops of moisture that contain the disease-causing organisms in your body enter the air.

**Contact With a Contaminated Object**  Some viruses and bacteria can survive for a while outside a person's body. They can be spread via objects, such as eating utensils, or in contaminated food or water. For example, drinking from a cup used by an infected person can spread diseases such as strep throat and mononucleosis. If you touch an object that an infected person has sneezed or coughed on, you may transfer some viruses or bacteria to yourself if you then touch your mouth or eyes. If you drink water or eat food that an infected person has contaminated, you may get sick. Drinking water that contains small amounts of sewage is a common way that disease is spread in many areas of the world.

**Contact With an Animal**  The bites of animals can transmit some serious infectious diseases to humans. For example, the deadly disease rabies can be transferred through the bite of an infected dog, raccoon, or some other animals. The bites of ticks can transmit the bacteria that cause Lyme disease. The bites of mosquitoes can spread the virus that causes encephalitis—a serious disease in which the brain tissues swell.

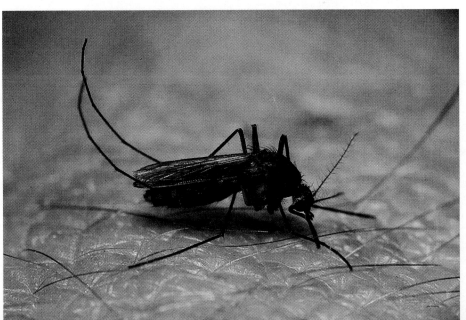

**Figure 15** This mosquito, *Culex nigripalpus*, is feeding on human blood. If this mosquito contains the virus that causes encephalitis, it can transmit the disease through its bite. *Applying Concepts What other diseases are spread by animal bites?*

In January 1925, two children died of diphtheria, a bacterial disease, in Nome, Alaska. The disease can be treated with an antitoxin that destroys the toxin that the bacteria produces. But Nome had no antitoxin and was snowbound. Antitoxin had to be rushed from Anchorage, over 1,500 kilometers away.

The antitoxin went by rail to Nenana, which was still 1,100 kilometers from Nome. Then twenty sled-dog owners organized a relay team. The drivers passed the antitoxin from one sled-dog team to the next, through storms and frigid weather. The sled-dog teams traveled along the Iditarod Trail, which was cut across the wilderness during the 1880s gold rush. After six grueling days, the last team arrived in Nome. The city was saved from the disease.

### In Your Journal

It is February 2, 1925, and you are the driver on the last leg of the antitoxin relay. Write a diary entry about your arrival in Nome.

**Contact With Environmental Sources**   Some viruses and bacteria live in food, water, and soil, or on the surfaces of objects. The places where they are naturally found are environmental sources of disease. For example, poultry, eggs, and meat often contain salmonella bacteria. Eating foods that contain these bacteria can lead to one type of food poisoning. Cooking the foods thoroughly kills the bacteria. A soil bacterium called *Clostridium botulinum* can grow in improperly processed canned foods. It produces a poison known as a **toxin**, which soaks into the food. Eating the food causes a serious, often deadly disease known as botulism. *Clostridium tetani*, another soil-dwelling bacteria, can enter a person's body through a wound and cause the deadly disease tetanus.

✓ *Checkpoint* *What is one thing you can do to reduce the risk of food poisoning?*

## Common Infectious Diseases

There are thousands of kinds of infectious diseases. Some are common in one part of the world but rare or absent in other places. Many infectious diseases are caused by viruses and bacteria. Others are caused by protists and fungi, which you will learn about in the next chapter. Figure 17 provides important information about some common viral and bacterial diseases in this country.

**Figure 16** Today, an event called the Iditarod Trail Dog Sled Race takes place in March each year. Sled-dog teams compete in a 1,930-kilometer race to celebrate the history of the Iditarod Trail.

## Common Infectious Diseases

| Disease | Disease-Causing Agent | Symptoms | How Spread | Treatment | Prevention |
|---------|-----------------------|----------|------------|-----------|------------|
| Acquired immuno-deficiency syndrome (AIDS) | Virus | Weight loss; chronic fatigue; fever; diarrhea; frequent infections | Sexual contact; contact with blood; pregnancy, birth, and breast-feeding | Drugs to slow viral multiplication | Avoid contact with infected body fluids |
| Chicken Pox | Virus | Fever; red itchy rash | Contact with rash; inhale droplets | Antiviral drug (for adults) | Vaccine |
| Influenza (flu) | Virus | High fever; sore throat; headache; cough | Contact with contaminated objects; inhale droplets | Bed rest; fluids | Vaccine (mainly for high-risk ill, elderly, and young) |
| Measles | Virus | High fever; sore throat; cough; white spots on cheek lining; rash; puffy eyelids | Inhale droplets | Bed rest, cough medicine | Vaccine |
| Poliomyelitis (polio) | Virus | Fever; muscle weakness; headache; difficulty swallowing | Inhale droplets | Bed rest | Vaccine |
| Rabies | Virus | Drooling; skin sensitivity; alternating periods of rage and calm; difficulty swallowing | Animal bite | Vaccine | Avoid wild animals and pets that act abnormally; keep track of pets outside |
| Food poisoning | Various bacteria | Vomiting; cramps; diarrhea; fever | Eating foods containing the bacteria | Antitoxin medicines; rest | Properly cook and store foods; avoid foods in rusted and swollen cans |
| Lyme disease | Bacterium | Rash at site of tick bite; chills; fever; body aches; joint swelling | Animal bite | Antibiotic | Tuck pants into socks; wear long-sleeved shirt |
| Strep throat | Bacterium | Fever; sore throat; swollen glands | Inhale droplets; contact with infected object | Antibiotic | Avoid contact with infected people |
| Tetanus (lockjaw) | Bacterium | Stiff jaw and neck muscles; spasms; difficulty swallowing | Deep puncture wound | Antibiotic; opening and cleaning wound | Vaccine |
| Tuberculosis (TB) | Bacterium | Fatigue; mild fever; weight loss; night sweats; cough | Inhale droplets | Antibiotic | Vaccine (for those in high risk occupations only) |

**Figure 17** Many common infectious diseases are caused by viruses and bacteria. Much is known about how these diseases are spread and how they can be treated or prevented.
*Interpreting Charts* Which diseases are spread by inhaling droplets in the air?

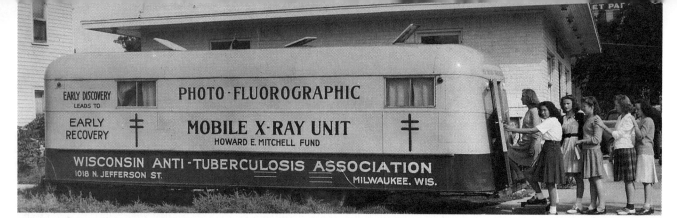

**Figure 18** Before antibiotics were available to treat tuberculosis, the deadly disease spread easily. People visited mobile X-ray vans to be screened for tuberculosis. *Relating Cause and Effect How has antibiotic resistance affected the number of tuberculosis cases?*

## Treating Infectious Diseases

Once you start to have symptoms of an infectious disease, your attention probably turns quickly to helping yourself feel better. For most infectious diseases, the best treatment is bedrest. Indeed, resting, drinking lots of fluids, and eating well-balanced meals may be all you can do while you recover from some infectious diseases.

**Viral Diseases** Unfortunately, there are no medications that can cure viral infections. However, while no cures exist, there are many over-the-counter medications that treat the symptoms. These medications are available without a prescription. Over-the-counter medications can make you feel better. But, they can also delay your recovery if you resume your normal routine while you are still sick. They can also hide symptoms that would normally cause you to go to a doctor.

**Bacterial Diseases** Unlike viral diseases, many bacterial diseases can be cured with medications known as antibiotics. An **antibiotic** is a chemical that can kill bacteria without harming a person's cells. Antibiotics are made naturally by some bacteria and fungi. Today, antibiotics such as penicillin are made in large quantities in factories. Penicillin works by weakening the cell walls of some bacteria and causing the cells to burst.

If you have ever had a strep throat infection, you know that the infection makes swallowing feel like you have a throat full of barbed wire. But soon after you begin taking the antibiotic that your doctor prescribes, your throat feels better. This is because the antibiotic quickly kills the bacteria that cause strep throat.

Unfortunately, antibiotics are less effective today than they once were. This is because many bacteria have become resistant to antibiotics over the years. Resistant bacteria are able to survive in the presence of an antibiotic. The recent increase in tuberculosis cases demonstrates the impact of antibiotic resistance. Between 1950 and 1980, the number of cases of tuberculosis dropped significantly as patients took antibiotics. Unfortunately, there were always a few tuberculosis bacteria that were resistant to the antibiotics. Those bacteria survived and reproduced, producing more bacteria like themselves. Today, many resistant bacteria exist. Since the mid-1980s, the number of tuberculosis cases has been on the rise despite the use of antibiotics.

## Preventing Infectious Diseases

One important tool that helps to prevent the spread of infectious diseases is vaccines. A **vaccine** is a substance that stimulates the body to produce chemicals that destroy viruses or bacteria. A vaccine may be made from dead or altered viruses or bacteria. The viruses or bacteria in the vaccine do not cause disease, but instead activate the body's natural defenses. In effect, the altered viruses or bacteria put the body "on alert." If that virus or bacterium ever invades the body, it is destroyed before it can produce disease. You may have been vaccinated against diseases such as tetanus, pertussis (whooping cough), measles, mumps, and polio. Now there is also a vaccine available for the viral disease chicken pox.

**Figure 19** By exercising and keeping your body healthy, you can help protect yourself from infectious diseases.

## Staying Healthy

The best way to protect against infectious diseases is to keep your body healthy. You need to eat nutritious food, as well as get plenty of rest, fluids, and exercise. You can also protect yourself by washing your hands often and by not sharing eating utensils or drink containers. You should also make sure that you have all recommended vaccinations. Storing food properly, keeping kitchen equipment and surfaces clean, and cooking meats well can prevent food poisoning.

Unfortunately, despite your best efforts, you'll probably get infectious diseases, such as colds, from time to time. When you do get ill, get plenty of rest, follow your doctor's recommendations, and try not to infect others.

## Section 3 Review

1. List four ways that infectious diseases can be spread.
2. What is an antibiotic? What types of infectious diseases do antibiotics cure?
3. What is a vaccine?
4. **Thinking Critically Inferring** Why is washing your hands an effective way to prevent the spread of some infectious diseases?

**Check Your Progress**

CHAPTER PROJECT 2

By now you should have nearly all of your questionnaires answered. You should be ready to tally your responses. Begin to think about how you will use graphs or other visual ways to organize your results. (*Hint:* You may need to review the research you did earlier to help you make sense of some survey data.)

## Antibiotic Resistance—An Alarming Trend

Penicillin, the first antibiotic, became available for use in 1943. Soon afterward, antibiotics became known as the "wonder drugs." Over the years, they have reduced the occurrence of many bacterial diseases and saved millions of lives. But each time an antibiotic is used, a few bacteria—those resistant to the drug—survive. They pass on their resistance to the next generation of bacteria. As more and more patients take antibiotics, the number of resistant bacteria increases.

In 1987, penicillin killed more than 99.9 percent of a type of bacteria that causes ear infections. By 1995, 25 percent of those bacteria were resistant to penicillin. Diseases such as tuberculosis are on the increase due in part to growing antibiotic resistance.

## The Issues

### What Can Doctors and Patients Do?

In a typical year, about 6 billion dollars worth of antibiotics are sold to drugstores and hospitals in the United States. One way to slow down the process that leads to resistance is to decrease the amount of antibiotics people use. About one out of five prescriptions for antibiotics is written for colds and other viral illnesses. Antibiotics, however, do not kill viruses. If doctors could better identify the cause of an infection, they could avoid prescribing unnecessary antibiotics.

Patients can also play an important role. If a doctor prescribes a ten-day course of antibiotics, all of the prescription should be taken. If a patient stops taking the antibiotic, the resistant bacteria will survive and reproduce. Then, a second antibiotic may be necessary. Patients also need to learn that some illnesses are best treated with rest and not with antibiotics.

### Limiting Non-medical Uses of Antibiotics

About forty percent of the antibiotics used each year are not given to people. Instead, the drugs are fed to food animals, such as cattle and chickens, to prevent illness and increase growth. Reducing this type of use would limit the amount of the drugs in food animals and in the people who eat them. But these actions might increase the risk of disease in animals and lead to higher meat prices.

### Finding New Antibiotics

Another way to slow the increase of antibiotic resistance might be through more research. Scientists are trying to identify new antibiotics. With more kinds of antibiotics, scientists hope that bacteria will not develop resistances as quickly.

## You Decide

### 1. Identify the Problem

Describe how the use of antibiotics can eventually make these medicines not work as well.

### 2. Analyze the Options

List all the ways to fight the development of antibiotic resistance in bacteria. For each action, tell who would carry it out and how it would work. Mention any costs or drawbacks.

### 3. Find a Solution

Make a persuasive poster about one way to deal with antibiotic resistance. Support your viewpoint with sound reasons. Target the group who could make the change.

# STUDY GUIDE

## SECTION 1 — Viruses

### Key Ideas

◆ Viruses are considered to be nonliving because viruses are not cells, and they do not use energy to grow and develop, or to respond to their surroundings.

◆ All viruses have two basic parts: an outer coat that protects the virus and an inner core made of genetic material.

◆ Once inside a cell, a virus uses the host cell's functions to make its own proteins and genetic material. The proteins and genetic material assemble into new viruses, which burst out, destroying the host.

### Key Terms

| | |
|---|---|
| virus | parasite |
| host | bacteriophage |

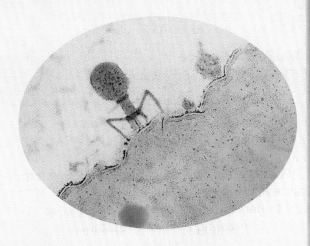

## SECTION 2 — Bacteria

### Key Ideas

◆ Bacteria are prokaryotes. Their cells do not have nuclei that contain the cell's genetic material. Instead, the genetic material floats freely in the cytoplasm.

◆ Bacteria reproduce asexually by binary fission, which results in the production of two cells exactly like the parent cell. Some bacteria have a simple form of sexual reproduction called conjugation. This process results in a cell with a new combination of genetic information.

◆ Bacteria play positive roles in the lives of humans. Bacteria are involved in fuel and food production, in environmental recycling and cleanup, and in the production of medicines.

### Key Terms

| | |
|---|---|
| cytoplasm | sexual reproduction |
| ribosome | conjugation |
| flagellum | respiration |
| binary fission | endospore |
| asexual reproduction | decomposer |

## SECTION 3 — Viruses, Bacteria, and Your Health

*INTEGRATING HEALTH*

### Key Ideas

◆ Infectious disease can spread through contact with an infected person, a contaminated object, an infected animal, or an environmental source.

◆ There is no cure for viral diseases. Bacterial diseases can be cured through the use of antibiotics. Vaccines can prevent some viral and bacterial diseases.

### Key Terms

| | |
|---|---|
| infectious disease | antibiotic |
| toxin | vaccine |

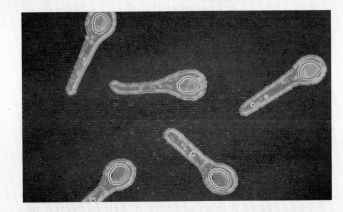

## USING THE INTERNET

**www.science-explorer.phschool.com**

*Chapter 2* **A ◆ 75**

**CHAPTER 2 REVIEW**

## Reviewing Content

*For more review of key concepts, see the Interactive Student Tutorial CD-ROM.*

### Multiple Choice
*Choose the letter of the best answer.*

1. Bacteriophages are viruses that attack and destroy
   a. other viruses.   b. bacteria.
   c. plants.          d. humans.
2. Which part of a virus determines which host cells it can infect?
   a. genetic material   b. ribosomes
   c. flagellum          d. outer coat
3. Viruses multiply
   a. slowly inside cells.   b. by binary fission.
   c. by taking over a cell's functions.   d. both asexually and sexually.
4. Most bacteria are surrounded by a rigid protective structure called the
   a. cell wall.      b. cell membrane.
   c. protein coat.   d. flagellum.
5. Which of the following statements about infectious diseases is *not* true?
   a. Some can be spread by contact with an infected person.
   b. Some can be spread by contact with animals.
   c. All can be treated with antibiotics.
   d. Some can be prevented with vaccines.

### True or False
*If the statement is true, write true. If it is false, change the underlined word or words to make the statement true.*

6. <u>Hidden viruses</u> enter a cell and immediately begin to multiply.
7. In gene therapy, scientists take advantage of a <u>bacteria's</u> ability to get inside a host cell.
8. Most <u>archaebacteria</u> live in extreme environments.
9. Bacteria form <u>endospores</u> to survive unfavorable conditions in their surroundings.
10. A <u>vaccine</u> is a chemical that can kill bacteria without harming a person's cells.

## Checking Concepts

11. List three ways that viruses are different from cells.
12. Explain why a certain virus will attach to only one or a few types of cells.
13. Describe how a bacteriophage multiplies.
14. What are the parts of a bacterial cell? Explain the role of each part.
15. Describe how bacteria reproduce.
16. How do the bacteria that live in your intestines help you?
17. Explain how antibiotics kill bacteria.
18. How do vaccines prevent the spread of some infectious diseases?
19. **Writing to Learn** Imagine you are a cold virus. The student you infected just sneezed you into the air in the cafeteria. Write a description of what happens to you until you finally attach to a cell in another student.

## Thinking Visually

20. Copy the Venn diagram comparing viruses and bacteria onto a separate sheet of paper. Then complete the Venn diagram. (For more on Venn diagrams, see the Skills Handbook.)

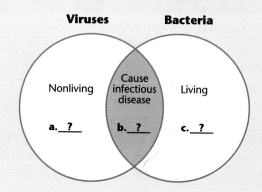

## Applying Skills

The graph shows how the number of bacteria that grow on a food source changes over time. Use the graph to answer Questions 21–23.

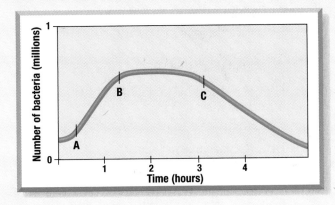

21. **Interpreting Data** Explain what is happening between points A and B.
22. **Developing Hypotheses** Develop a hypothesis that explains why the number of bacteria stays constant between points B and C.

23. **Designing Experiments** How could you test the hypothesis you developed in Question 22? What would your results show?

## Thinking Critically

24. **Classifying** You know that viruses vary in shape, size, and the kinds of organisms they infect. Which one of these three characteristics would you use as a basis for a classification system for viruses? Explain your answer.
25. **Comparing and Contrasting** Describe the similarities and differences between active and hidden viruses.
26. **Problem Solving** Bacteria will grow in the laboratory on a gelatin-like substance called agar. Viruses will not grow on agar. If you needed to grow viruses in the laboratory, what kind of substance would you have to use? Explain.

## Performance Assessment

### CHAPTER PROJECT 2 — Wrap Up

**Present Your Project** Your presentation should lead your audience through your project—from your survey to your conclusions. Make sure to explain why you chose the questions and survey group that you did. Use graphs or other visual displays to highlight important similarities or differences you found. Make sure that you support your conclusions with data.

**Reflect and Record** Do you think that a survey like this one is similar to a science experiment? What makes them alike or different? In your journal, describe what you did to make your survey accurate and complete.

### Getting Involved

**In Your School** With your classmates plan a "Bacteria in Food" display for the other students in your school. Arrange for a place to set up your display. Put out samples of foods that require bacteria for their production. Make posters and models to inform students how bacteria are involved in each food's production. Be prepared to answer questions about the foods and about the bacteria that are used to make the foods.

# CHAPTER
# 3 Protists and Fungi

## WHAT'S AHEAD

### SECTION
### 1 Protists

Discover **What Lives in a Drop of Pond Water?**
Try This **Feeding Paramecia**
Sharpen Your Skills **Predicting**

### SECTION
### 2 Algal Blooms
*Integrating Environmental Science*

Discover **How Can Algal Growth Affect Pond Life?**
Real-World Lab **An Explosion of Life**

### SECTION
### 3 Fungi

Discover **Do All Molds Look Alike?**
Try This **Making Spore Prints**
Try This **Spreading Spores**
Skills Lab **What's for Lunch?**

# A Mushroom Farm

**H**ave you ever seen mushrooms growing in a local park or on a forest floor? Over the centuries, people have been curious about these organisms because they seem to sprout up without warning, often after a rainfall. Mushrooms are the most familiar type of fungi. In some ways, they resemble plants, often growing near or even on them like small umbrellas. But mushrooms are very different from plants in some important ways. In this project, you'll learn these differences.

As you read the chapter, you'll also learn about other fungi and about the diverse kingdom known as protists. You'll find out how these organisms carry out their life activities and how important they are to people and to the environment.

**Your Goal** To determine the conditions needed for mushrooms to grow.

To complete this project successfully, you must
- ◆ choose one variable, and design a way to test how it affects mushroom growth
- ◆ make daily observations, and record them in a data table
- ◆ prepare a poster that describes the results of your experiment
- ◆ follow the safety guidelines in Appendix A

**Get Started** With your partners, brainstorm possible hypotheses about the way variables such as light or moisture could affect the growth of mushrooms. Write your own hypothesis and the reasons why you chose it. Write out a plan for testing the variable that you chose. Then start growing your mushrooms!

**Check Your Progress** You'll be working on this project as you study the chapter. To keep your project on track, look for Check Your Progress boxes at the following points.

**Section 2 Review,** page 92: Make observations and collect data.
**Section 3 Review,** page 104: Plan a poster about your discoveries.

**Wrap Up** At the end of the chapter (page 107), you will display your poster that details what you learned about mushroom growth.

Although these scarlet waxy cap mushrooms are quite tasty, beware. There are poisonous mushrooms that look just like them.

### What Lives in a Drop of Pond Water?

1. Use a plastic dropper to place a drop of pond water on a microscope slide.
2. Put the slide under your microscope's low-power lens. Focus on the objects you see.
3. Find at least three different objects that you think might be organisms. Observe them for a few minutes.
4. Draw the three organisms in your notebook. Below each sketch, describe the movements or behaviors of the organism. Wash your hands thoroughly when you have finished.

**Think It Over**

*Observing* What characteristics did you observe that made you think that each organism was alive?

◆ What are the characteristics of animal-like, funguslike, and plantlike protists?

*Reading Tip* As you read, use the headings to make an outline of the different kinds of protists.

ook at the objects in Figure 1. What do they look like to you? Jewels? Stained glass windows? Crystal ornaments? You might be surprised to learn that these beautiful, delicate structures are the walls of unicellular organisms called diatoms. Diatoms live in both salt water and fresh water. Believe it or not, these tiny organisms provide food for some of Earth's largest organisms—whales.

## What Is a Protist?

Diatoms are only one type of organism classified in the protist kingdom. Protists are so different from each other that you can think of this kingdom as the "junk drawer" kingdom. You may have a drawer in your room where you store ticket stubs, postcards, and other odds and ends. Just as these items don't really fit anywhere else in your room, protists don't really fit into any other biological kingdom. Protists do share some characteristics. They are all eukaryotes, or organisms that have cells with nuclei. In addition, all protists live in moist surroundings.

Despite these common characteristics, the word that best describes the protist kingdom is diversity. For example, most protists are unicellular like the diatoms. On the other hand, some

**Figure 1** These delicate-looking diatoms are classified in the protist kingdom.

protists are multicellular. In fact, the protists known as giant kelps can be over 100 meters long. Protists also vary in how they obtain food—some are heterotrophs, some are autotrophs, and others are both. Some protists cannot move, while others zoom around their moist surroundings.

Because of the great variety of protists, scientists have proposed different ways of grouping these organisms. One useful way of grouping protists is to divide them into three categories: animal-like protists, funguslike protists, and plantlike protists.

✓ *Checkpoint* *What characteristics do all protists share?*

## Animal-like Protists

What image pops into your head when you think of an animal? A tiger chasing its prey? A snake slithering onto a rock? Most people immediately associate animals with movement. In fact, movement is often involved with an important characteristic of animals—obtaining food. All animals are heterotrophs that must obtain food by consuming other organisms.

**Like animals, animal-like protists are heterotrophs.** And most animal-like protists, or **protozoans** (proh tuh ZOH unz), are able to move from place to place to obtain their food. Unlike animals, however, protozoans are unicellular. Some scientists distinguish between four types of protozoans based on the way these organisms move and live.

**Protozoans With Pseudopods** The ameba in *Exploring Protozoans* on the next page belongs to the group of protozoans called sarcodines. Sarcodines move and feed by forming **pseudopods** (SOO doh pahdz)—temporary bulges of the cell membrane that fill with cytoplasm. The word *pseudopod* means "false foot." Pseudopods form when the cell membrane pushes outward in one location. The cytoplasm flows into the bulge

**Figure 2** The protist kingdom includes animal-like, plantlike, and funguslike organisms. **A.** These shells contained unicellular, animal-like protists called foraminifera. **B.** This red alga is a multicellular, plantlike protist found on ocean floors. **C.** This yellow slime mold is a funguslike protist. *Comparing and Contrasting In what way are animal-like protists similar to animals? How do they differ?*

and the rest of the organism follows. Pseudopods enable sarcodines to move in response to changes in the environment. For example, amebas use psuedopods to move away from bright light. Sarcodines also use pseudopods to trap food. The organism extends a pseudopod on each side of the food particle. The two pseudopods then join together, trapping the particle inside.

Organisms that live in fresh water, such as amebas, have a problem. Small particles, like those of water, pass easily through the cell membrane into the cytoplasm. If the excess water were to build up inside the cell, the ameba would burst. Fortunately, amebas have a **contractile vacuole** (kun TRAK til  VAK yoo ohl), a structure that collects the extra water and then expels it from the cell.

# EXPLORING Protozoans

Amebas are sarcodines that live either in water or soil. They feed on bacteria and smaller protists in the surroundings. Paramecia are ciliates that live mostly in fresh water. Like amebas, paramecia feed on bacteria and smaller protists.

## AMEBA

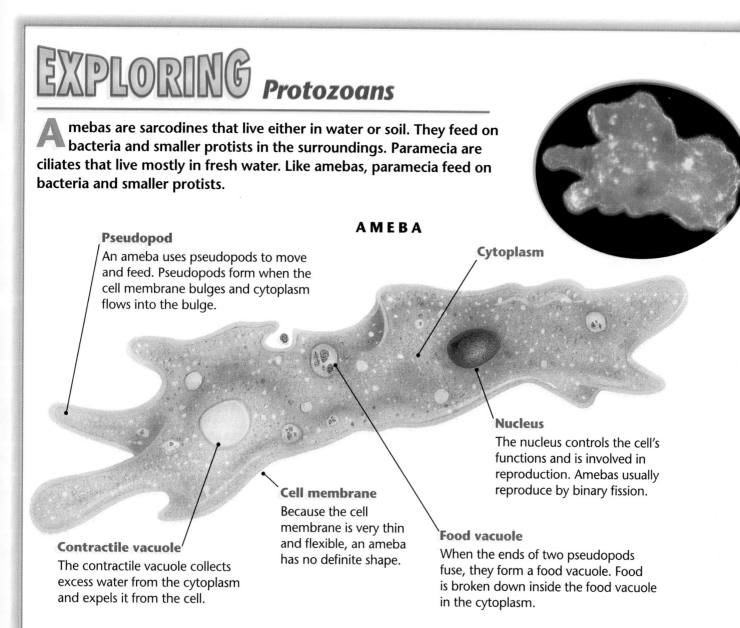

**Pseudopod**
An ameba uses pseudopods to move and feed. Pseudopods form when the cell membrane bulges and cytoplasm flows into the bulge.

**Cytoplasm**

**Nucleus**
The nucleus controls the cell's functions and is involved in reproduction. Amebas usually reproduce by binary fission.

**Cell membrane**
Because the cell membrane is very thin and flexible, an ameba has no definite shape.

**Food vacuole**
When the ends of two pseudopods fuse, they form a food vacuole. Food is broken down inside the food vacuole in the cytoplasm.

**Contractile vacuole**
The contractile vacuole collects excess water from the cytoplasm and expels it from the cell.

**Protozoans With Cilia**  The second type of animal-like protist is the ciliate. Ciliates have structures called **cilia** (SIL ee uh) which are hairlike projections from cells that move with a wavelike pattern. They use cilia to move, obtain food, and sense the environment. Cilia act something like tiny oars to move a ciliate. Their movement sweeps food into the organism.

Ciliates have complex cells. In *Exploring Protozoans*, you see a ciliate called a paramecium. Notice that the paramecium has two nuclei. The large nucleus controls the everyday tasks of the cell. The small nucleus functions in reproduction. Paramecia usually reproduce asexually by binary fission. Sometimes, they reproduce by conjugation. This occurs when two paramecia join together and exchange genetic material.

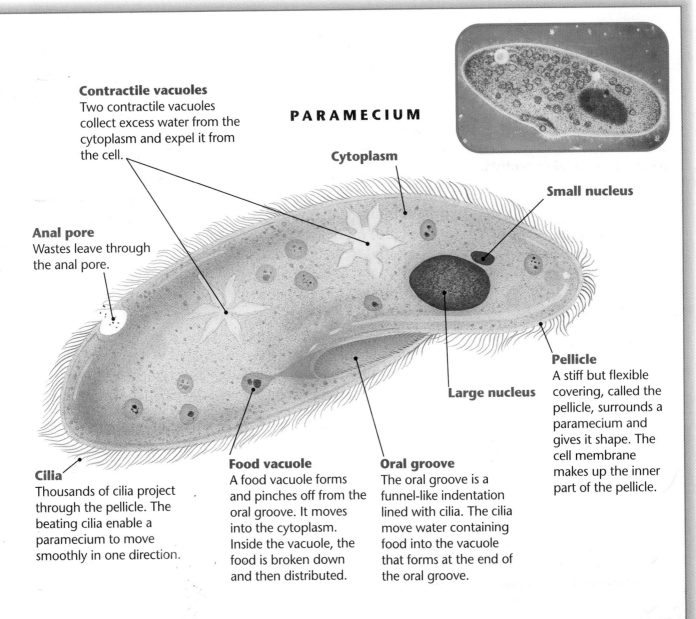

**PARAMECIUM**

**Contractile vacuoles**
Two contractile vacuoles collect excess water from the cytoplasm and expel it from the cell.

**Cytoplasm**

**Small nucleus**

**Anal pore**
Wastes leave through the anal pore.

**Pellicle**
A stiff but flexible covering, called the pellicle, surrounds a paramecium and gives it shape. The cell membrane makes up the inner part of the pellicle.

**Large nucleus**

**Cilia**
Thousands of cilia project through the pellicle. The beating cilia enable a paramecium to move smoothly in one direction.

**Food vacuole**
A food vacuole forms and pinches off from the oral groove. It moves into the cytoplasm. Inside the vacuole, the food is broken down and then distributed.

**Oral groove**
The oral groove is a funnel-like indentation lined with cilia. The cilia move water containing food into the vacuole that forms at the end of the oral groove.

**Figure 3** When people drink from freshwater streams and lakes, they can get hiker's disease. Below you see the organism responsible for the disease, a protozoan called *Giardia lamblia.*

**Feeding Paramecia**

In this activity you will feed *Chlorella*, a plantlike protist, to paramecia. **ACTIVITY**

1. 🔧 Use a plastic dropper to place one drop of paramecium culture on a micrscope slide. Add some cotton fibers to slow down the paramecia.

2. Use the microscope's low-power objective to find some paramecia.

3. Add one drop of *Chlorella* to the paramecium culture on your slide.

4. Switch to high power and locate a paramecium. Observe what happens. Then wash your hands.

*Inferring* What evidence do you have that paramecia are heterotrophs? That *Chlorella* are autotrophs?

**Protozoans With Flagella** The third type of protozoans are called zooflagellates (zoh uh FLAJ uh lits)—animal-like protists that use flagella to move. Most zooflagellates have one to eight long, whiplike flagella that help them move.

Many zooflagellates live inside the bodies of other organisms. For example, one type of zooflagellate lives in the intestines of termites. The zooflagellates produce chemicals that help the termites digest the wood that they eat. In turn, the termites protect the zooflagellates. The interaction between these two species is an example of **symbiosis** (sim bee OH sis)—a close relationship where at least one of the species benefits. When both partners benefit from living together, the relationship is a type of symbiosis called **mutualism.**

**INTEGRATING HEALTH** Sometimes a zooflagellate harms the animal in which it lives. In Figure 3 you see a zooflagellate called *Giardia.* This zooflagellate is a parasite in humans. Wild animals, such as beavers, deposit *Giardia* organisms in freshwater streams, rivers, and lakes. When a person drinks water containing *Giardia,* the zooflagellates attach to the person's intestine, where they feed and reproduce. The person develops a serious intestinal condition commonly called hiker's disease.

**Other Protozoans** The fourth type of protozoans, the sporozoans, are characterized more by the way they live than by the way they move. Sporozoans are parasites that feed on the cells and body fluids of their hosts. They move in a variety of ways. Some have flagella and some depend on hosts for transport. One even slides from place to place on a layer of slime that it produces.

Many sporozoans have more than one host. For example, *Plasmodium* is a sporozoan that causes malaria, a serious disease of the blood. Two hosts are involved in *Plasmodium's* life cycle—humans and a species of mosquitoes found in tropical areas. The disease spreads when a healthy mosquito bites a person with malaria, becomes infected, and then bites a healthy person. Symptoms of malaria include high fevers that alternate with severe chills. These symptoms can last for weeks, then disappear, only to reappear a few months later.

☑ *Checkpoint* **What structures do protozoans use to move?**

## Funguslike Protists

The second group of protists are the funguslike protists. Recall from Chapter 1 that fungi include organisms such as mushrooms and yeast. Until you learn more about fungi in Section 3, you can think of fungi as the "sort of like" organisms. Fungi are "sort of like" animals because they are heterotrophs. They are "sort of like" plants because their cells have cell walls. In addition, most fungi use spores to reproduce. A **spore** is a tiny cell that is able to grow into a new organism.

**Like fungi, funguslike protists are heterotrophs, have cell walls, and use spores to reproduce. Unlike fungi, however, all funguslike protists are able to move at some point in their lives.** The three types of funguslike protists are water molds, downy mildews, and slime molds.

**Water Molds and Downy Mildews** Most water molds and downy mildews live in water or in moist places. These organisms grow as tiny threads that look like a fuzzy covering. Figure 5 shows a fish attacked by a water mold.

Water molds and downy mildews also attack food crops, such as potatoes, cabbages, corn, and grapes. A water mold destroyed the Irish potato crops in 1845 and 1846. The loss of these crops led to a famine that resulted in the deaths of over one million Irish people. Many others left Ireland and moved to other countries, such as Canada and the United States.

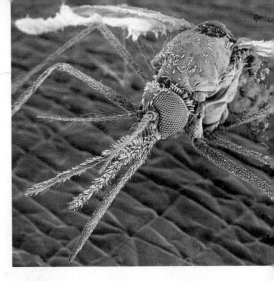

**Figure 4** *Anopheles* mosquitoes can carry a sporozoan, *Plasmodium*, which causes malaria in people. *Relating Cause and Effect* Why do you think it is difficult to control the spread of malaria?

**Figure 5** This threadlike water mold is a parasite that grows on fish. The water mold eventually kills the fish.

**Figure 6** Slime molds, like the chocolate tube slime mold (left), feed on microorganisms on the surfaces of decaying materials. When food runs low, they grow stalks that produce spores (right).

**Slime Molds** Slime molds live in moist soil and on decaying plants and trees. Slime molds are often beautifully colored. Many are bright yellow, like the one in Figure 6. Their glistening bodies creep over fallen logs and dead leaves on shady, moist forest floors. They move in an amebalike way by forming pseudopods and oozing along the surfaces of decaying materials. Slime molds feed on bacteria and other microorganisms.

Some slime molds are large enough to be seen with the naked eye. Many, however, are so small that you need a microscope to see them. When the food supply decreases or other conditions change, some tiny slime molds creep together and form a multicellular mass. Spore-producing structures grow out of the mass and release spores, which can develop into a new generation of slime molds.

☑ *Checkpoint* *In what environments are slime molds found?*

## Plantlike Protists

If you've ever seen seaweed at a beach, then you are familiar with a type of plantlike protist. Plantlike protists, which are commonly called **algae** (AL jee), are even more varied than the animal-like and funguslike protists. **The one characteristic that all algae share is that, like plants, they are autotrophs.**

Some algae live in the soil, others live on the barks of trees, and still others live in fresh water and salt water. Algae that live on the surface of ponds, lakes, and oceans are an important food source for other organisms in the water. In addition, most of the oxygen in Earth's atmosphere is made by these algae.

Algae range greatly in size. Some algae, such as diatoms, are unicellular. Others are groups of unicellular organisms that live together in colonies. Still others, such as seaweeds, are multicellular. Recall from Chapter 1 that a unicellular organism carries out all the functions necessary for life. But the cells of a multi-cellular organism are specialized to do certain tasks. When single-celled algae come together to form colonies, some of the cells may become specialized to perform certain functions, such as reproduction. However, most cells in a colony continue to carry out all functions. Colonies can contain from four up to thousands of cells.

Algae exist in a wide variety of colors because they contain many types of **pigments**—chemicals that produce color. Depending on their pigments, algae can be green, yellow, red, brown, orange, or even black. Read on to learn about the types of algae that live on Earth.

**Euglenoids** Euglenoids are green, unicellular algae that are found mostly in fresh water. Unlike other algae, euglenoids have one animal-like characteristic—they can be heterotrophs under certain conditions. When sunlight is available, euglenoids are autotrophs that produce their own food. However, when sunlight is not available, euglenoids will act like heterotrophs by finding and taking in food from their environment.

In Figure 7 you see a euglena, which is a common euglenoid. Notice the long whiplike flagellum that helps the organism move. Locate the eyespot near the flagellum. Although the eyespot is not really an eye, it contains pigments. These pigments are sensitive to light and help a euglena recognize the direction of a light source. You can imagine how important this response is to an organism that needs light to make food.

**Figure 7** Euglenas are unicellular algae that live in fresh water. In sunlight, euglenas make their own food. Without sunlight, they obtain food from their environment.
*Interpreting Diagrams* What structures help a euglena find and move toward light?

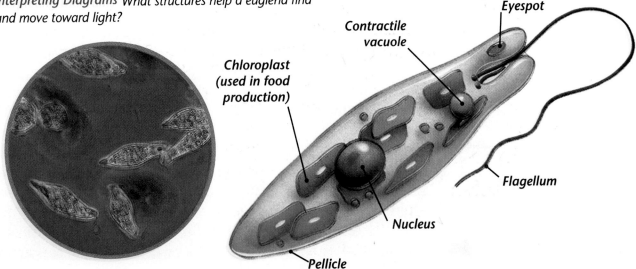

Contractile vacuole

Eyespot

Chloroplast (used in food production)

Flagellum

Nucleus

Pellicle

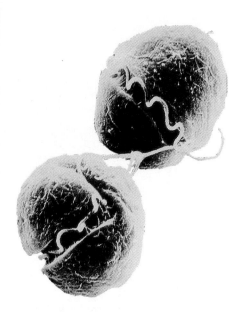

**Figure 8** Dinoflagellates, such as these *Gonyaulax*, have rigid plates for protection. They use flagella to move through the water.

**Dinoflagellates** Dinoflagellates are unicellular algae covered by stiff plates that look like a suit of armor. Because they have different amounts of green, red, and other pigments, dinoflagellates exist in a variety of colors.

All dinoflagellates have two flagella held in grooves between their plates. When the flagella beat, the dinoflagellates twirl like toy tops through the water. Many glow in the dark and look like miniature fireflies dancing on the ocean's surface at night.

**Diatoms** Diatoms are unicellular protists with beautiful glasslike cell walls. Some float on the surface of freshwater and saltwater environments. Others attach to objects such as rocks in shallow water. Diatoms move by shooting chemicals out of slits in their cell walls. This gives them a kind of jet propulsion. Diatoms are a food source for heterotrophs in the water.

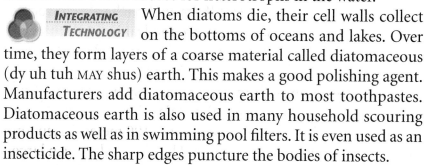

**INTEGRATING TECHNOLOGY** When diatoms die, their cell walls collect on the bottoms of oceans and lakes. Over time, they form layers of a coarse material called diatomaceous (dy uh tuh MAY shus) earth. This makes a good polishing agent. Manufacturers add diatomaceous earth to most toothpastes. Diatomaceous earth is also used in many household scouring products as well as in swimming pool filters. It is even used as an insecticide. The sharp edges puncture the bodies of insects.

**Green Algae** As their name suggests, all green algae contain green pigments. Otherwise, green algae are quite diverse, as you can see in Figure 9. Although most green algae are unicellular, some form colonies, and a few are multicellular. You might have seen multicellular green algae, or green seaweed, washed up on a beach. Most green algae live in either freshwater or saltwater surroundings. The few that live on land are found along the bases of trees or in moist soils.

**Figure 9** Green algae range in size from unicellular organisms to multicellular seaweeds. **A.** The multicellular sea lettuce, *Ulva*, lives in oceans. **B.** This unicellular algae, *Closterium*, lives in fresh water.

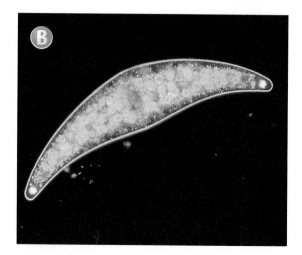

**Red Algae**  Almost all red algae are multicellular seaweeds. Divers have found red algae growing at depths greater than 260 meters below the ocean's surface. Their red pigments are especially good at absorbing the small amount of light that enters deep ocean waters.

Red algae are used by humans in a variety of ways. Carrageenan (kar uh JEE nun), a substance extracted from red algae, is used in products such as ice creams and hair conditioners. For people in many Asians cultures, red algae is a nutrient-rich delicacy that is eaten fresh, dried, or toasted.

**Brown Algae**  Many of the organisms that are commonly called seaweeds are brown algae. In addition to their brown pigment, brown algae also contain green, yellow, and orange pigments. As you can see in Figure 10, a typical brown alga has many plantlike structures. Holdfasts anchor the alga to rocks. Stalks support the blades, which are the leaflike structures of the alga. Brown algae also have gas-filled sacs called bladders that allow the algae to float upright in the water.

Brown algae flourish in cool, rocky waters. Brown algae called rockweed live along the Atlantic coast of North America. Giant kelps, which can grow to 100 meters in length, live in some Pacific coastal waters. The giant kelps form large underwater "forests" where many organisms, including sea otters and abalone, live. Some people eat brown algae for their nutrients. Substances called algins are extracted from brown algae and used as thickeners in foods such as puddings and salad dressings.

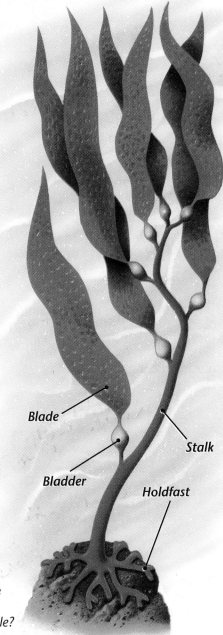

Blade

Bladder

Stalk

Holdfast

**Figure 10** Giant kelps have many plantlike structures. *Applying Concepts What plant structures do the holdfasts and blades resemble?*

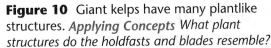

# Section 1 Review

1. What characteristic do all protozoans share?
2. What are three characteristics of the funguslike protists?
3. What characteristic do algae share with plants?
4. **Thinking Critically  Making Judgments** Would you classify euglena as an animal-like protist or as a plantlike protist? Explain your answer.

## Science at Home

Look through your kitchen with a family member to find products that contain substances made from algae. Look at both food and non-food items. Before you begin, tell your family member that words such as diatomaceous earth, algin, and carrageenan are substances that come from algae. Make a list of the products and the algae-based ingredient they contain. Share your list with the class.

# INTEGRATING ENVIRONMENTAL SCIENCE

## SECTION 2 Algal Blooms

### DISCOVER •••••••••••••••••••••••••••••••••••••• ACTIVITY

#### How Can Algal Growth Affect Pond Life?

1. Pour water into a plastic petri dish until the dish is half full. The petri dish will represent a pond.

2. Sprinkle a spoonful of green paper punches into the water in the petri dish to represent green algae growing in the pond water.

3. Sprinkle two more spoonfuls of paper punches into the water to represent one cycle of algae reproduction.

4. Sprinkle four more spoonfuls of paper punches into the water to represent the next reproduction cycle of the algae.

**Think It Over**

*Predicting* How might algae growing on the surface affect organisms living deep in a pond?

### GUIDE FOR READING

◆ What makes red tides dangerous?

◆ How does the rapid growth of algae affect a pond or lake?

*Reading Tip* As you read, look for evidence of the dangers of algal blooms.

Over a five-week period one year, the bodies of 14 humpback whales washed up along beaches on Cape Cod, Massachusetts. The whales showed no outward signs of sickness. Their stomachs were full of food. Their bodies contained plenty of blubber to insulate them from changes in water temperature. What caused such healthy-looking animals to die?

When biologists examined the dead whales' tissues, they identified the cause of the puzzling deaths. The whales' cells contained a deadly toxin produced by a dinoflagellate called *Alexandrium tamarense.* For reasons that scientists don't fully understand, the population of these algae grew rapidly in the ocean waters through which the whales were migrating. When the whales fed on the toxin-producing algae or on fishes that had eaten the algae, the toxins reached a deadly level and killed the whales.

Algae are common in both saltwater and freshwater environments on Earth. They float on the surface of the waters and use sunlight to make food. The rapid growth of a population of algae is called an **algal bloom.** The deaths of the humpbacks is one example of the damage that an algal bloom can cause.

◀ A humpback whale

**Figure 11** Rapid algae growth has caused a red tide in this small bay off the coast of California. *Relating Cause and Effect What organisms are most often responsible for causing red tides?*

## Saltwater Blooms

In Figure 11, you see an algal bloom in ocean water. Saltwater algal blooms are commonly called **red tides.** This is because the algae that grow rapidly often contain red pigments and turn the color of the water red. But red tides do not always look red. Some red tides are brown, green, or colorless depending on the species of algae that blooms. Dinoflagellates and diatoms are two algae that frequently bloom in red tides.

Scientists are not sure why some saltwater algal populations increase rapidly at times. But red tides occur most often when there is an increase in nutrients in the water. Increases in ocean temperature due to climate changes also affect the occurrence of red tides. Some red tides occur regularly in certain seasons. The cold bottom layers of the ocean contain a lot of nutrients. When the cold water mixes with the surface waters, more nutrients become available to surface organisms. With excess nutrients present in the surface waters, blooms of algae occur.

**Red tides are dangerous when the toxins that the algae produce become concentrated in the bodies of organisms that consume the algae.** Shellfish feed on large numbers of the algae and store the toxins in their cells. Fishes may also feed on the algae and store the toxins. When people or other large organisms eat these shellfish and fishes, it may lead to serious illness or even death. Public health officials close beaches in areas of red tides and prohibit people from gathering shellfish or fishing.

**INTEGRATING TECHNOLOGY** Red tides occur more frequently worldwide today than they did a decade ago. Scientists cannot yet predict when red tides will occur. They use images taken by satellites in space to track how red tides move with ocean currents. Satellite images can also detect increases in ocean temperatures, which may put an area at risk for red tide.

✓ *Checkpoint* *Why are red tides often red in color?*

**Figure 12** Increased nutrient levels in lakes and ponds can lead to algal blooms. The thick layer of algae on the surface can threaten other organisms in the water. *Problem Solving Outline a series of steps that could help slow down the rapid growth of algae in a lake.*

## Freshwater Blooms

Algal blooms also occur in bodies of fresh water. Have you ever seen a pond or lake that looked as if it was coated with a layer of green paint? The green layer of surface scum usually consists of huge numbers of unicellular green algae.

Lakes and ponds undergo natural processes of change over time. In a process called **eutrophication** (yoo troh fih KAY shun), nutrients, such as nitrogen and phosphorus, build up in a lake or pond over time, causing an increase in the growth of algae.

Certain natural events and human activities can increase the rate of eutrophication. For example, when farmers spread fertilizers on fields, some of these chemicals can run off into nearby lakes and ponds. In addition, poorly designed or aging septic systems can leak their contents into the soil. The nutrients make their way from the soil into water that leads into lakes and ponds. These events cause a rapid increase in algae growth.

**The rapid growth of algae in a pond or lake triggers a series of events with serious consequences.** First, the layer of algae prevents sunlight from reaching plants and other algae beneath the surface. Those organisms die and sink to the bottom. Then organisms, such as bacteria, which break down the bodies of the dead plants and algae, increase in number. Soon the bacteria use up the oxygen in the water. Fishes and other organisms in the water die without the oxygen they need to survive. About the only life that survives is the algae on the surface.

Algal blooms in fresh water can be easier to control than those in salt water because lakes and ponds have definite boundaries. To slow eutrophication, scientists first need to find the sources of the excess nutrients and then eliminate them. If the source can be eliminated and the nutrients used up, eutrophication slows to its natural rate.

# Section 2 Review

1. Why are red tides dangerous?
2. What causes a freshwater bloom?
3. How does the death of bottom plants in a shallow pond affect the rest of the pond?
4. **Thinking Critically  Problem Solving** A new housing development is to be built along a recreational lake. What factors should the developers consider to protect the lake from rapid eutrophication?

*Check Your Progress*

By now, you should have your teacher's approval for your plan, and you should have started growing your mushrooms. Make careful observations of growth every day. Include sketches and measurements as appropriate. Use a data table to organize the data you collect. *(Hint: As you make your observations, be careful not to disturb the experiment or introduce any new variables.)*

CHAPTER PROJECT
**3**

## You and Your Environment

# AN EXPLOSION OF LIFE

Living things are interconnected with their surroundings in many ways. In this lab, you will investigate how one change in a freshwater environment can affect everything that lives in that environment.

## Problem

How does the amount of fertilizer affect algae growth?

## Skills Focus

controlling variables, predicting, drawing conclusions

## Materials

4 glass jars with lids          marking pen
aged tap water                  aquarium water
graduated cylinder              liquid fertilizer

## Procedure

1. Read through the steps in the procedure. Then write a prediction describing what you think will happen in each of the four jars.
2. Copy the data table into your notebook. Be sure to allow enough lines to make entries for a two-week period.
3. Label four jars A, B, C, and D. Fill each jar half full with aged tap water.
4. Add aquarium water to each jar until the jar is three-fourths full.
5. Add 3 mL of liquid fertilizer to jar B; 6 mL to jar C; and 12 mL to jar D. Do not add any fertilizer to jar A. Loosely screw the lid on each jar. Place all the jars in a sunny location where they will receive the same amount of direct sunlight.

### DATA TABLE

| Date | Observations | | | |
|------|------|------|------|------|
| | Jar A<br>no<br>fertilizer | Jar B<br>3 mL<br>fertilizer | Jar C<br>6 mL<br>fertilizer | Jar D<br>12 mL<br>fertilizer |
| Day 1 | | | | |
| Day 2 | | | | |

6. Observe the jars every day for two weeks. Compare the color of the water in the four jars. Record your observations in your data table.

## Analyze and Conclude

1. How did the color in the four jars compare at the end of the two-week period? How can you account for any differences that you observed?
2. What was the purpose of jar A?
3. Describe the process that led to the overall color change in the water. What organisms were responsible for causing that color change?
4. Predict what would have happened if you placed the four jars in a dark location instead of in sunlight. Explain your prediction.
5. **Apply** What do you think might happen to fish and other living organisms when fertilizer gets into a body of fresh water? What are some ways that fertilizer might get into a body of water?

## Design an Experiment

Some detergents contain phosphates, which are an ingredient in many kinds of fertilizer. Design an experiment to compare how regular detergent and low-phosphate detergent affect the growth of algae.

## Eutrophication — The Threat to Clear, Clean Water

**W**eiss Lake, on the Georgia-Alabama border, is a popular vacation area. People come to this lake to fish, boat, and swim. But every year about 2 million pounds of phosphorus pour into Weiss Lake from rivers. These excess nutrients are threatening the lake's good fishing and clean, clear water.

Weiss Lake is just one of thousands of lakes and ponds in the United States threatened by eutrophication. The threat is not just to recreation. Drinking water for nearly 70 percent of Americans comes from lakes, reservoirs, and other surface water.

## The Issues

### Where Does the Pollution Come From?
The two main sources of excess nutrients are wastes and fertilizers from farms and wastewater from sewage treatment plants. When farmers fertilize crops, the plants absorb only some of these nutrients. The excess nutrients can be washed with soil into lakes and ponds. When wastewater from homes and factories is treated, large amounts of nutrients still remain in the water. For example, about 380 million liters of treated wastewater flow toward Weiss Lake daily. This treated wastewater still contains large amounts of phosphorus produced by many factories.

### What Are the Costs of Eutrophication?
People who live near Weiss Lake depend on the lake for jobs and money. But as the fish die in the oxygen-poor waters, swimming and boating in the murky water become less appealing and possibly unsafe. Over 4,000 jobs and millions of dollars each year would be lost if Weiss Lake were to close down. But upgrading or building new water-treatment plants would cost millions of dollars in higher taxes to citizens.

### What Can Be Done?
Even as cities, farms, and factories grow, the amount of nutrients reaching lakes and ponds can be reduced. Factories can install water-treatment facilities that remove more nitrogen and phosphorus from their wastewater. Farmers can often reduce the use of fertilizers. People can plant trees along the banks of lakes to reduce the amount of soil entering the lake. These solutions can cost millions of dollars, but they can reverse the problem.

## You Decide

### 1. Identify the Problem
In your own words, describe the eutrophication issues that affect Weiss Lake.

### 2. Analyze the Options
Make a chart of different ways to slow the eutrophication process. How would each work? What groups of people would be affected?

### 3. Find a Solution
Create a "prevention plan" advising town leaders how to reduce eutrophication in lakes and ponds.

## SECTION 3 Fungi

### DISCOVER

**Do All Molds Look Alike?**

1. Your teacher will give you two sealed, clear plastic bags—one containing moldy bread and another containing moldy fruit. **CAUTION:** *Do not open the sealed bags at any time.*

2. Examine each mold. In your notebook, describe what you see.

3. Then, use a hand lens to examine each mold. Sketch each mold in your notebook and list its characteristics.

4. Return the sealed bags to your teacher. Wash your hands.

**Think It Over**
*Observing* How are the molds similar? How do they differ?

---

Unnoticed, a speck of dust lands on a cricket's back. But this is no ordinary dust—it is alive! Tiny glistening threads emerge from the dust and begin to grow into the cricket's moist body. As they grow, the threads release chemicals that slowly dissolve the cricket's living tissues. The threads continue to grow deeper into the cricket's body. Within a few days, the cricket's body is little more than a hollow shell filled with a tangle of the deadly threads. Then the threads begin to grow up and out of the dead cricket. They produce long stalks with knobs at their tips. When one of the knobs breaks open, it will release thousands of dustlike specks, which the wind can carry to new victims.

### What Are Fungi?

The strange cricket-killing organism is a member of the fungi kingdom. Although you may not have heard of a cricket-killing fungus before, you are probably familiar with other kinds of fungi. For example, the molds that grow on stale bread or on decaying fruit are all fungi. Mushrooms that sprout in forests or yards are also fungi.

### GUIDE FOR READING

◆ What characteristics do fungi share?

◆ How do fungi obtain food?

◆ What roles do fungi play in the living world?

*Reading Tip* Before you read, preview the headings. Record them in outline form, leaving space for writing notes.

▼ A bush cricket attacked by a killer fungus

*Chapter 3* **A ◆ 95**

Fungi vary in size from the unicellular yeasts to the multicellular fungi, such as mushrooms and the bracket fungi that look like shelves growing on tree trunks. **Most fungi share three important characteristics: They are eukaryotes, use spores to reproduce, and are heterotrophs that feed in a similar way.** In addition, fungi need moist, warm places in which to grow. They thrive on moist foods, damp tree barks, lawns coated with dew, damp forest floors, and even wet bathroom tiles.

## Cell Structure

Except for yeast cells, which are unicellular, the cells of fungi are arranged in structures called hyphae. **Hyphae** (HY fee) (singular *hypha*) are the branching, threadlike tubes that make up the bodies of multicellular fungi. The hyphae of some fungi are continuous threads of cytoplasm that contain many nuclei. Substances move quickly and freely through the hyphae.

The appearance of a fungus depends on how its hyphae are arranged. In some fungi, the threadlike hyphae are loosely tangled. Fuzzy-looking molds that grow on old foods have loosely tangled hyphae. In other fungi, hyphae are packed tightly together. For example, the stalk and cap of the mushrooms in Figure 13 are made of hyphae packed so tightly that they appear solid. Underground, however, a mushroom's hyphae form a loose, threadlike maze in the soil.

☑ *Checkpoint* *What structures make up the bodies of multicellular fungi?*

Cap

Gills

Stalk

Hyphae

Underground hyphae

**Figure 13** The hyphae in the stalk and cap of a mushroom are packed tightly to form very firm structures. Underground hyphae, on the other hand, are arranged loosely. *Inferring What function do you think the underground hyphae perform?*

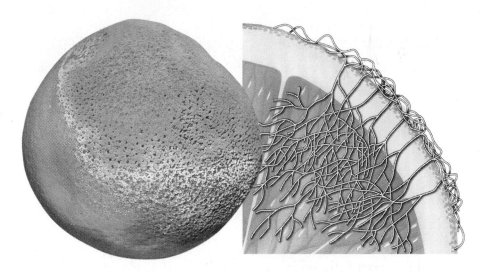

**Figure 14** The mold *Penicillium* often grows on old fruits such as this orange. Notice that some hyphae grow deep inside the orange. These hyphae digest the food and absorb the smaller chemicals.

## How Do Fungi Obtain Food?

Although fungi are heterotrophs, they do not take food into their bodies as you do. Instead fungi absorb food through hyphae that grow into the food source.

Look at Figure 14 to see how a fungus feeds. **First, the fungus grows hyphae into a food source. Then digestive chemicals ooze from the tips of the hyphae into the food. The digestive chemicals break down the food into small substances that can be absorbed by the hyphae.** Imagine yourself sinking your fingers down into a chocolate cake and dripping digestive chemicals out of your fingertips. Then imagine your fingers absorbing the digested particles of the cake. That's how a fungus feeds.

Some fungi feed on the remains of dead organisms. Other fungi are parasites that break down the chemicals in living organisms. For example, athlete's foot is a disease caused by a fungus that feeds on chemicals in a person's skin. Dutch elm disease is caused by a fungus that feeds on elm trees and eventually kills the trees.

## Reproduction in Fungi

Like it or not, fungi are everywhere. The way they reproduce guarantees their survival and spread. Fungi usually reproduce by producing lightweight spores that are surrounded by a protective covering. Spores can be carried easily through air or water to new sites. Fungi produce many more spores than will ever grow into new fungi. Only a few of the thousands of spores that a fungus releases will fall where conditions are right for them to grow into new organisms.

**Making Spore Prints**

In this activity, you will examine the reproductive structures of a mushroom.

1. Place a fresh mushroom cap, gill side down, on a sheet of white paper. **CAUTION:** *Do not eat the mushroom.*

2. Cover the mushroom cap with a plastic container. Wash your hands with soap.

3. After two days, carefully remove the container and then the cap. You should find a spore print on the paper.

4. Examine the print with a hand lens. Then wash your hands with soap.

*Predicting* Use your spore print to estimate how many spores a mushroom could produce. Where would spores be most likely to grow into new mushrooms?

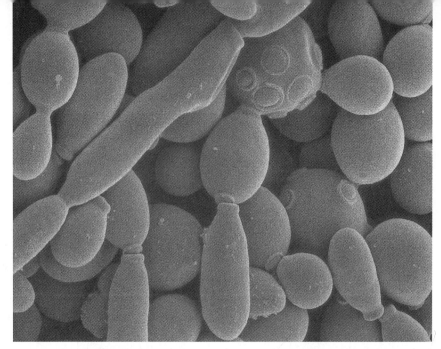

**Figure 15** Budding is a form of asexual reproduction that occurs in yeast. The small yeast cell that grows from the body of a parent cell is identical to the parent.

Fungi produce spores in structures called **fruiting bodies,** which are reproductive hyphae that grow out of a fungus. The appearances of fruiting bodies vary from one type of fungus to another. For some fungi, such as mushrooms and puffballs, the part of the fungus that you see is the fruiting body. In other fungi, such as bread molds, the stalklike fruiting bodies grow upward from the hyphae on the surface of the bread. The knoblike structure, or spore case, at the tip of a stalk contains the spores.

**Asexual Reproduction** Most fungi reproduce both asexually and sexually. When there is adequate moisture and food, most fungi reproduce asexually by growing fruiting bodies that release thousands of spores.

Unicellular yeast cells undergo a form of asexual reproduction called **budding.** In budding, no spores are produced. Instead, a small yeast cell grows from the body of a large, well-fed parent cell in a way that might remind you of a bud forming on the branch of a tree. The new cell then breaks away and lives on its own.

**Sexual Reproduction** When growing conditions become unfavorable, fungi may reproduce sexually. In sexual reproduction, the hyphae of two fungi grow together. A new spore-producing structure grows from the joined hyphae. The new structure produces spores, which can develop into fungi that differ from either parent.

☑ *Checkpoint* **What is a fruiting body?**

## Classification of Fungi

Fungi are classified into groups based on the shape of the spore-producing structures and on their ability to reproduce sexually. The four groups of fungi—the threadlike fungi, the sac fungi, the club fungi, and the imperfect fungi—are shown in Figure 16.

▲ **Threadlike Fungi**

This group contains about 600 different species of molds, including many common bread molds, such as this *Rhizopus nigrens*. These fungi produce spores in their threadlike hyphae.

▲ **Sac Fungi**

This group contains over 30,000 diverse species of fungi, including yeast, morels, truffles, and some fungi that cause plant diseases, such as Dutch elm disease. They are called sac fungi because they produce spores in structures that look like sacks. The sac fungi in the photo are called bird's nest fungi.

◀ **Club Fungi**

This group includes about 25,000 species of mushrooms, bracket fungi, plant parasites, and puffballs. Club fungi produce spores in structures that look like clubs. One of the puffballs in the photo is shooting out its spores.

▲ **Imperfect Fungi**

The 25,000 species in this group include this *Penicillium*, the source of an important antibiotic. The fungi in this group are not known to reproduce sexually.

**Figure 16** The four groups of fungi differ in the appearance of their spore-producing structures and in how they reproduce. *Classifying  To which group do mushrooms belong?*

# What's for Lunch?

**I**n this lab, you will draw conclusions about the effects of two substances on the activity of yeast.

## Problem

How does the presence of sugar or salt affect the activity of yeast?

## Materials

marking pen
5 plastic straws
salt
beaker
graduated cylinder
5 small narrow-necked bottles

5 round balloons
sugar
warm water (40–45°C)
dry powdered yeast

## Procedure

1. Copy the data table into your notebook. Then read over the entire procedure to see how you will test the activity of the yeast cells in bottles A through E. Write a prediction about what will happen in each bottle.

2. Gently stretch each of the 5 balloons so that they will inflate easily.

3. Using the marking pen, label the bottles A, B, C, D, and E.

4. Use a beaker to fill each bottle with the same amount of warm water. **CAUTION:** *Glass is fragile. Handle the bottles and beaker gently to avoid breakage. Do not touch broken glass.*

5. Put 5 mL of salt into bottle B.

6. Put 5 mL of sugar into bottles C and E.

7. Put 30 mL of sugar into bottle D.

8. Put 2 mL of powdered yeast into bottle A, and stir the mixture with a clean straw. Remove the straw and discard it.

9. Immediately place a balloon over the opening of bottle A. Make sure that the balloon opening fits very tightly around the neck of the bottle.

10. Repeat Steps 8 and 9 for bottle B, bottle C, and bottle D.

## DATA TABLE

| Bottle | Contents | Prediction | Observations |
|--------|----------|------------|--------------|
| A | Yeast alone | | |
| B | Yeast and 5 mL of salt | | |
| C | Yeast and 5 mL of sugar | | |
| D | Yeast and 30 mL of sugar | | |
| E | No yeast and 5 mL of sugar | | |

**Skills Lab**

11. Place a balloon over bottle E without adding yeast to the bottle.
12. Place the 5 bottles in a warm spot away from drafts. Observe and record what happens.

## Analyze and Conclude

1. Which balloons changed in size during this lab? How did they change?
2. Explain why the balloon changed size in some bottles and not in others. What caused that change in size?
3. Do yeast cells use sugar as a food source? How do you know?
4. Do yeast cells use salt as a food source? How do you know?
5. What did the results from bottle C show, compared with the results from bottle D?
6. **Think About It** If you removed bottle E from your experiment, would you be able to conclude whether or not sugar is a food source for the yeast cells? Why or why not?

## Design an Experiment

Develop a hypothesis about whether yeast cells need light to carry out their life activities. Then design an experiment to test your hypothesis. Obtain your teacher's permission before you carry out the experiment.

## Fungi and the Living World

Fungi affect humans and other organisms in many ways. **Fungi play an important role as decomposers on Earth. In addition, many fungi provide foods for people. Some cause disease and some fight disease. Still other fungi live in symbiosis with other organisms.**

**Environmental Recycling**  Like bacteria, fungi are decomposers—organisms that break down the chemicals in dead organisms. For example, many fungi live in the soil and break down the chemicals in dead plant matter. This process returns important nutrients to the soil. Without fungi and bacteria, Earth would be buried under dead plants and animals.

**Food and Fungi**  When you eat a slice of bread, you benefit from the work of yeast. Bakers add yeast to bread dough to make it rise. Yeast cells use the sugar in the dough for food and produce carbon dioxide gas as they feed. The gas forms bubbles, which cause the dough to rise. You see these bubbles as holes in a slice of bread. Without yeast, bread would be flat and solid. Yeast is also used to make wine from grapes. Yeast cells feed on the sugar in the grapes and produce carbon dioxide and alcohol.

Other fungi are also important sources of foods. Molds are used in the production of foods such as some cheeses. The blue streaks in blue cheese, for example, are actually growths of *Penicillium roqueforti*. People enjoy eating mushrooms in salads and soups and on pizza. Because some mushrooms are poisonous, however, you should never pick or eat wild mushrooms.

*Checkpoint* *What are three foods that fungi help to produce?*

**Disease-Causing Fungi**  Many fungi cause serious diseases in plants that result in huge crop losses every year. Corn smut and wheat rust are two club fungi that cause diseases in important food crops. Fungal plant diseases also affect other crops, including rice, cotton, and soybeans.

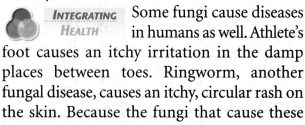

**INTEGRATING HEALTH**  Some fungi cause diseases in humans as well. Athlete's foot causes an itchy irritation in the damp places between toes. Ringworm, another fungal disease, causes an itchy, circular rash on the skin. Because the fungi that cause these

**Figure 17** Many food crops are lost each year due to fungal diseases. The ear of corn in the photo has been attacked by a fungus called corn smut. *Making Generalizations Why is the spread of fungal diseases difficult to control?*

diseases produce spores at the site of infection, the diseases can spread easily from person to person. Both diseases can be treated with antifungal medications.

**Disease-Fighting Fungi** In 1928 a Scottish biologist, Alexander Fleming, was examining petri dishes in which he was growing bacteria. To his surprise, Fleming noticed a spot of a bluish-green mold growing in one dish. Curiously, no bacteria were growing near the mold. Fleming hypothesized that the mold, a fungus named *Penicillium*, produced a substance that killed the bacteria growing near it. Fleming's work led to the development of the first antibiotic, penicillin. It has saved the lives of millions of people with bacterial infections. Since the discovery of penicillin, many additional antibiotics have been isolated from both fungi and eubacteria.

**Fungus-Plant Root Associations** Some fungi help plants grow larger and healthier when their hyphae grow among the plant's roots. The hyphae spread out underground and absorb water and nutrients from the soil for the plant. With more water and nutrients, the plant grows larger than it would have grown without its fungal partner. The plant is not the only partner that benefits. The fungi get to feed on the extra food that the plant makes and stores.

Many plants are so dependent on their fungal partners that they cannot survive well without them. For example, orchids cannot grow without their fungal partners.

## Language Arts
### CONNECTION

Folk tales are ancient stories that were passed down by word of mouth over many generations. Folk tales often involve magical elements, such as fairies—supernatural beings with powers to become invisible, change form, and affect the lives of people.

The circle of mushrooms in Figure 18 was often mentioned in folk tales. These circles were said to be the footprints of fairies who danced there at midnight. These mushroom circles were given the name "fairy rings"—a name that is still used today. People believed that the area inside a fairy ring was a magical location. Cutting down the tree inside a fairy ring was believed to bring bad luck.

*In Your Journal*

A type of mushroom called a toadstool is mentioned in some folk tales. Write a paragraph that could be part of a folk tale that reveals how toadstools got their name.

**Figure 18** The fruiting bodies of these mushrooms have emerged in an almost perfect circular pattern. This pattern is called a fairy ring. The mushrooms share the same network of underground hyphae.

**Figure 19** Lichens consist of a fungus living together with either algae or autotrophic bacteria.
**A.** This lichen—a British soldier—probably gets its name from its scarlet red tops, which stand upright. **B.** The lichens covering these rocks are slowly breaking down the rocks to create soil.

**Lichens** A **lichen** (LY kun) consists of a fungus and either algae or autotrophic bacteria that also live together in a mutualistic relationship. You have probably seen some familiar lichens—irregular, flat, crusty patches that grow on tree barks or rocks. The fungus benefits from the food produced by the algae or bacteria. The algae or bacteria, in turn, obtain water and minerals from the fungus.

*INTEGRATING EARTH SCIENCE* Lichens are often called "pioneer" organisms because they are the first organisms to appear on the bare rocks in an area after a volcano, fire, or rock slide has occurred. Over time, the lichens break down the rock into soil in which other organisms can grow. Lichens are also useful as indicators of air pollution. Many species of lichens are very sensitive to pollutants and die when pollution levels rise. By monitoring the growth of lichens, scientists can assess the air quality in an area.

## Section 3 Review

1. List three characteristics that fungi share.
2. Explain how a fungus feeds. What do fungi feed on?
3. Describe three roles that fungi play in the world.
4. **Thinking Critically Classifying** Explain why mushrooms are classified as fungi rather than as plants.

**Check Your Progress**

CHAPTER PROJECT 3

Continue to observe your mushrooms and collect data. Begin to review your data to see which conditions favored mushroom growth. How do your results compare with your hypothesis? Begin to plan your poster now. Think about how you can use graphs and diagrams to display your results. *(Hint:* Draw a rough sketch of your poster, and show it to your teacher. Include a labeled drawing of a mushroom.)

## SECTION 1 Protists

### Key Ideas

◆ Animal-like protists, or protozoans, include sarcodines, ciliates, zooflagellates, and sporozoans. Like animals, these protists are heterotrophs. Most protozoans move by using pseudopods, cilia, or flagella.

◆ Funguslike protists include water molds, downy mildews, and slime molds. Like fungi, these protists are heterotrophs, have cell walls, and use spores to reproduce.

◆ Plantlike protists, or algae, include euglenoids, dinoflagellates, diatoms, green algae, red algae, and brown algae. Like plants, these organisms are autotrophs.

### Key Terms

protozoan
pseudopod
contractile vacuole
cilia
symbiosis

mutualism
spore
algae
pigment

## SECTION 2 Algal Blooms

INTEGRATING ENVIRONMENTAL SCIENCE

### Key Ideas

◆ Red tides occur when a population of algae increases quickly in ocean waters. Some algae can secrete toxins that poison animals.

◆ Nutrients in a lake or pond build up over time, causing an increase in the numbers of algae. An accelerated rate of eutrophication can lead to the deaths of many organisms in the lake or pond.

### Key Terms

algal bloom
red tide

eutrophication

## SECTION 3 Fungi

### Key Ideas

◆ Most fungi are eukaryotes, use spores to reproduce, and are heterotrophs.

◆ Most fungi feed by absorbing food through their hyphae. The hyphae secrete digestive chemicals into a food source, which is broken down into small substances that are absorbed by the hyphae.

◆ Fungi produce spores in structures called fruiting bodies. The majority of fungi reproduce both asexually and sexually.

◆ Fungi are decomposers that recycle Earth's chemicals. In addition, some fungi cause disease while some fight disease. Many produce important foods for people. Some fungi live in symbiotic relationships with other organisms.

### Key Terms

hypha
fruiting body
budding
lichen

USING THE INTERNET
www.science-explorer.phschool.com

# Reviewing Content

For more review of key concepts, see the Interactive Student Tutorial CD-ROM.

## Multiple Choice
*Choose the letter of the best answer.*

1. Which of the following characteristics describes *all* protists?
   a. They are unicellular.
   b. They can be seen with the unaided eye.
   c. Their cells have nuclei.
   d. They are unable to move on their own.

2. Which protist uses cilia to move?
   a. euglena
   b. ameba
   c. paramecium
   d. diatom

3. Which statement is true of slime molds?
   a. They are always unicellular.
   b. They are autotrophs.
   c. They are animal-like protists.
   d. They use spores to reproduce.

4. An overpopulation of saltwater algae is called a(n)
   a. pigment.
   b. lichen.
   c. red tide.
   d. eutrophication.

5. A lichen is a symbiotic association between which of the following?
   a. fungi and plant roots
   b. algae and fungi
   c. algae and bacteria
   d. protozoans and algae

## True or False
*If the statement is true, write true. If it is false, change the underlined word or words to make the statement true.*

6. Sarcodines use <u>flagella</u> to move.

7. <u>Eutrophication</u> is the process by which nutrients in a lake build up over time, causing an increase in the growth of algae.

8. Most fungi are made up of threadlike structures called <u>hyphae</u>.

9. All mushrooms are classified as <u>sac</u> fungi.

10. Most fungi that live among the roots of plants are <u>beneficial</u> to the plants.

# Checking Concepts

11. Describe how an ameba obtains its food.
12. How do algae differ in terms of size?
13. Compare how animal-like, funguslike, and plantlike protists obtain food.
14. How does sexual reproduction occur in fungi?
15. Explain how both organisms in a lichen benefit from their symbiotic relationship.
16. **Writing to Learn** Imagine you are a spore in a ripe puffball. An animal passing by punctures the outer covering of your spore case. Describe what happens to you next.

# Thinking Visually

17. **Flowchart** Copy this flowchart about changes in a lake onto a separate sheet of paper. Then complete the flowchart and add a title. (For more on flowcharts, see the Skills Handbook.)

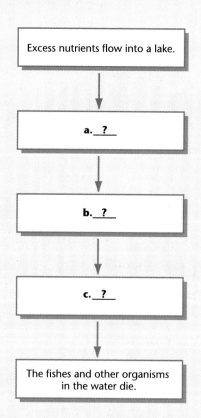

Excess nutrients flow into a lake.

a. ____?____

b. ____?____

c. ____?____

The fishes and other organisms in the water die.

## Applying Skills

When yeast is added to bread dough, the yeast cells produce carbon dioxide, which causes the dough to rise. The graph below shows how temperature affects the amount of carbon dioxide that is produced. Use the graph to answer Questions 18–20.

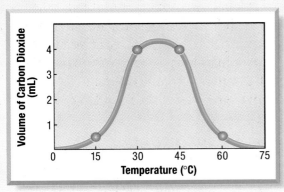

18. **Interpreting Data** Explain how temperature affects the amount of carbon dioxide that the yeast cells produce.
19. **Inferring** Use the graph to explain why yeast is dissolved in warm water rather than cold water when it is used to make bread.

20. **Predicting** Based on the graph, would you expect bread dough to continue to rise if it were placed in a refrigerator (about 2°–5°C)? Explain.

## Thinking Critically

21. **Comparing and Contrasting** How are amebas and paramecia similar to one another? How are they different?
22. **Relating Cause and Effect** You see a layer of green scum growing on the walls of your aquarium at home. List some possible reasons why this growth has occurred.
23. **Predicting** If algae disappeared from Earth's waters, what would happen to living things on Earth? Explain your answer.
24. **Problem Solving** What actions could homeowners take to discourage the growth of mildew in their basement? Explain why these actions might help solve the problem.

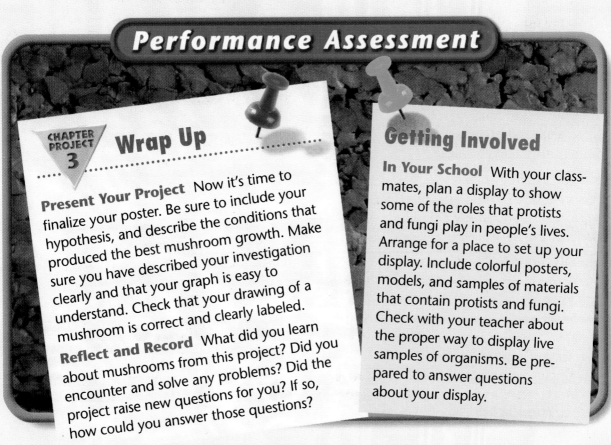

## Performance Assessment

### CHAPTER PROJECT 3 — Wrap Up

**Present Your Project** Now it's time to finalize your poster. Be sure to include your hypothesis, and describe the conditions that produced the best mushroom growth. Make sure you have described your investigation clearly and that your graph is easy to understand. Check that your drawing of a mushroom is correct and clearly labeled.

**Reflect and Record** What did you learn about mushrooms from this project? Did you encounter and solve any problems? Did the project raise new questions for you? If so, how could you answer those questions?

### Getting Involved

**In Your School** With your classmates, plan a display to show some of the roles that protists and fungi play in people's lives. Arrange for a place to set up your display. Include colorful posters, models, and samples of materials that contain protists and fungi. Check with your teacher about the proper way to display live samples of organisms. Be prepared to answer questions about your display.

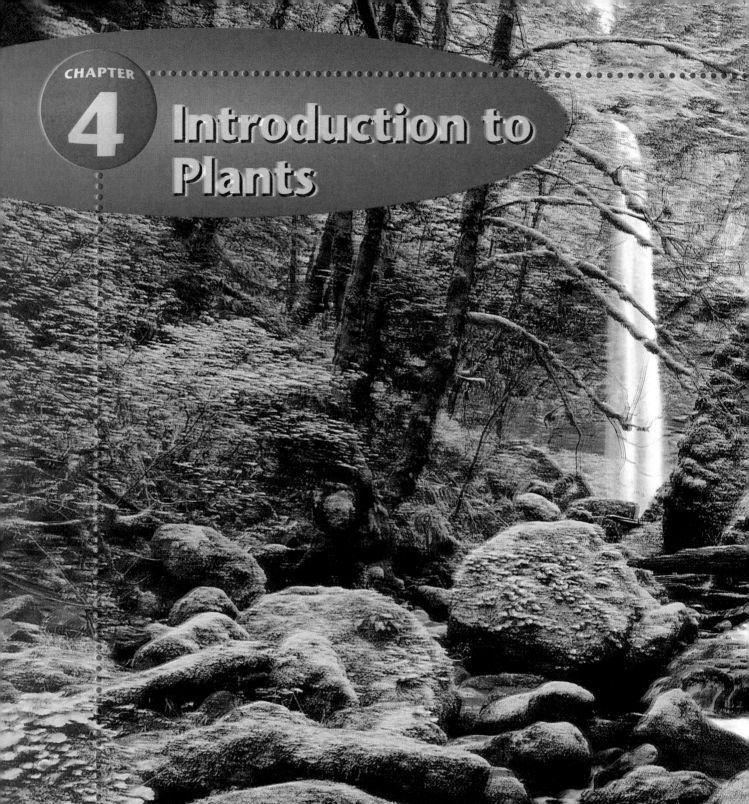

# CHAPTER 4 Introduction to Plants

## WHAT'S AHEAD

### 1 The Plant Kingdom

Discover **What Do Leaves Reveal About Plants?**
Sharpen Your Skills **Interpreting Data**

*Integrating Physics*
### 2 Photosynthesis and Light

Skills Lab **Eye on Photosynthesis**
Discover **What Colors Make Up Sunlight?**

### 3 Mosses, Liverworts, and Hornworts

Discover **Will Mosses Absorb Water?**
Skills Lab **Masses of Mosses**

# Become a Moss Expert

I n a shady valley, mosses cover the banks of a stream. Over-head, trees stretch their branches toward the light. Each type of plant has its own requirements for growth. In this project, you'll care for one type of plant, a moss similar to the ones growing on these rocks. By the time you're finished, you'll be able to tell others what conditions are needed for mosses to grow.

**Your Goal** To create a brochure titled "How to Raise Mosses" to share with an audience of your choice.

To successfully complete this project you must
◆ grow moss in a terrarium you construct from a 2-liter bottle
◆ observe the moss daily, and keep a log of the amount of light, water, and other conditions you provide for it
◆ publish information about caring for mosses
◆ follow the safety guidelines in Appendix A

**Get Started** In a small group, create a list of places where you've seen mosses growing. Compare the list your group makes with those from other groups. What are some locations that many groups identified? What do you notice about the environments where mosses are found? List possible ways to create a similar environment in a terrarium. Start to write out a plan for making the terrarium.

**Check Your Progress** You'll be working on this project as you study this chapter. To keep your project on track, look for Check Your Progress boxes at the following points.

**Section 1 Review**, page 117: Plan your terrarium.
**Section 3 Review**, page 128: Provide the proper conditions as you care for your moss.
**Section 4 Review**, page 134: Plan and produce your brochure.

**Wrap Up** At the end of the chapter (page 137), you'll share your brochure about mosses with your audience.

Mosses carpet the rocks along this stream in Pennsylvania's Pocono Mountains.

**SECTION 4** **Ferns and Their Relatives**

**Discover** How Quickly Can Water Move Upward?
**Try This** Examining a Fern

# SECTION 1 The Plant Kingdom

## DISCOVER ···································· ACTIVITY····

### What Do Leaves Reveal About Plants?

1. Your teacher will give you two leaves from plants that grow in two very different environments: a desert and an area with average rainfall.

2. Carefully observe the color, size, shape, and texture of the leaves. Touch the surfaces of each leaf. Examine each leaf with a hand lens. Record your observations in your notebook.

3. When you have finished, wash your hands thoroughly with soap and water.

**Think It Over**
*Inferring* Use your observations to determine which plant lives in the desert and which does not. Give at least one reason to support your inference.

---

### GUIDE FOR READING

◆ What characteristics do all plants share?

◆ What do plants need to live successfully on land?

*Reading Tip* Before you read, list the boldfaced vocabulary words in your notebook. Leave space to add notes as you read.

Imagine a forest where a thick growth of fungi, mosses, and ferns carpets the floor. Because there is no bare soil, seedlings start their lives on fallen logs. Ferns hang like curtains from the limbs of giant hemlock trees. Douglas fir trees grow taller than 20-story buildings. Other plants with strange names—scouler willow, vanilla leaf, self-heal, and licorice fern—also grow in the forest.

Such a forest exists on the western slopes of the Olympic Mountains in Washington State. Native Americans named the forest *Hoh*, which means "fast white water," after a river there. In some areas of the forest, over 300 centimeters of rain fall each year, which makes the area a rain forest. But unlike rain forests in the tropics, the most common trees in the Hoh rain forest are maples, spruces, red cedars, and firs.

▼ **The Hoh rain forest**

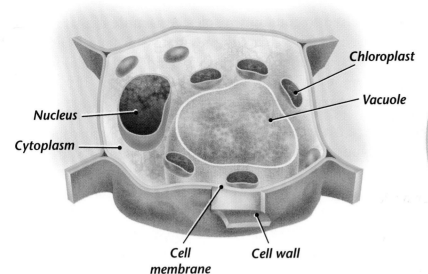

Nucleus

Cytoplasm

Chloroplast

Vacuole

Cell membrane

Cell wall

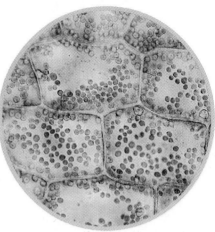

**Figure 1** Plants have eukaryotic cells that are enclosed by a cell wall. *Interpreting Photographs Which plant cell structures can you find in the photograph on the right? What roles do these structures play?*

## What Is a Plant?

You would probably recognize many of the plants that grow in the Hoh rain forest. You encounter other familiar plants when you pick flowers, run across freshly cut grass, or eat vegetables such as carrots. Members of the plant kingdom share some important characteristics. **Plants are autotrophs that produce their own food. In addition, all plants are eukaryotes that contain many cells.**

**Plants Are Autotrophs** You can think of a plant as a sun-powered, food-making factory. The process by which plants make food is called **photosynthesis** (foh toh SIN thuh sis). The word *photosynthesis* comes from two Greek words. *Photo* means "light," and *synthesis* means "to make." During photosynthesis, a plant uses carbon dioxide gas and water to make food and oxygen. The process occurs in a series of complex chemical reactions. Sunlight provides the energy that powers the entire process. You will learn more about the process of photosynthesis in the next section.

**Plant Cells** If you were to look at a plant's cells under a microscope, you would see that plants are eukaryotes. But unlike the cells of some other eukaryotes, a plant's cells are enclosed by a cell wall. The **cell wall** is a boundary that surrounds the cell membrane and separates the cell from the environment. Plant cell walls are made mostly of **cellulose** (SEL yuh lohs), a chemical that makes the walls rigid. Because of the rigid cell walls, plant cells look something like boxes, as Figure 1 shows.

Plant cells also contain many structures called chloroplasts. **Chloroplasts** (KLAWR uh plasts), which look similar to green jelly beans, are the structures in which food is made. The Greek word *chloro* means "green."

Plant cells also contain vacuoles. A **vacuole** is a large, sack-like storage area. The vacuole stores many substances, including water, wastes, and food. A vacuole expands like a balloon when water enters it and shrinks when water leaves it. If too much water leaves a plant's vacuoles, the plant wilts.

**Plants Are Multicellular** You don't need a microscope to see plants because they are multicellular. Plants do vary greatly in size, however. For example, mosses are among the smallest plants—many are only a few millimeters tall. But some redwood trees can grow over 80 meters tall.

No matter how large or small a plant is, its cells are organized into **tissues**—groups of similar cells that perform a specific function in an organism. For example, most plants that live on land have tissues that transport materials throughout their bodies. You will learn about some important plant tissues later in this chapter.

☑ *Checkpoint* *What is the function of the vacuole in a plant cell?*

## Origin of Plants

Which organisms were the ancestors of today's plants? To answer this question, biologists study fossils, the traces of ancient life forms preserved in rock and other substances. The oldest plant fossils are about 400 million years old. These fossils show that early plants resembled small algae.

Other clues to the origin of plants come from analyzing the chemical makeup of plants. In particular, biologists study a green pigment called **chlorophyll** (KLAWR uh fil), which is found in the chloroplasts of plants as well as in algae and some bacteria. Like ice cream, chlorophyll comes in different "flavors," or forms, that have slightly different chemical structures. Scientists have found that plants and green algae contain the same form of chlorophyll. For this reason, biologists infer that ancient green algae were the ancestors of today's plants.

**Figure 2** These fossils are from two plants that lived about 300 million years ago. The larger fossil is of a fern's leaf. The small star-shaped fossil is of a plant called a horsetail. *Inferring What organisms do scientists think gave rise to today's plants?*

**Figure 3** Plants have adaptations that help them retain water. The shiny, waterproof cuticle on this leaf slows down evaporation.

## Living on Land

Unlike algae, most plants live on land. How is living on land different from living in water? Imagine multicellular green algae floating in the ocean. Their bodies are held up toward the sunlight by the water around them. The algae obtain water and other materials directly from their watery surroundings. When algae reproduce, sperm cells swim to egg cells through the water.

Now imagine the same green algae living on land. Would the algae be able to stand upright? Could they absorb water and other materials from their surroundings? Could their sperm cells swim to egg cells? The answer to all of these questions is no. **For plants to survive on land, they must have ways to obtain water and other materials from their surroundings, retain water, transport materials throughout the plant, support their bodies, and reproduce successfully.** In *Exploring Plant Adaptations* on the next page, you can see some of the ways in which plants are adapted to live on land.

**Obtaining Water and Other Materials** Recall that all organisms need water to survive. Obtaining water is easy for algae because water surrounds them. To live on land, though, plants need adaptations for obtaining water from the soil. Plants must also have ways of obtaining other nutrients from the soil.

**Retaining Water** Have you ever noticed that a puddle of rainwater gradually shrinks and then disappears after the rain stops? This happens because there is more water in the puddle than in the air. As a result, the water evaporates into the air. The same principle explains why a plant on land can dry out. Because there is more water in plant cells than in air, water evaporates into the air. Plants need adaptations to reduce water loss to the air. One common adaptation is a waxy, waterproof layer called the **cuticle** that covers the leaves of most plants.

## Sharpen your Skills

**Interpreting Data**

**ACTIVITY**

The table shows how much water a certain plant loses during the hours listed.

| Time | Water Loss (grams) |
|---|---|
| 7 to 8 AM | 190 |
| 9 to 10 AM | 209 |
| 11 to Noon | 221 |
| 1 to 2 PM | 233 |
| 3 to 4 PM | 227 |
| 5 to 6 PM | 213 |
| 7 to 8 PM | 190 |
| 9 to 10 PM | 100 |
| 11 to Midnight | 90 |

When does the plant lose the most water? The least water? How could you account for the pattern you see?

# EXPLORING *Plant Adaptations*

Today, plants are found in almost every environment on Earth—deserts, lakes, jungles, and even the polar regions. As you read about each plant, notice how it is adapted to living in its specific environment.

**◄ Pasque Flower**
Pasque flowers, such as this *Anemone patens,* often grow on cold, rocky mountain slopes. The flower's petals trap sunlight, keeping the flower up to 10° C warmer than the surrounding air. This feature enables the plant to survive in cold environments.

**▲ Bristlecone Pine**
Because the needles of bristlecone pines live more than 15 years, the trees survive long periods of drought. Bristlecone pine trees can live more than 4,000 years. This is because they grow slowly in high altitude areas where there are few harmful insects or other disease-causing organisims.

**Staghorn Fern ►**
Staghorn ferns do not grow in soil. Instead, they cling to the bark of trees in tropical areas. The leaves that hug the bark store water and nutrients. The leaves that hang down are involved in reproduction.

**◄ Water Lily**
Water lilies live only in fresh water. Large, flat leaves and sweet-smelling flowers float on the water's surface. The plants have long stems under the water. Roots anchor the plant in the mud at the bottom of the pond.

**Rafflesia** ▶
The rafflesia plant produces the largest flowers on Earth. This flower that grew in Borneo measures over 83 centimeters in diameter. Rafflesia flowers have a foul odor—something like rotting meat. The odor attracts insects that help the plant reproduce.

▲ **Mangrove**
Mangrove trees, such as these on Guadalcanal Island in the Pacific Ocean, grow in salt water in tropical areas. The tree's huge root system makes the tree appear as if it is on stilts. The roots trap soil and sand around them, providing a material in which to anchor as they grow.

◀ **Date Palm**
Date palms, such as these growing on a date farm in southern California, grow in warm climates. These flowering trees can grow up to 23 meters tall. The leaves are long and narrow, reducing the amount of surface area for evaporation. The female trees produce dates that hang from the stems in large clusters.

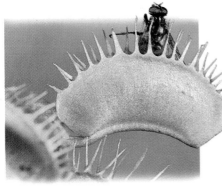

◀ **Venus Fly Trap**
The Venus fly trap can grow in soil that is low in nitrogen. This is because the plant obtains its nitrogen by digesting insects that it traps. When an insect touches sensitive hairs on the inner surface of a leaf, the two parts of the leaf quickly snap shut. It takes about ten days for the plant to digest an insect.

**Transporting Materials** A plant needs to transport food, water, minerals, and other materials from one part of its body to another. In general, water and minerals are taken up by the bottom part of the plant. Food is made in the top part. But all the plant's cells need water, minerals, and food. To supply all cells with the materials they need, water and minerals must be transported up to the top of the plant. Then food must be transported throughout the plant.

Some plants have transporting tissue called **vascular tissue.** Vascular tissue is an internal system of tubelike structures through which water and food move inside the plant. Plants that have vascular tissue are called vascular plants. Vascular plants can grow quite tall because they have an effective way of transporting substances to distant cells.

**Support** While algae are supported by the surrounding water, a plant on land must support its own body. Because plants need sunlight for photosynthesis, the food-making parts of the plant must be exposed to as much sunlight as possible. In vascular plants, vascular tissue strengthens and supports the large bodies of the plants.

**Reproduction** All plants undergo sexual reproduction that involves fertilization. **Fertilization** occurs when a sperm cell unites with an egg cell. The fertilized egg is called a **zygote.** For algae and some plants, fertilization can only occur if there is water in the environment. This is because sperm cells swim through the water to egg cells. Other plants, however, have an adaptation that make it possible for fertilization to occur in dry environments. You will learn more about this adaptation in the next chapter.

**Figure 4** The vascular tissue in these tree ferns transports water and nutrients inside the plants. Vascular tissue also strengthens and supports the plants' stems and leaves.

*Checkpoint* *Why do plants need adaptations to prevent water loss?*

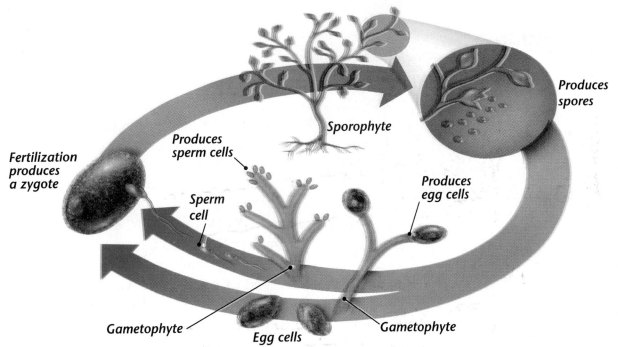

Fertilization
produces
a zygote

Produces
sperm cells

Sporophyte

Produces
spores

Sperm
cell

Produces
egg cells

Gametophyte

Egg cells

Gametophyte

## Complex Life Cycles

Unlike most animals, plants have complex life cycles that are made up of two different stages, or generations. In one stage, called the **sporophyte** (SPAWR uh fyt), the plant produces spores, the tiny cells that can grow into new organisms. A spore develops into the plant's other stage, called the gametophyte. In the **gametophyte** (guh MEE tuh fyt) stage, the plant produces two kinds of sex cells, or **gametes**—sperm cells and egg cells.

Figure 5 shows a typical plant life cycle. A sperm cell and egg cell join to form a zygote. The zygote then develops into a sporophyte. The sporophyte produces spores, which develop into the gameophyte. Then the gameophyte produces sperm cells and egg cells and the cycle starts again. The sporophyte of a plant usually looks quite different than the gametophyte.

**Figure 5** Plants have complex life cycles that consist of two stages—the sporophyte stage and the gametophyte stage. *Interpreting Diagrams* During which stage are sperm and egg cells produced?

## Section 1 Review

1. List three characteristics that all plants share.
2. What are five adaptations that plants need to survive on land?
3. What evidence led scientists to think that green algae were the ancestors of plants?
4. **Thinking Critically** **Classifying** Suppose you found a tall plant living in the desert. Do you think it would be a vascular plant? Explain.

**Check Your Progress**

**CHAPTER PROJECT 4**

At this point, your plan for creating a terrarium should be complete. On a sheet of paper, list the conditions that will affect moss growth. Explain how you'll provide those conditions in your terrarium. (*Hint:* Use a sketch to show what your bottle terrarium will look like.)

# Eye on Photosynthesis

I n this lab, you'll design an experiment to investigate what substances and conditions are needed for photosynthesis.

## Problem

What raw materials and conditions are involved in photosynthesis?

## Materials

Elodea plants                 2 test tubes
water (boiled, then cooled)   2 wax pencils
wide-mouthed container        lamp (optional)
sodium bicarbonate solution

## Procedure

### Part 1 Observing Photosynthesis

1. Use a wax pencil to label two test tubes *1* and *2*. Fill test tube 1 with sodium bicarbonate solution, which provides a source of carbon dioxide.

2. Fill the container about three-fourths full of sodium bicarbonate solution.

3. Hold your thumb over the mouth of test tube 1. Turn the test tube over, and lower the tube to the bottom of the container. Do not let in any air. If necessary, repeat this step so that test tube 1 contains no air pockets. **CAUTION:** *Glass test tubes are fragile. Handle the test tubes carefully. Do not touch broken glass.*

4. Fill test tube 2 with sodium bicarbonate solution. Place an *Elodea* plant in the tube with the cut stem at the bottom. Put your thumb over the mouth of the test tube, and lower it into the container without letting in any air. Wash your hands.

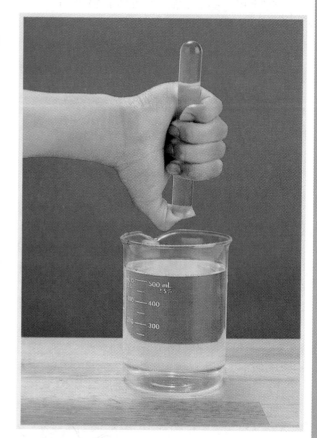

5. Place the container with the two test tubes in bright light. After a few minutes, examine both test tubes for bubbles.

6. If bubbles form in test tube 2, observe the *Elodea* stem to see if it is producing the bubbles. The bubbles are oxygen bubbles. The production of oxygen signals that photosynthesis is taking place.

7. Leave the setup in bright light for thirty minutes. Observe what happens to any bubbles that form. Record your observations.

## Part 2  Is Carbon Dioxide Needed for Photosynthesis?

8. Your teacher will provide a supply of water that has been boiled and then cooled. Boiling drives off gases that are dissolved in the water, including carbon dioxide.

9. Based on what you learned in Part 1, design an experiment to show whether or not carbon dioxide is needed for photosynthesis. Obtain your teacher's approval before carrying out your experiment. Record all your observations.

## Part 3  What Other Conditions Are Needed for Photosynthesis?

10. Make a list of other factors that may affect photosynthesis. For example, think about conditions such as light, the size of the plant, and the number of leaves.

11. Choose one factor from your list. Then design an experiment to show how the factor affects photosynthesis. Obtain your teacher's approval before carrying out your experiment. Record all your observations.

## Analyze and Conclude

1. What process produced the bubbles you observed in Part 1?
2. In Part 1, what was the purpose of test tube 1?
3. Based on your results in Part 2, is carbon dioxide necessary for photosynthesis?
4. Explain what you learned about photosynthesis from the investigation you did in Part 3.
5. **Think About It**  For the experiments you carried out in Parts 2 and 3, identify the manipulated variable and the responding variable. Explain whether or not your experiments were controlled experiments.

## More to Explore

A small animal in a closed container will die, even if it has enough water and food. A small animal in a closed container with a plant, water, and food will not die. Use what you have learned from this experiment to explain those facts.

## SECTION 2 Photosynthesis and Light

### What Colors Make Up Sunlight?

1. Glue a piece of white paper onto the inside bottom of a shoebox.

2. Place the box on its side near a window or outside in a sunny area.

3. [icon] Hold a mirror in front of the open side of the box. Adjust the mirror until it reflects sunlight onto the paper in the box. **CAUTION:** *Do not direct the sunlight into your eyes.*

4. Hold a prism between the mirror and the box as shown in the photo. Adjust the location of the prism so that sunlight passes through the prism.

5. Describe what you see on the paper in the box.

**Think It Over**

*Observing* What did you learn about light by carrying out this investigation?

---

### GUIDE FOR READING

◆ What happens when light strikes a green leaf?

◆ How do scientists describe the overall process of photosynthesis?

*Reading Tip* As you read, make a list of the main ideas and the supporting details about photosynthesis.

The year was 1883. T. W. Engelmann, a German biologist, was at work in his laboratory. He peered into the microscope at some strands of algae on a slide. The microscope had a prism located between the light source and the algae. As Engelmann watched the algae, he saw gas bubbles forming in the water around some of the cells. Curiously, no gas bubbles formed around other cells. Although Engelmann did not know it at the time, his experiment provided a clue about how light is involved in photosynthesis. To understand what Engelmann observed, you need to know more about the nature of light.

### The Nature of Light

The sun is the source of energy on Earth. If you take a walk outside on a sunny day, you feel the sun's energy as the sun heats your skin. You see the energy in the form of light on objects around you. The light that you see is called white light. But when white light passes through a prism, you can see that it is made up of the colors of the rainbow—red, orange, yellow, green, blue, and violet. Scientists refer to these colors as the visible spectrum.

**Figure 6** When sunlight passes through a prism, it separates into its parts—the colors of the rainbow.

In addition to prisms, white light strikes many other objects. Some objects such as glass and other transparent materials transmit light, or allow the light to pass through. Shiny surfaces such as mirrors reflect, or bounce back, light. Dark objects such as street pavements absorb, or take in and hold, light.

Most objects, however, reflect some colors of the visible spectrum while they absorb other colors. For example, when white light strikes a red shirt, the shirt absorbs most of the light's colors. However, the shirt reflects red light. The shirt looks red because your eyes see the reflected color.

✓ *Checkpoint* *What are the colors of the visible spectrum?*

## Plants and Light

Like red shirts and most other objects around you, plants absorb some colors of the visible spectrum and reflect others. **When light strikes the green leaves of a plant, most of the green part of the spectrum is reflected. Most of the other colors of light are absorbed.**

**Plant Pigments** When light strikes a leaf, it is absorbed by pigments found in the chloroplasts of the cells. Chlorophyll, the most abundant pigment in plants, absorbs most of the blue and red light. Green light, on the other hand, is reflected rather than absorbed. This explains why chlorophyll appears green in color, and why plants appear green.

Other pigments, called **accessory pigments,** include yellow, orange, and red pigments. These pigments absorb colors of light that chlorophyll does not. Most accessory pigments are not visible in plants for most of the year because they are masked by the chlorophyll. However, in some areas during the fall season, cool temperatures break down the chlorophyll in many plants. The colors of the accessory pigments become visible and produce the beautiful orange, red, and yellow colors of fall leaves.

**Figure 7** When chlorophyll breaks down in some trees in the fall, the accessory pigments in the leaves become visible. *Applying Concepts Which colors do the accessory pigments in leaves reflect?*

**Capturing Energy**   Because light is a form of energy, a substance that absorbs light absorbs energy. Just as a car requires the energy in gasoline to move, the process of photosynthesis in plants requires energy in the form of light. Photosynthesis begins when light strikes the chlorophyll in the chloroplasts of the plant's cells. The light energy that is absorbed powers the process of photosynthesis.

☑ *Checkpoint*   *What colors of light does chlorophyll absorb?*

## Unraveling the Mysteries of Photosynthesis

**What do plants need to make their own food? What substances do plants produce in the process of photosynthesis? Over time, the work of many scientists has provided answers to these questions.**

### 1771
### Joseph Priestley

When Joseph Priestley, an English scientist, placed a burning candle in a covered jar, the flame went out. When he placed both a plant and a candle in a covered jar, the candle kept burning. Priestley concluded that the plant released something into the air that kept the candle burning. Today we know that plants produce oxygen, a product of photosynthesis.

| 1650 | 1750 |
| --- | --- |

### 1643
### Jean-Baptiste Van Helmont

A Dutch scientist, Jean-Baptiste Van Helmont, planted a willow tree in a tub of soil. After five years of adding only water, the tree gained 74 kilograms. Van Helmont concluded that trees need only water to grow. Today it is known that water is one of the raw materials of photosynthesis.

### 1779
### Jan Ingenhousz

Jan Ingenhousz, a Dutch scientist, placed branches with leaves in water. In sunlight, the leaves produced oxygen bubbles. In the dark, the leaves produced no oxygen. Ingenhousz concluded that plants need sunlight to produce oxygen, a product of photosynthesis.

# The Chemistry of Photosynthesis

**INTEGRATING CHEMISTRY** Light energy is just one of the things that plants need to carry out photosynthesis. Just as you need flour and eggs to make cookies, a plant also needs raw materials to make its own food. Plants use carbon dioxide gas and water as raw materials for photosynthesis.

During photosynthesis, plants use the energy absorbed by the chlorophyll to power a series of complex chemical reactions.

*In Your Journal*

Find out more about the experiments conducted by one of these scientists. Then write a summary of one experiment as it might appear in a front-page newspaper story of the time. Be sure to give your story a headline.

## 1883
### T. W. Engelmann

T. W. Engelmann studied how different colors of light affect photosynthesis in green algae. He found that cells bathed in blue and red light had the fastest rates of photosynthesis. Today scientists know that the chlorophyll in both green algae and plants absorbs mostly blue and red light.

**1850**

**1950**

## 1864
### Julius Sachs

A German biologist, Julius Sachs, observed living leaf cells under a microscope. As he watched, he tested the cells for the presence of carbohydrates. Sachs discovered that plants produce carbohydrates during photosynthesis.

## 1948
### Melvin Calvin

The American scientist Melvin Calvin traced the chemical path that the carbon from carbon dioxide follows during photosynthesis. By doing this, Calvin learned about the complex chemical reactions of photosynthesis.

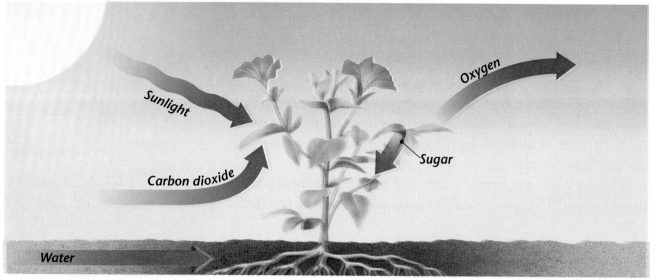

**Figure 8** In photosynthesis, the energy in sunlight is used to make sugar and oxygen from carbon dioxide and water. *Classifying Which substances are the raw materials of photosynthesis? Which are the products?*

In these reactions, carbon dioxide from the air and water from the soil combine to produce sugar, a type of carbohydrate. Another product, oxygen gas, is also produced. The events of photosynthesis are pictured in Figure 8.

One way that scientists describe chemical reactions is to write equations. A chemical equation shows the raw materials and the products. **The many chemical reactions of photosynthesis can be summarized by the following equation.**

$$\text{carbon dioxide} + \text{water} \xrightarrow{\text{light energy}} \text{sugar} + \text{oxygen}$$
$$(CO_2) \qquad (H_2O) \qquad\qquad (C_6H_{12}O_6) \quad (O_2)$$

**Carbon dioxide and water combine in the presence of light to produce sugar and oxygen.**

Like all organisms, plants need a steady supply of energy to grow and develop, respond, and reproduce. Some of the food made by plants supplies the energy for these activities. The excess food is stored by the plants in their roots, stems, or leaves. Carrot plants, for example, store excess food in their roots. When you eat a carrot, you are eating the plant's stored food.

 **Section 2 Review**

1. Describe what happens when light strikes a green leaf.
2. What is the overall equation for photosynthesis? What information does the equation provide?
3. What happens when light passes through a prism? What does this reveal about white light?
4. **Thinking Critically Relating Cause and Effect** Sometimes you see a rainbow during a rain shower. What might act as a prism to separate the light into its colors?

**Science at Home**

With a family member, look around your kitchen for objects that transmit, reflect, and absorb white light. Explain to your family member what happens to white light when it strikes each type of object. Then use one object to explain why you see it as the color you do.

# SECTION 3 Mosses, Liverworts, and Hornworts

## DISCOVER

ACTIVITY

### Will Mosses Absorb Water?

1. Place 20 milliliters (mL) of sand into a plastic graduated cylinder. Place 20 mL of peat moss into a second plastic graduated cylinder.

2. Predict what would happen if you were to slowly pour 10 mL of water into each of the two graduated cylinders and then wait five minutes.

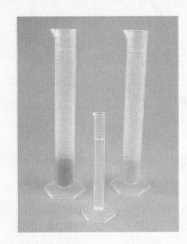

3. To test your prediction, use a third graduated cylinder to slowly add 10 mL of water to the sand. Then add 10 mL of water to the moss. After 5 minutes, record your observations.

### Think It Over

*Predicting* How did your prediction compare with your results? What did you learn about moss from this investigation?

---

If you enjoy gardening, you know that a garden requires time, effort, and knowledge. Before you start to plant your garden, you need to know how much water and sun your plants will need. You also need to know whether the soil in your garden can supply the plants with the water and nutrients they need.

Many gardeners add peat moss to the soil in their gardens. Peat moss improves the texture of soil and increases the soil's ability to hold water. When peat moss is added to claylike soil, it loosens the soil so that the plant's roots can easily grow through it. When peat moss is added to sandy soil, the soil stays moist for a longer time after it is watered.

## GUIDE FOR READING

◆ What characteristics do nonvascular plants share?

*Reading Tip* As you read, make a table comparing and contrasting mosses, liverworts, and hornworts.

### Characteristics of Nonvascular Plants

Peat moss contains one type of **nonvascular plant.** Some other nonvascular plants are liverworts and hornworts. **All nonvascular plants are low-growing plants that lack vascular tissue.**

Nonvascular plants do not have vascular tissue—a system of tubelike structures that transport water and other materials. Nonvascular plants can only pass materials from one cell to the next. That means that the materials do not travel very far or very quickly. Also, these plants have only their rigid cell walls to provide support. With this type of structure, these plants cannot grow very wide or tall. As a result, nonvascular plants are small and grow low to the ground.

Like all plants, nonvascular plants require water to survive. These plants lack roots, but they can obtain water and minerals directly from their surroundings. Many nonvascular plants live where water is plentiful. But even nonvascular plants that live in drier areas need enough water to let the sperm cells swim to the egg cells during reproduction.

## Mosses

Have you ever seen mosses growing in the crack of a sidewalk, on a tree trunk, or on rocks that are misted by waterfalls? With over 10,000 species, mosses are by far the most diverse group of nonvascular plants.

**The Structure of a Moss** If you were to look closely at a moss, you would see a plant that looks something like the one in Figure 9. The familiar green fuzzy moss is the gametophyte generation of the plant. Structures that look like tiny leaves grow off a small stemlike structure. Thin rootlike structures called **rhizoids** anchor the moss and absorb water and nutrients from the soil. The sporophyte generation grows out of the gametophyte. It consists of a slender stalk with a capsule at the end. The capsule contains spores.

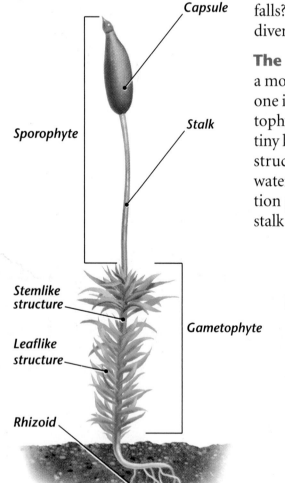

Capsule

Sporophyte

Stalk

Stemlike structure

Leaflike structure

Gametophyte

Rhizoid

**Figure 9** A moss gametophyte is low-growing and has structures that look like roots, stems, and leaves. The stalklike sporophyte generation remains attached to the gametophyte.
*Interpreting Diagrams* What structure anchors the gametophyte in the soil?

**The Importance of Mosses**  Many people use peat moss in agriculture and gardening. The peat moss that gardeners use contains sphagnum (SFAG num) moss. Sphagnum moss grows in a type of wetland called a **bog.** The still water in a bog is so acidic that decomposing organisms cannot live in the water. Thus when the plants die, they do not decay. Instead, the dead plants accumulate at the bottom of the bog. Over time, the mosses become compressed into layers and form a blackish-brown material called **peat.** Large deposits of peat exist in North America, Europe, and Asia. In Europe and Asia, people use peat as a fuel to heat homes and to cook food.

*INTEGRATING EARTH SCIENCE*  Like the lichens you learned about in Chapter 3, many mosses are pioneer plants. They are among the first organisms to grow in areas destroyed by volcanoes or in burnt-out forests. Like lichens, mosses trap wind-blown soil. Over time, enough soil accumulates to support the growth of other plants whose spores or seeds are blown there.

✓ *Checkpoint*  *What does a moss sporophyte look like?*

## Social Studies
### CONNECTION

Historians have found many items preserved in the acidic water of peat bogs. Weapons more than 1,600 years old have been recovered from bogs in northern Europe. In addition, about 700 human bodies have been found in bogs. Most are as well preserved as the body that you see in the photo. This man, who lived 2,000 years ago, was found in a bog in Denmark.

*In Your Journal*

Imagine that you have just recovered an old wooden tool from a bog. Write a letter to a natural history museum explaining why the tool is so well preserved.

**Figure 10**  The sphagnum moss that grew in this bog is being harvested as peat.

## Liverworts and Hornworts

Figure 11 shows examples of two other groups of nonvascular plants—liverworts and hornworts. There are more than 8,000 species of liverworts. This group of plants is named for the shape of the plant's body, which looks somewhat like a human liver. *Wort* is an old English word for "plant." Liverworts are often found growing as a thick crust on moist rocks or soil along the sides of a stream. Unlike mosses, most liverworts grow flat along the ground. In Figure 11, you can see the gametophyte generation of one type of liverwort.

There are fewer than 100 species of hornworts. At first glance, these plants resemble liverworts. But if you look closely, you can see slender, curved structures that look like horns growing out of the gametophytes. These hornlike structures, which give these plants their names, are the sporophytes. Unlike mosses or liverworts, hornworts are seldom found on rocks or tree trunks. Instead, hornworts live in moist soil, often mixed in with grass plants.

**Figure 11** Like mosses, liverworts and hornworts are nonvascular plants. **A.** Liverworts grow flat along the ground on moist soil and rocks. **B.** Hornworts grow only in soil and are often found growing among grasses.

## Section 3 Review

1. Describe two characteristics that nonvascular plants share. Explain how the two characteristics are related.
2. Describe the structure of a moss plant.
3. How does peat form?
4. **Thinking Critically  Comparing and Contrasting**  In what ways are mosses, liverworts, and hornworts similar? How do they differ?

**Check Your Progress**
You should now be caring for your moss, and providing the best conditions for its survival and growth. Be sure to keep in mind how mosses differ from other familiar kinds of plants. (*Hint:* Keep your terrarium warm, but not hot, and make sure it remains moist.)

CHAPTER PROJECT 4

# Masses of Mosses

I n this lab, you will look closely at some tiny members of the plant kingdom.

## Problem

How is a moss plant adapted to carry out its life activities?

## Materials

| | |
|---|---|
| clump of moss | hand lens |
| metric ruler | toothpicks |
| plastic dropper | water |

## Procedure

1. Your teacher will give you a clump of moss. Examine the clump from all sides. Draw a diagram of what you see. Measure the size of the overall clump and the main parts of the clump. Record your observations.

2. Using toothpicks, gently separate five individual moss plants from the clump. Be sure to pull them totally apart so that you can observe each plant separately. If the moss plants appear to dry up as you are working, moisten them with a few drops of water.

3. Measure the length of the leaflike, stemlike, and rootlike structures on each plant. If brown stalks and capsules are present, measure them. Find the average length of each structure.

4. Make a life-size drawing of a moss plant. Label the parts, give their sizes, and record the color of each part. When you are finished observing the moss, return it to your teacher. Wash your hands thoroughly.

5. Obtain class averages for the sizes of the structures you measured in Step 3. Also, if the moss that you observed had brown stalks and capsules, share your observations about those structures.

## Analyze and Conclude

1. Describe the typical size of the leaflike portion of moss plants, the typical height of the stemlike portion, and the typical length of the rootlike portion.

2. In which part(s) of the moss does photosynthesis occur? How do you know?

3. Why are mosses unable to grow very tall?

4. **Think About It** What did you learn by observing a moss up close and in detail?

## More to Explore

Select a moss plant with stalks and capsules. Use toothpicks to release some of the spores, which can be as small as dust particles. Examine the spores under a microscope.

# SECTION 4 Ferns and Their Relatives

## DISCOVER ······························ ACTIVITY

### How Quickly Can Water Move Upward?

1. Put on your goggles. Your teacher will give you a plastic petri dish as well as a narrow glass tube that is open at both ends.

2. Fill the petri dish half full of water. Add a drop of food coloring to the water.

3. Stand the tube on end in the water and hold it upright. Observe what happens. Record your observations.

**Think It Over**

*Inferring* Why might it be an advantage for the transporting cells of plants to be arranged in a tubelike way?

---

### GUIDE FOR READING

◆ What are the main characteristics of seedless vascular plants?

*Reading Tip* As you read, create a table comparing ferns, club mosses, and horsetails.

The time is 340 million years ago—long before the dinosaurs lived. The place is somewhere in the forests that covered most of Earth's land. If you could have walked through one of these ancient forests, it would have looked very strange to you. You might have recognized the mosses and liverworts that carpeted the moist soil. But overhead you would have seen odd-looking trees, some towering 25 meters above the ground. Among the trees were ancient ferns—huge versions of the ferns you find in today's florist shops. Other trees resembled giant stick figures with leaves up to one meter long. The huge leaves hugged the branches, looking something like the scales that cover a fish.

*INTEGRATING EARTH SCIENCE* As the trees and other plants died, they formed thick layers and partially decomposed. Over millions of years, the layers became compressed under the weight of the layers above them. Eventually, these layers became the coal deposits that we use for fuel today.

## Characteristics of Seedless Vascular Plants

The odd-looking plants in the ancient forests were the ancestors of three groups of plants that are alive today—ferns, club mosses, and horsetails. **Ferns and their relatives share two characteristics. They have vascular tissue and use spores to reproduce.**

**Vascular Tissue** What adaptations allowed plants to grow very tall? Unlike the mosses, the ancient trees were **vascular plants**—plants that have vascular tissue. Vascular plants are better suited to life on land than are nonvascular plants. This is because vascular tissue solves the problems of support and transportation. Vascular tissue transports water quickly and efficiently throughout the plant's body. It also transports the food produced in the leaves to other parts of the plant, including the roots.

In addition, vascular tissue strengthens the plant's body. Imagine a handful of drinking straws bundled together with rubber bands. The bundle of straws would be stronger and more stable than a single straw would be. In a similar way, vascular tissue provides strength and stability to a plant.

**Figure 12** Ferns and their relatives dominated the ancient forests on Earth.

**Spores for Reproduction** Ferns, club mosses, and horsetails still need to grow in moist surroundings. This is because the plants release spores into their surroundings, where they grow into gametophytes. When the gametophytes produce egg cells and sperm cells, there must be enough water available for fertilization to occur.

☑ *Checkpoint* *What adaptation allowed plants to grow tall?*

## Ferns

Fossil records indicate that ferns first appeared on land about 400 million years ago. There are over 12,000 species of ferns alive today. They range in size from tiny plants about the size of this letter "M" to large tree ferns that grow up to 5 meters tall in moist, tropical areas.

**The Structure of Ferns** Like other vascular plants, ferns have true stems, roots, and leaves. The stems of most ferns are underground. Leaves grow upward from the top side of the stems, and roots grow downward from the bottom of the stems. Roots are structures that anchor the fern to the ground and absorb water and nutrients from the soil. These substances enter the root's vascular tissue and travel through the tissue into the stems and leaves. In Figure 13 you can see the fern's structure.

**Figure 13** Most ferns have underground stems in addition to underground roots. The leaves, or fronds, grow above ground.

Figure 14 Spores are produced on the undersides of mature fronds. *Applying Concepts What happens to spores that are released?*

Look closely at the fern's leaves, or **fronds.** Notice that the frond is divided into many smaller parts that look like small leaves. Many other ferns have a similar divided-leaf structure. The upper surface of each frond is coated with a cuticle that helps the plant retain water. In many types of ferns, the developing leaves are coiled at first. Because they resemble the top of a violin, these young leaves are often called fiddleheads. As they mature, the fiddleheads uncurl.

**Reproduction in Ferns** The familiar fern with its visible fronds is the sporophyte stage of the plant. On the underside of mature fronds, spores develop in tiny spore cases. When the spores are released, wind and water can carry them great distances. If a spore lands in moist, shaded soil, it develops into a gametophyte. Fern gametophytes are tiny plants that grow low to the ground.

**The Importance of Ferns** Ferns are useful to people in many ways. They are popular houseplants because they are attractive and easy to grow. Ferns are also used to grow other kinds of houseplants. For example, orchids are often grown on the tangled masses of fern roots.

People eat some ferns. During the spring, fiddleheads are sold in supermarkets and farm stands. Fiddleheads make a nutritious vegetable dish. But because some ferns are not safe to eat, you should never gather wild fiddleheads for food.

In Southeast Asia, farmers grow a small aquatic fern alongside rice plants in their rice fields. Tiny pockets in the fern's leaves provide a home for some bacteria. The bacteria produce a natural fertilizer that helps the rice plants grow.

Figure 15 Fiddleheads are the developing leaves of a fern.

Figure 16 Club mosses and horsetails are other seedless vascular plants. **A.** This club moss looks like a tiny pine tree. **B.** These horsetail plants have jointed stems. Needle-like branches grow out of each joint.

## Club Mosses and Horsetails

Two other groups of seedless, vascular plants are the club mosses and horsetails. Like ferns, club mosses and horsetails have true leaves, stems, and roots. They also have a similar life cycle. However, there are relatively few species of club mosses and horsetails alive today.

Unlike their larger ancestors, today's club mosses are small. Do not be confused by the name *club mosses*. Unlike the true mosses, the club mosses have vascular tissue. You may be familiar with the club moss you see in Figure 16. The plant, which looks like the small branch of a pine tree, is sometimes called ground pine or princess pine. It grows in moist woodlands and near streams.

There are 30 species of horsetails on Earth today. As you can see in Figure 16, the stems of horsetails are jointed. Long, coarse, needlelike branches grow in a circle around each joint. Small leaves grow flat against the stem just above each joint. The stems contain silica, a gritty substance also found in sand. During colonial times, Americans called horsetails "scouring rushes" because they used the plants to scrub their pots and pans.

# Section 4 Review

1. What two characteristics do ferns, club mosses, and horsetails share? How do these characteristics differ from those of mosses?

2. Describe the structure of a fern plant. What do its leaves, stems, and roots look like?

3. List three ways that ferns are useful to people today.

4. **Thinking Critically  Applying Concepts** Although ferns have vascular tissue, they still must live in moist, shady environments. Explain why this is true.

*Check Your Progress*

CHAPTER PROJECT 4

Begin planning your brochure as you continue caring for your moss. What's the best way to give clear directions for making a terrarium? What must you say about the amount of light, water, and other conditions that mosses need to survive? (*Hint:* Be sure to include important information about mosses, such as how tall they grow and how they reproduce.)

## SECTION 1 The Plant Kingdom

### Key Ideas

◆ Plants are autotrophs. All plants are also multicellular eukaryotes.

◆ Plant cells have cell walls that are made mostly of cellulose. Plant cells contain chloroplasts, in which food is made, and vacuoles that store water, food, and other substances.

◆ All plants have complex life cycles. In the sporophyte stage, plants produce spores. In the gametophyte stage, plants produce sperm cells and egg cells.

◆ For plants to survive on land, they need ways to obtain water and other materials from their surroundings, retain moisture, support their bodies, transport materials throughout the plant, and reproduce successfully.

### Key Terms

| | | |
|---|---|---|
| photosynthesis | cuticle | sporophyte |
| cell wall | vascular tissue | gametophyte |
| cellulose | fertilization | gamete |
| chloroplast | zygote | |
| vacuole | | |
| tissue | | |
| chlorophyll | | |

## SECTION 2 Photosynthesis and Light

INTEGRATING PHYSICS

### Key Ideas

◆ White light is made up of the different colors of the rainbow—red, orange, yellow, green, blue, and violet.

◆ Most of the light that strikes a leaf is absorbed by pigments in the chloroplasts of the cells. Chlorophyll, the main pigment, absorbs red and blue light. Light energy powers the process of photosynthesis.

◆ In photosynthesis, carbon dioxide and water are converted into sugars and oxygen using the light energy.

### Key Term

accessory pigment

## SECTION 3 Mosses, Liverworts, and Hornworts

### Key Ideas

◆ Nonvascular plants are small, low-growing plants that lack vascular tissue. Most nonvascular plants transport materials by passing them from one cell to the next. They live in areas where there is enough moisture for them to survive.

◆ Mosses, liverworts, and hornworts are three types of nonvascular plants.

### Key Terms

| | |
|---|---|
| nonvascular plant | bog |
| rhizoid | peat |

## SECTION 4 Ferns and Their Relatives

### Key Ideas

◆ Seedless vascular plants have vascular tissue and use spores to reproduce. These plants include ferns, club mosses, and horsetails.

◆ Although seedless vascular plants grow taller than nonvascular plants, they still need to live in moist places. The plants' spores are released into the environment, where they grow into gametophytes.

### Key Terms

| | |
|---|---|
| vascular plant | frond |

USING THE INTERNET

ACTIVITY

www.science-explorer.phschool.com

## Reviewing Content

 *For more review of key concepts, see the Interactive Student Tutorial CD-ROM.*

### Multiple Choice

*Choose the letter of the best answer.*

1. Mosses and ferns are both
   a. vascular plants.
   b. nonvascular plants.
   c. seed plants.
   d. plants.
2. The ancestors of plants were probably
   a. fungi.
   b. brown algae.
   c. green algae.
   d. bacteria.
3. When visible light strikes a green leaf, green light is
   a. reflected.
   b. absorbed.
   c. transmitted.
   d. stored.
4. The familiar green, fuzzy moss is the
   a. frond.
   b. rhizoid.
   c. gametophyte.
   d. sporophyte.
5. The leaves of ferns are called
   a. rhizoids.
   b. sporophytes.
   c. fronds.
   d. cuticles.

### True or False

*If the statement is true, write true. If it is false, change the underlined word or words to make the statement true.*

6. Plants are <u>autotrophs</u>.
7. In the fall, leaves turn colors because <u>accessory pigments</u> become visible as the chlorophyll breaks down.
8. <u>Carbon dioxide and water</u> are the products of photosynthesis.
9. Mosses are <u>vascular</u> plants.
10. The young leaves of <u>liverworts</u> are known as fiddleheads.

## Checking Concepts

11. Describe three structures that characterize the eukaryotic cells of plants. Explain the role of each structure.
12. In what two ways is vascular tissue important to a plant?
13. Briefly describe the life cycle of a typical plant.
14. Explain why a yellow school bus appears yellow.
15. What role does chlorophyll play in photosynthesis?
16. In what ways do mosses and club mosses differ from each other? In what ways are they similar?
17. **Writing to Learn** Imagine that you are a beam of white light traveling through the air. Write a paragraph to explain what happens to you when a green leaf gets in your way.

## Thinking Visually

18. **Compare/Contrast Table** Copy the table comparing mosses and ferns onto a separate sheet of paper. Complete the table by filling in the missing information. Then add a title. (For more on compare/contrast tables, see the Skills Handbook.)

| Characteristic | Moss | Fern |
|---|---|---|
| Size | a. ? | Can be tall |
| Environment | Moist | b. ? |
| Body parts | Rootlike, stemlike, and leaflike | c. ? |
| Familiar generation | d. ? | sporophyte |
| Vascular tissue present? | e. ? | f. ? |

## Applying Skills

*A scientist exposed a green plant to different colors of light. She then measured how much of each light the plant absorbed. Use the data to answer Questions 19–22.*

| Absorption of Light by a Plant | |
|---|---|
| **Color of Light** | **Percentage of Light Absorbed** |
| Red | 55 |
| Orange | 10 |
| Yellow | 2 |
| Green | 1 |
| Blue | 85 |
| Violet | 40 |

**19. Graphing** Construct a bar graph using the information in the data table. (For information on constructing bar graphs, see the Skills Handbook.)

**20. Drawing Conclusions** List the three colors of light that are most important for photosynthesis in this plant.

**21. Predicting** If the plant were exposed only to yellow light, how might the plant be affected? Explain.

**22. Inferring** If a plant with reddish leaves were used in a similar experiment, how might the results differ? Explain.

## Thinking Critically

**23. Applying Concepts** A friend tells you that he has seen moss plants that are about 2 meters tall. Is your friend correct? Explain.

**24. Comparing and Contrasting** How does the sporophyte generation of a plant differ from the gametophyte generation?

**25. Relating Cause and Effect** People have observed that mosses tend to grow on the north side of a tree rather than the south side. Why do you think this is so?

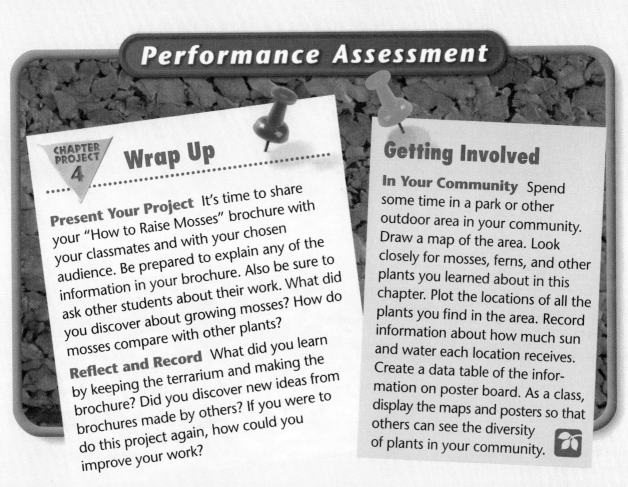

## Performance Assessment

### CHAPTER PROJECT 4  Wrap Up

**Present Your Project** It's time to share your "How to Raise Mosses" brochure with your classmates and with your chosen audience. Be prepared to explain any of the information in your brochure. Also be sure to ask other students about their work. What did you discover about growing mosses? How do mosses compare with other plants?

**Reflect and Record** What did you learn by keeping the terrarium and making the brochure? Did you discover new ideas from brochures made by others? If you were to do this project again, how could you improve your work?

### Getting Involved

**In Your Community** Spend some time in a park or other outdoor area in your community. Draw a map of the area. Look closely for mosses, ferns, and other plants you learned about in this chapter. Plot the locations of all the plants you find in the area. Record information about how much sun and water each location receives. Create a data table of the information on poster board. As a class, display the maps and posters so that others can see the diversity of plants in your community.

WHAT'S AHEAD

SECTION

**1** The Characteristics of
Seed Plants

Discover  Which Plant Part Is It?
Try This  The In-Seed Story
Sharpen Your Skills  Calculating

SECTION

**2** Gymnosperms

Discover  Are All Leaves Alike?
Try This  The Scoop on Cones

SECTION

**3** Angiosperms

Discover  What Is a Fruit?
Real-World Lab  A Close Look at Flowers

# PROJECT 5

# Cycle of a Lifetime

How long is a seed plant's life? Redwood trees can live for thousands of years. Tomato plants die after one growing season. Can organisms that seem so different have anything in common? In this chapter, you'll find out. Some answers will come from this chapter's project. In this project, you'll grow some seeds, then care for the plants until they, in turn, produce their own seeds.

**Your Goal** To care for and observe a plant throughout its life cycle. To complete this project successfully you must

◆ grow a plant from a seed
◆ observe and describe key parts of your plant's life cycle, such as seed germination and pollination
◆ harvest and plant the seeds that your growing plant produces
◆ follow the safety guidelines in Appendix A

**Get Started** Observe the seeds that your teacher gives you. In a small group, discuss what conditions the seeds might need to grow. What should you look for after you plant the seeds? What kinds of measurements could you make? Will it help to make drawings? When you are ready, plant your seeds.

**Thistle plants depend on bees for pollination.**

**Check Your Progress** You'll be working on this project as you study this chapter. To keep your project on track, look for Check Your Progress boxes at the following points.

Section 1 Review, page 149: Observe the developing seedlings.
Section 3 Review, page 161: Pollinate your flowers.
Section 5 Review, page 170: Collect the seeds from your plant and plant some of them.

**Wrap Up** At the end of the chapter (page 173), you'll present an exhibit showing the plant's life cycle.

**SECTION 4** Plant Responses and Growth

Discover **Can a Plant Respond to Touch?**
Skills Lab **Which Way Is Up?**

**SECTION 5** Integrating Technology 🔵
Feeding the World

Discover **Will There Be Enough to Eat?**

# The Characteristics of Seed Plants

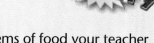

### Which Plant Part Is It?

1. With a partner, carefully observe the items of food your teacher gives you.

2. Make a list of the food items.

3. For each food item, write the name of the part of the plant—root, stem, or leaf—from which you think the food is obtained.

**Think It Over**

*Classifying* Classify the items into groups depending on the plant part from which the food is obtained. Compare your groupings with those of your classmates.

---

**GUIDE FOR READING**

◆ What characteristics do seed plants share?

◆ What are the main parts of a seed?

◆ What are the functions of leaves, stems, and roots?

*Reading Tip* As you read, make a list of the boldfaced terms. Write a definition for each term in your own words.

---

Chances are you've seen dandelions. But how much do you know about these common plants? For example, do you know that dandelion blossoms open only in sunlight? Or that each blossom is made up of hundreds of tube-shaped flowers? Do you know that a seed develops in each of these tiny flowers? And that, just like apple seeds, dandelion seeds are enclosed in structures that biologists call fruits?

The next time you see a dandelion's fluffy "seed head," examine it closely. It is made up of hundreds of individual fruits, each containing a seed. Each fruit has a hooklike structure at one end. Like tiny parachutes, the fruits ride in currents of air. When one hooks into moist soil, the seed inside can grow into a new dandelion plant.

## What Is a Seed Plant?

Dandelions are seed plants. So are most of the other plants on Earth. In fact, seed plants outnumber seedless plants by more than ten to one. You eat many seed plants—rice, tomatoes, peas, and squash, for example. You may also eat the meat of animals that eat seed plants. You wear clothes made from seed plants, such as cotton and flax. You may even live in a home built from seed plants—oak, pine, or maple trees. In addition, seed plants produce much of the oxygen you breathe.

**Figure 1** Some of these dandelions are releasing tiny parachute-like fruits, which carry the seeds inside to new areas.

**All seed plants share two characteristics. They have vascular tissue and use seeds to reproduce.** In addition, they all have body plans that include leaves, stems, and roots. Like seedless plants, seed plants have complex life cycles that include the sporophyte and the gametophyte. In seed plants, the plants that you see are the sporophytes. The gametophytes are microscopic.

## Vascular Tissue

Most seed plants live on land. Recall from Chapter 4 that land plants face many challenges, including standing upright and supplying all their cells with water and food. Like ferns, seed plants meet these two challenges with vascular tissue. The thick walls of the cells in the vascular tissue help support the plants. In addition, water, food, and nutrients are transported throughout the plants in vascular tissue.

There are two types of vascular tissue. **Phloem** (FLOH um) is the vascular tissue through which food moves. When food is made in the plant's leaves, it enters the phloem and travels to the plant's stems and roots. Water and nutrients, on the other hand, travel in the vascular tissue called **xylem** (ZY lum). The plant's roots absorb water and nutrients from the soil. These materials enter the root's xylem and move upward into the plant's stems and leaves.

☑ *Checkpoint* *What material travels in phloem? What materials travel in xylem?*

**Figure 2** Seed plants are diverse and live in many environments. **A.** Wheat is an important food for people. **B.** Organpipe cacti, here surrounded by other flowering plants, live in deserts. **C.** Lodgepole pines thrive in the mountains of the western United States.
*Applying Concepts* *What two roles does vascular tissue play in these plants?*

## The In-Seed Story

1. Your teacher **ACTIVITY** will give you a hand lens and two different seeds that have been soaked in water.

2. Carefully observe the outside of each seed. Draw what you see.

3. Gently remove the coverings of the seeds. Then carefully separate the parts of each seed. Use a hand lens to examine the inside of each seed. Draw what you see.

*Observing* Based on your observations, label the parts of each seed. Then describe the function of each part next to its label.

## Seeds

One reason why seed plants are so numerous is that they produce seeds. **Seeds** are structures that contain a young plant inside a protective covering. As you learned in Chapter 4, seedless plants need water in the surroundings for fertilization to occur. Seed plants do not need water in the environment to reproduce. This is because the sperm cells are delivered directly to the regions near the eggs. After sperm cells fertilize the eggs, seeds develop and protect the young plant from drying out.

If you've ever planted seeds in a garden, you know that seeds look different from each other. Despite their differences, however, all seeds have a similar structure. **A seed has three important parts—an embryo, stored food, and a seed coat.**

The young plant that develops from the zygote, or fertilized egg, is called the **embryo.** The embryo already has the beginnings of roots, stems, and leaves. In the seeds of most plants, the embryo stops growing when it is quite small. When the embryo begins to grow again, it uses the food stored in the seed until it can make its food. In some plants, food is stored inside one or two seed leaves, or **cotyledons** (kaht uh LEED unz). You can see the cotyledons in the seeds in Figure 3.

The outer covering of a seed is called the seed coat. Some familiar seed coats are the "skins" on lima beans, peanuts, and peas. The seed coat acts like plastic wrap, protecting the embryo and its food from drying out. This allows a seed to remain inactive for a long time. For example, after finding some 10,000-year-old seeds in the Arctic, scientists placed them in warm water. Two days later, the seeds began to grow!

☑ *Checkpoint* *What is the function of the seed coat?*

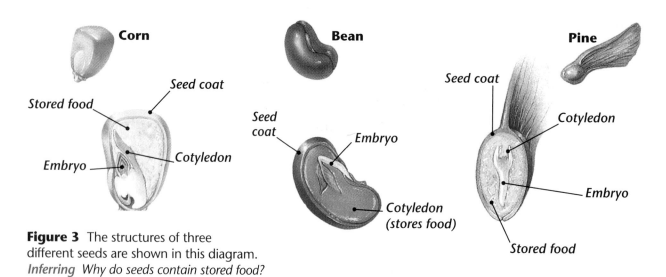

**Figure 3** The structures of three different seeds are shown in this diagram. *Inferring* Why do seeds contain stored food?

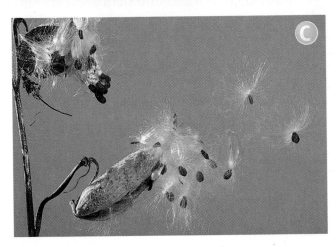

**Figure 4** Plants have different ways of dispersing their seeds. **A.** Both grass seeds and spiny parsley seeds are hitching a ride on this dog's fur. **B.** Water transports coconut palm seeds to new areas. **C.** The wind carries milkweed seeds through the air. **D.** Witch hazel plants shoot out seeds when their pods explode.

## Seed Dispersal

To develop into a new plant, a seed needs light, water, and nutrients. After seeds have formed, they are usually scattered, sometimes far from where they were produced. When seeds land in a suitable area, they can sprout, or begin to grow.

The scattering of seeds is called seed dispersal. Seeds, or the fruits that enclose the seeds, are dispersed in many ways. One method involves animals. Some animals eat fruits, such as cherries and grapes. The seeds inside pass through the animal's digestive system and are deposited in new areas. Other seeds are enclosed in barblike structures that hook onto an animal's fur or a person's clothes. The structures then fall off in a new area. Water disperses other seeds when the seeds float in oceans, rivers, and streams. The seeds inside a coconut, for example, are carried from one area to another by ocean currents.

A third dispersal method involves wind. Wind disperses lightweight seeds, such as those of milkweed plants and pine trees. Finally, some plants shoot out their seeds, in a way that might remind you of popping popcorn. For example, the seedpods of wisteria and impatiens plants burst suddenly. The force scatters the seeds away from the pods in many directions.

**Figure 5** The embryo in this peanut seed uses stored food to germinate. **A.** The peanut's root is the first structure to begin growing. **B.** After the root anchors the germinating plant, the peanut's stem and first two leaves emerge from the seed.

## Germination

After seeds are dispersed, they may remain inactive for a while, or they may begin to grow immediately. **Germination** (jur muh NAY shun) is the early growth stage of the embryo. Germination begins when the seed absorbs water from the environment. Then the embryo uses its stored food to begin to grow. First, the embryo's roots grow downward, then its leaves and stem grow upward.

Seeds that are dispersed far away from the parent have a better chance of survival. This is because these young plants do not have to compete with their parent for light, water, and nutrients as they begin to grow.

☑ *Checkpoint* *What must happen before germination can begin?*

## Leaves

The most numerous parts on many plants are their leaves. Plant leaves vary greatly in size and shape. Pine trees, for example, have needle-shaped leaves. Birch trees have small rounded leaves with jagged edges. Yellow skunk cabbages, which grow in the northwestern United States, have oval leaves that can be more than one meter wide. No matter what their shape, leaves play an important role in a plant. **Leaves capture the sun's energy and carry out the food-making process of photosynthesis.**

**The Structure of a Leaf** If you were to cut through a leaf and look at the edge under a microscope, you would see the structures in *Exploring a Leaf.* The leaf's top and bottom surface layers protect the cells inside. Between the layers of cells inside the leaf are veins that contain xylem and phloem. The underside of the leaf has small openings, or pores, called **stomata** (STOH muh tuh) (singular *stoma*). The Greek word *stoma* means "mouth"—and stomata do look like tiny mouths. The stomata open and close to control when gases enter and leave the leaf. When the stomata are open, carbon dioxide enters the leaf and oxygen and water vapor exit.

**The Leaf and Photosynthesis** The structure of a leaf is ideal for carrying out photosynthesis. Recall from Chapter 4 that photosynthesis occurs in the chloroplasts of plant cells. The cells that contain the most chloroplasts are located near the leaf's upper surface, where they are exposed to the sun. The chlorophyll in the chloroplasts traps the sun's energy.

Carbon dioxide enters the leaf through open stomata. Water, which is absorbed by the plant's roots, travels up the stem to the leaf through the xylem. During photosynthesis, sugar and oxygen are produced from the carbon dioxide and water. Oxygen passes out of the leaf through the open stomata. The sugar enters the phloem and then travels throughout the plant.

# EXPLORING *a Leaf*

**A** leaf is a well-adapted food factory. Each structure helps the leaf produce food.

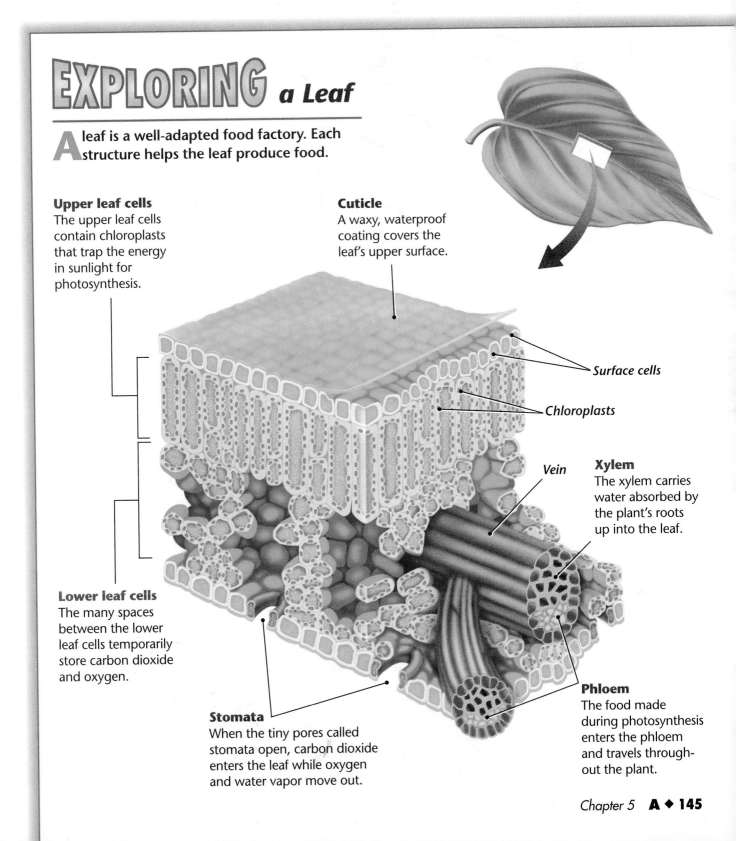

**Upper leaf cells**
The upper leaf cells contain chloroplasts that trap the energy in sunlight for photosynthesis.

**Cuticle**
A waxy, waterproof coating covers the leaf's upper surface.

*Surface cells*

*Chloroplasts*

*Vein*

**Xylem**
The xylem carries water absorbed by the plant's roots up into the leaf.

**Lower leaf cells**
The many spaces between the lower leaf cells temporarily store carbon dioxide and oxygen.

**Stomata**
When the tiny pores called stomata open, carbon dioxide enters the leaf while oxygen and water vapor move out.

**Phloem**
The food made during photosynthesis enters the phloem and travels through-out the plant.

**Controlling Water Loss** Because such a large area of a leaf is exposed to the air, water can quickly evaporate, or be lost, from a leaf into the air. The process by which water evaporates from a plant's leaves is called **transpiration**. A plant can lose a lot of water through transpiration. A corn plant, for example, can lose as much as 3.8 liters of water on a hot summer day. Without a way to slow down the process of transpiration, a plant would shrivel up and die.

Fortunately, plants have ways to slow down transpiration. One way that plants retain water is by closing the stomata. The stomata often close when the temperature is very hot.

☑ *Checkpoint* *How does carbon dioxide get into a leaf?*

## Stems

The stem of a plant has two important functions. **The stem carries substances between the plant's roots and leaves. The stem also provides support for the plant and holds up the leaves so they are exposed to the sun.** In addition, some stems, such as those of asparagus, also store food.

Stems vary in size and shape. Some stems, like those of the baobab trees in Figure 6, are a prominent part of the plant. Other stems, like those of cabbages, are short and hidden.

**The Structure of a Stem** Stems can be either herbaceous (hur BAY shus) or woody. Herbaceous stems are soft. Dandelions, dahlias, peppers, and tomato plants have herbaceous stems.

**Figure 6** This road in Madagascar is called Baobab Avenue. Tall, fat stems and stubby branches give baobab trees an unusual appearance.

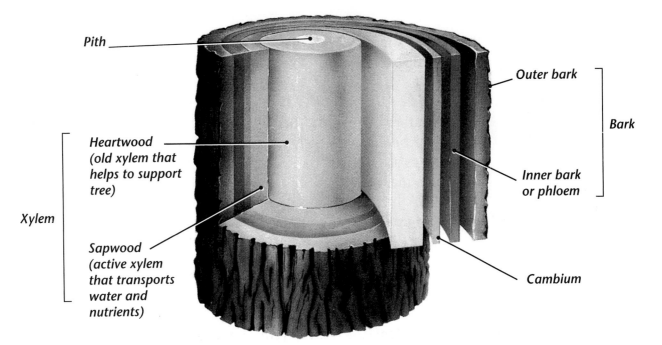

Pith

Outer bark

Bark

Heartwood
(old xylem that
helps to support
tree)

Inner bark
or phloem

Xylem

Sapwood
(active xylem
that transports
water and
nutrients)

Cambium

**Figure 7** A typical woody stem is made up of many cell layers. *Interpreting Diagrams Where is the cambium located? What is the function of this layer of cells?*

In contrast, woody stems are hard and rigid. Maple trees, pine trees, and roses all have woody stems.

Herbaceous and woody stems consist of phloem and xylem tissue as well as many other supporting cells. However, unlike herbaceous stems, woody stems have an outer layer of material called bark, which helps protect the cells inside it, and inner layers of heartwood for additional support.

In Figure 7 you can see the inner structure of a woody stem. Bark covers the outer part of the stem. Just inside the bark is the phloem. Inside the phloem is a layer of cells called the **cambium** (KAM bee um). The cells of the cambium divide to produce new phloem and xylem. This process increases the stem's width. Just inside the cambium is a layer of active xylem that transports water and nutrients. Inside that layer is a layer of xylem cells that no longer carries water and nutrients. This layer, which is called heartwood, strengthens the stem, providing it with additional support. In the center of the stem is a material called the pith. In young trees, the pith stores food and water.

**Annual Rings** Have you ever looked at a tree stump and seen a pattern of circles that looks something like a target? These circles are called annual rings because they represent one year of a tree's growth. Annual rings are made of xylem. Xylem cells that form in the spring are large and have thin walls because they grow rapidly. They produce a wide, light brown ring. Xylem cells that form in the summer grow slowly and, therefore, are small and have thick walls. They produce a thin, dark ring. One pair of light and dark rings represents one year's growth. You can estimate a tree's age by counting its annual rings.

**INTEGRATING EARTH SCIENCE** The width of a tree's annual rings can provide important clues about past weather conditions, such as rainfall. In rainy years, more xylem is produced, so the tree's annual rings are wide. In dry years, rings are narrow. By examining a tree's annual rings, scientists can make inferences about the weather conditions during the tree's life. For example, when scientists examined annual rings from trees in the southwestern United States, they inferred that severe droughts occurred in the years 840, 1067, 1379, and 1632.

✓ *Checkpoint* *What function does bark perform?*

## Roots

Have you ever tried to pull a dandelion out of the soil? It's not easy, is it? That is because most roots are good anchors. **Roots anchor a plant in the ground and absorb water and nutrients from the soil.** The more root area a plant has, the more water and nutrients it can absorb. The roots of an oak tree, for example, may be twice as long as the aboveground tree. In addition, for plants such as carrots and beets, roots function as a storage area for food.

**Types of Roots** As you can see in Figure 9, there are two types of root systems: taproot and fibrous. A taproot system consists of a long, thick main root. Thin, branching roots grow off the main root. Turnips, radishes, dandelions, and cacti have taproots. In contrast, fibrous root systems consist of several main roots that branch

**Figure 8** Tree rings tell more than just the age of a tree. For example, thick rings that are far apart indicate years in which growing conditions were favorable.
*Interpreting Photographs What was the weather like during the early years of this locust tree's life?*

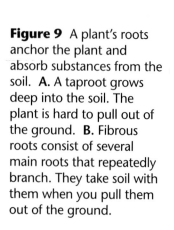

**Figure 9** A plant's roots anchor the plant and absorb substances from the soil. **A.** A taproot grows deep into the soil. The plant is hard to pull out of the ground. **B.** Fibrous roots consist of several main roots that repeatedly branch. They take soil with them when you pull them out of the ground.

repeatedly to form a tangled mass. Lawn grass, corn, and most trees have fibrous roots.

**The Structure of a Root** In Figure 10 you see the structure of a typical root. Notice that the tip of the root is rounded and is covered by a structure called the **root cap.** The root cap, which contains dead cells, protects the root from injury from rocks and other material as the root grows through the soil.

Behind the root cap are the cells that divide to form new root cells. These dividing cells cause the root to lengthen. Root hairs grow out of the root's surface. These hairs increase the surface area of the root that touches the soil. When more surface area is in contact with the soil, more water and nutrients can be absorbed. The root hairs also help to anchor the plant.

Locate the vascular tissue in the center of the root. The water and nutrients that are absorbed from the soil quickly move into the xylem. From there, these substances are transported upward to the plant's stems and leaves.

Phloem tissue transports food manufactured in the leaves to the root. The root tissues may then use the food for growth or store it for future use by the plant. The root also contains a layer of cambium, which produces new xylem and phloem.

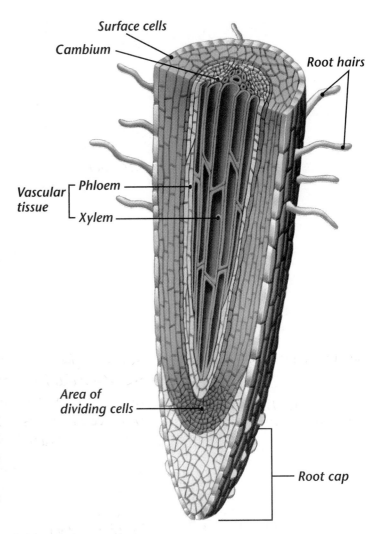

**Figure 10** The root cap protects the root as it grows into the soil. Root hairs absorb water and nutrients, which are transported through the root's vascular tissue.

# Section 1 Review

1. What two characteristics do all seed plants share?
2. List the three main parts of a seed. Describe the function of each part in producing a new plant.
3. What are the main functions of a plant's leaves, stems, and roots?
4. **Thinking Critically  Predicting** Predict what would happen to a plant if you were to coat the underside of each leaf with wax. Explain your prediction.

*Check Your Progress*

CHAPTER PROJECT 5

If your seeds haven't germinated yet, they soon will. For the next few days keep a close watch on your young plants to see how they grow. How do they change in height? How do the leaves appear and grow? (*Hint:* Consider using drawings or photographs as part of your record keeping.)

# SECTION 2 Gymnosperms

## DISCOVER 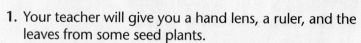 ACTIVITY

### Are All Leaves Alike?

1. Your teacher will give you a hand lens, a ruler, and the leaves from some seed plants.

2. Using the hand lens, examine each leaf. Sketch each leaf in your notebook.

3. Measure the length and width of each leaf. Record your measurements in your notebook.

**Think It Over**

*Classifying* Divide the leaves into two groups on the basis of your observations. Explain why you grouped the leaves as you did.

## GUIDE FOR READING

◆ What are the characteristics of gymnosperms?

◆ How do gymnosperms reproduce?

*Reading Tip* Before you read, preview *Exploring the Life Cycle of a Gymnosperm* on page 154. List any unfamiliar terms. As you read, write definitions for the terms.

Have you ever seen a tree that has grown wider than a car? Do trees this huge really exist? The answer is yes. Some giant sequoia trees, which grow almost exclusively in central California, are over ten meters wide. You can understand why giant sequoias are commonly referred to as "big trees." It takes a long time for a tree to grow so big. Scientists think that the largest giant sequoias may be about 2,000 years old. One reason they live so long is because their bark is fire-resistant.

## What Are Gymnosperms?

The giant sequoia trees belong to the group of seed plants known as gymnosperms. A **gymnosperm** (JIM nuh spurm) is a seed plant that produces naked seeds. The seeds of gymnosperms are "naked" because they are not enclosed by any protective covering.

**Every gymnosperm produces naked seeds. In addition, many gymnosperms also have needlelike or scalelike leaves, and deep-growing root systems.** Although a few kinds of gymnosperms are shrubs or vines, most are trees.

◄ A giant sequoia in California

## Types of Gymnosperms

Gymnosperms are the oldest type of seed plant. According to fossil evidence, gymnosperms first appeared on Earth about 360 million years ago. Fossils also indicate that there were many more species of gymnosperms in the past than today. Today, gymnosperms are classified into four groups—the cycads, the ginkgo, the gnetophytes, and the conifers.

**Cycads** About 175 million years ago, the majority of plants on Earth were cycads (SY kadz). Today, cycads are found only in tropical areas. As you can see in Figure 11, cycads look like palm trees with cones. A cycad cone can grow as large as a football. In Mexico people grind seeds from the cones of one cycad to make a type of flour for tortillas.

**Ginkgo** Like cycads, ginkgoes (GING kohz) are also hundreds of millions of years old. Only one species of ginkgo, *Ginkgo biloba*, exists today. It probably survives only because the Chinese and Japanese cared for the species in their gardens. Ginkgoes can grow as tall as 25 meters. Today, ginkgo trees are planted along many city streets because they can tolerate the air pollution produced by city traffic.

**Gnetophytes** Gnetophytes (NEE tuh fyts) are the gymnosperms that you are least likely to see. These gymnosperms live only in the hot, dry deserts of southern Africa, the deserts of the western United States, and the tropical rain forests. Some gnetophytes are trees, some are shrubs, and others are vines.

**Figure 11** Gymnosperms are the oldest seed plants. **A.** Cycads, similar to this sago palm, were quite common during the age of dinosaurs. **B.** Only one kind of ginkgo, *Ginkgo biloba*, lives today. **C.** Gnetophytes, such as *Welwitschia mirabilis* shown here, grow in the very dry deserts of west Africa.

**Figure 12** Ponderosa pines (A) are conifers that grow in the Rocky Mountains. Both male cones (B) and female cones (C) are produced on a single tree.
*Comparing and Contrasting How do the male and female cones differ?*

**Conifers** Conifers (KAHN uh furz), or cone-bearing plants, are the largest and most diverse group of gymnosperms on Earth today. Most conifers, such as pines, redwoods, cedars, hemlocks, and junipers, are evergreen plants. Evergreen plants keep their leaves, or needles, year round. Old needles drop off and are replaced by new ones throughout the life of the plant.

If someone were to write a Book of Records for plants, conifers would get many awards. As you already know, giant sequoia trees would win the widest tree on Earth award. New Zealand pygmy pines, in contrast, are among the shortest trees on Earth. They grow only 8 centimeters tall. A bristlecone pine tree in Nevada holds the record for being the oldest organism on Earth. Its annual rings indicate that the tree is about 4,900 years old!

## Reproduction

Most gymnosperms have reproductive structures called **cones.** Cones are covered with scales. Most gymnosperms produce two types of cones: male cones and female cones. Usually, a single plant produces both male and female cones. In some types of gymnosperms, however, individual trees produce either male cones or female cones. A few types of gymnosperms produce no cones at all.

Figure 12 shows the male and female cones of a Ponderosa pine. Notice that the male cones are smaller than the female cones. Male cones produce tiny grains of pollen. **Pollen** contains the microscopic cells that will later become sperm cells. Male cones produce so many pollen grains that they can overflow the spaces between the cone's scales.

Female cones contain at least one ovule at the base of each scale. An **ovule** (OH vyool) is a structure that contains an egg cell. After fertilization occurs, the ovule develops into a seed.

You can learn how gymnosperms reproduce in *Exploring the Life Cycle of a Gymnosperm* on the next page. **First, pollen falls from a male cone onto a female cone. In time, a sperm cell and an egg cell join together in an ovule on the female cone.** After fertilization occurs, the zygote develops into the embryo part of the seed.

**Pollination and Fertilization** The transfer of pollen from a male reproductive structure to a female reproductive structure is called **pollination.** In gymnosperms, wind often carries the pollen from the male cones to the female cones. The pollen collects in a sticky substance produced by each ovule. The scales of the female cone close and seal in the pollen. Inside the closed scale, fertilization occurs. The seed then develops on the scale.

Female cones stay on the tree until the seeds mature. It can take up to two years for the seeds of some gymnosperms to mature. Male cones, however, usually fall off the tree after they have shed their pollen.

**Seed Dispersal** As the seeds develop, the female cone increases in size. The cone's position on the branch may change as well. Cones that contain immature seeds point upward, while cones that contain mature seeds point downward. When the seeds are mature, the scales open. The wind shakes the seeds out of the cone and carries them away. Only a few seeds will land in a suitable place and grow into new plants.

*Checkpoint* *What is pollen and where is it produced?*

**The Scoop on Cones**

In this activity, **ACTIVITY** you will observe the structure of a female cone.

1. Use a hand lens to look closely at the female cone. Gently shake the cone over a piece of white paper. Observe what happens.

2. Break off one scale from the cone. Examine its base. If the scale contains a seed, remove the seed.

3. With a hand lens, examine the seed from Step 2, or examine a seed that fell on the paper in Step 1.

4. Wash your hands.

*Inferring* How does the structure of the cone protect the seeds?

# EXPLORING the Life Cycle of a Gymnosperm

**P**ine trees have a typical life cycle for a gymnosperm. Follow the steps of pollination, fertilization, and seed development in the pine tree.

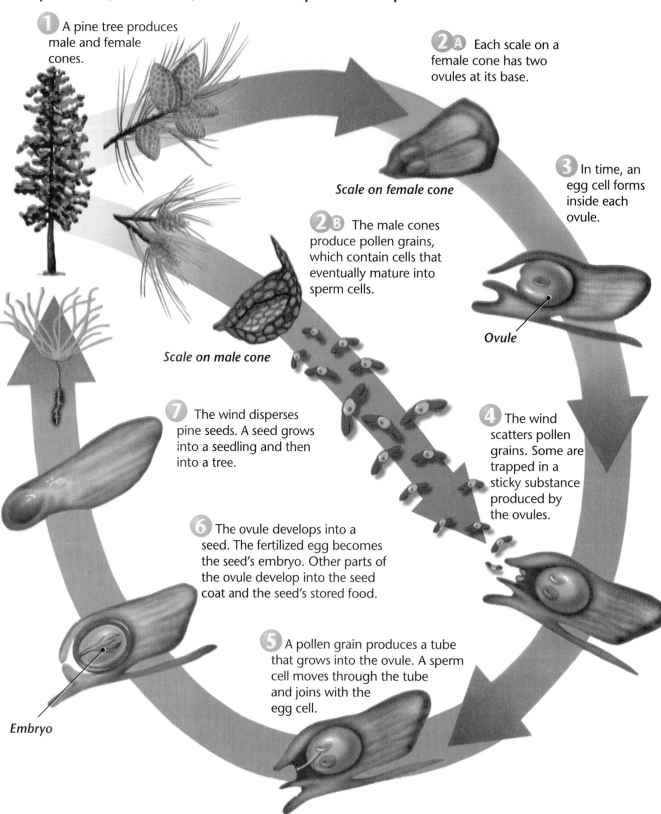

**1** A pine tree produces male and female cones.

**2A** Each scale on a female cone has two ovules at its base.

*Scale on female cone*

**3** In time, an egg cell forms inside each ovule.

**2B** The male cones produce pollen grains, which contain cells that eventually mature into sperm cells.

*Scale on male cone*

*Ovule*

**7** The wind disperses pine seeds. A seed grows into a seedling and then into a tree.

**4** The wind scatters pollen grains. Some are trapped in a sticky substance produced by the ovules.

**6** The ovule develops into a seed. The fertilized egg becomes the seed's embryo. Other parts of the ovule develop into the seed coat and the seed's stored food.

**5** A pollen grain produces a tube that grows into the ovule. A sperm cell moves through the tube and joins with the egg cell.

*Embryo*

**Figure 13** Conifers provided the lumber for this playground.

## Gymnosperms and the Living World

Paper and other wood products, such as the lumber used to build homes, come from conifers. Conifers are also used to make the rayon fibers in clothes as well as the cellophane wrappers on some food products. Other products, such as turpentine and the rosin used by baseball pitchers and musicians, are made from the sap produced by some conifers.

 **INTEGRATING ENVIRONMENTAL SCIENCE** Because conifers are so useful to humans, they are grown in large forests in many regions of the United States. One method that is sometimes used to obtain lumber is called clear cutting. In this method all of the trees in a large area of a forest are cut down at once. This practice can leave forest animals homeless and cause the soil to be washed away by rains. Sometimes, other less-damaging cutting methods are used. For example, loggers may cut down trees in a long, narrow strip and then plant new trees in the strips. This method allows forests to regrow more quickly without the loss of soil and homes for wildlife.

## Section 2 Review

1. What are three characteristics of many gymnosperms?
2. Describe how gymnosperms reproduce.
3. List four products that are produced from gymnosperms. Which group of gymnosperms are used to make the products in your list?
4. **Thinking Critically Comparing and Contrasting** Compare the functions of male and female cones.

### Science at Home

With a family member, make a list of things in your home that are made from gymnosperms. Then describe the characteristics of gymnosperms to your family member. What gymnosperms grow where you live?

# SECTION
## 3 Angiosperms

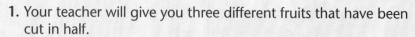

### What Is a Fruit?

1. Your teacher will give you three different fruits that have been cut in half.

2. Use a hand lens to carefully observe the outside of each fruit. For each fruit, record its color, shape, size, and external features. Record your observations in your notebook.

3. Carefully observe the structures inside the fruit. Record your observations.

**Think It Over**

**Forming Operational Definitions** Based on your observations, how would you define the term *fruit*?

---

### GUIDE FOR READING

◆ What characteristics do angiosperms share?

◆ How do angiosperms reproduce?

***Reading Tip*** Before you read, preview the photographs in this section. Predict how angiosperms differ from gymnosperms.

▼ Kudzu vines

Americans who visited the Japanese pavilion at the United States Centennial Exhibition in 1876 were introduced to kudzu, an attractive Asian vine. Soon, many Americans began planting kudzu in their communities. Little did they know that this creeping vine would become a huge problem.

Kudzu is one of the world's fastest-growing plants. Although it is nicknamed the "mile-a-minute vine," kudzu really does not grow that fast. But it can grow as much as 30 centimeters a day. In the southern United States, kudzu now covers an area twice the size of Connecticut. Unfortunately, there is no effective way to control the growth of this fast-growing plant.

### What Are Angiosperms?

Kudzu is a type of seed plant known as an angiosperm. An **angiosperm** (AN jee uh spurm) is a plant that produces seeds that are enclosed in a fruit. The word *angiosperm* comes from two Greek words that mean "seed in a vessel." The protective "vessel"

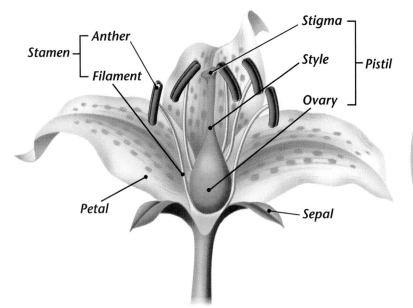

**Figure 14** Like most flowers, this lily contains both male and female reproductive structures. *Interpreting Photographs* What structures in the diagram can you find in the photograph?

where seeds develop is called the **ovary.** The ovary is located within an angiosperm's **flower**—the reproductive structure of an angiosperm. **Two characteristics of angiosperms are that they produce flowers and fruits.**

Most of the familiar plants around you are angiosperms. Angiosperms live almost everywhere on Earth. They grow in frozen areas in the Arctic, tropical jungles, and barren deserts. A few angiosperms, such as mangrove trees and some sea grasses, even live in the oceans.

## The Structure of Flowers

Like the plants that produce them, flowers come in all sorts of shapes, sizes, and colors. But all flowers have the same function—reproduction. Look at Figure 14 to see the parts of a typical flower. As you read about the parts, keep in mind that the description does not apply to all flowers. For example, some flowers have only male reproductive parts, and some flowers lack **petals**—the colorful structures that you see when flowers open.

When a flower is still a bud, it is enclosed by leaflike structures called **sepals** (SEE pulz). Sepals protect the developing flower. After the sepals fold back, the petals are revealed. The colors and shapes of the petals and the odors produced by the flower attract insects and other animals. These organisms ensure that pollination occurs.

Within the petals are the flower's male and female reproductive parts. Locate the thin stalks topped by small knobs inside the flower in Figure 14. These are the **stamens** (STAY munz), the male reproductive parts. The thin stalk is called the filament. Pollen is produced in the knob, or anther, at the top of the stalk.

<h1>Visual Arts<br>CONNECTION</h1>

The American artist Georgia O'Keeffe (1887–1986) is best known for her paintings of the landscape and wildlife in the western United States. Below you see an O'Keeffe painting of a red poppy. O'Keeffe painted the flower with accurate detail. Look carefully at the red poppy. At first it may not appear to have a lot of detail. But if you look more closely, you can see such structures as petals and reproductive parts.

*In Your Journal*

Write a paragraph describing the red poppy's adaptations for attracting animals for pollination.

The female parts, or **pistils** (PIS tulz), are usually found in the center of the flower. Some flowers have two or more pistils; others have only one. The sticky tip of the pistil is called the stigma. A slender tube, called a style, connects the stigma to a hollow structure at the base of the flower. This hollow structure is the ovary, which contains one or more ovules.

## Reproduction

You can learn how angiosperms reproduce in *Exploring the Life Cycle of an Angiosperm*. **First, pollen falls on a stigma. In time, the sperm cell and egg cell join together in the flower's ovule. The zygote develops into the embryo part of the seed.**

**Pollination and Fertilization** A flower is pollinated when a grain of pollen falls on the stigma. Like gymnosperms, some angiosperms are pollinated by the wind. But most angiosperms rely on birds, bats, or insects for pollination. Nectar, a sugar-rich food, is located deep inside a flower. When an animal enters a flower to obtain the nectar, it brushes against the anthers and becomes coated with pollen. Some of the pollen can drop onto the flower's stigma as the animal leaves the flower. The pollen can also be brushed onto the sticky stigma of the next flower the animal visits. If the pollen falls on the stigma of a similar plant, fertilization can occur. The zygote then begins to develop into the seed's embryo. Other parts of the ovule develop into the rest of the seed.

**Seed Dispersal** As the seed develops, the ovary changes into a **fruit**—a ripened ovary and other structures that enclose one or more seeds. Apples and cherries are fruits. So are many foods you usually call vegetables, such as tomatoes and squash. For an angiosperm, a fruit is a way to disperse its seeds. Animals that eat fruits help to disperse their seeds.

☑ *Checkpoint* *What attracts pollinators to angiosperms?*

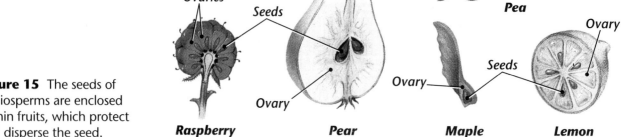

**Figure 15** The seeds of angiosperms are enclosed within fruits, which protect and disperse the seed.

# EXPLORING the Life Cycle of an Angiosperm

**A**ll angiosperms have a similar life cycle. Follow the steps of pollination, fertilization, and fruit development in this typical angiosperm.

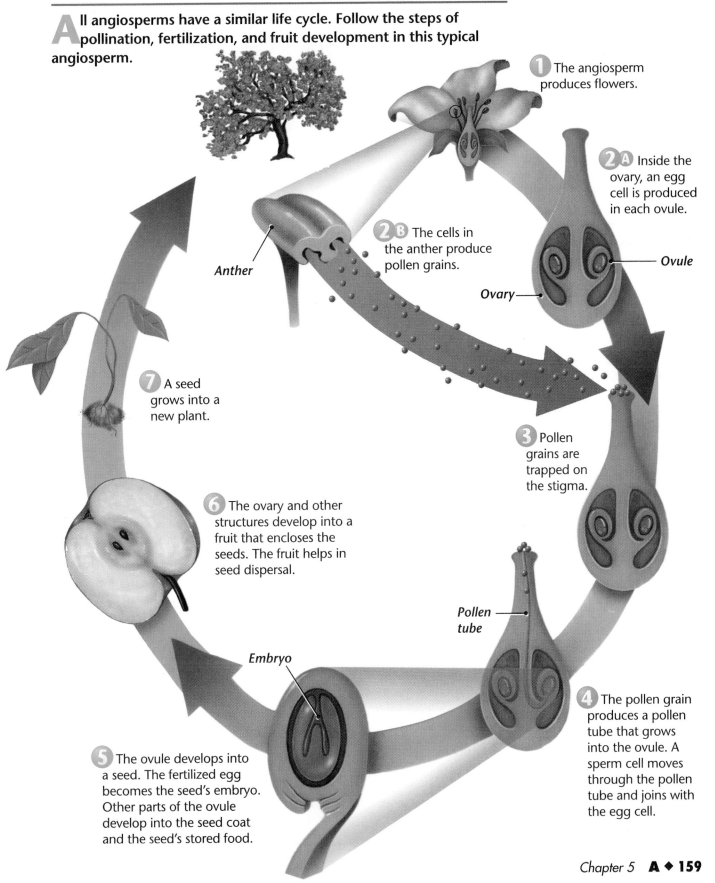

**1** The angiosperm produces flowers.

**2A** Inside the ovary, an egg cell is produced in each ovule.

*Ovule*

*Ovary*

**2B** The cells in the anther produce pollen grains.

*Anther*

**7** A seed grows into a new plant.

**3** Pollen grains are trapped on the stigma.

**6** The ovary and other structures develop into a fruit that encloses the seeds. The fruit helps in seed dispersal.

*Pollen tube*

*Embryo*

**5** The ovule develops into a seed. The fertilized egg becomes the seed's embryo. Other parts of the ovule develop into the seed coat and the seed's stored food.

**4** The pollen grain produces a pollen tube that grows into the ovule. A sperm cell moves through the pollen tube and joins with the egg cell.

**Monocots**

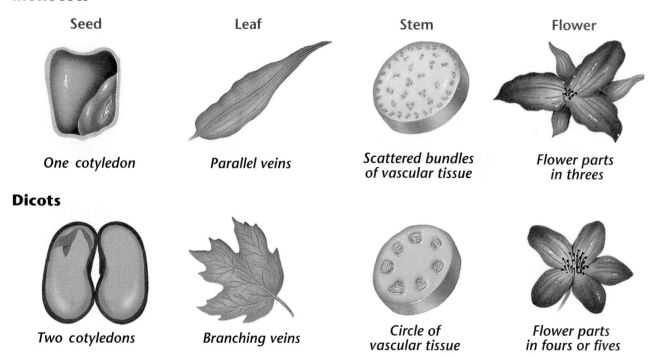

| Seed | Leaf | Stem | Flower |
| --- | --- | --- | --- |
| One cotyledon | Parallel veins | Scattered bundles of vascular tissue | Flower parts in threes |

**Dicots**

| | | | |
| --- | --- | --- | --- |
| Two cotyledons | Branching veins | Circle of vascular tissue | Flower parts in fours or fives |

**Figure 16** Monocots and dicots are the two groups of angiosperms. The groups differ in the number of cotyledons, the arrangement of veins and vascular tissue, and the number of petals.
*Classifying Would a plant whose flowers have 20 petals be a monocot or a dicot?*

## Types of Angiosperms

Angiosperms are divided into two major groups: monocots and dicots. "Cot" is short for *cotyledon*. Recall from Section 1 that the cotyledon, or seed leaf, provides food for the embryo. *Mono* means "one" and *di* means "two". **Monocots** are angiosperms that have only one seed leaf. **Dicots,** on the other hand, produce seeds with two seed leaves. Look at Figure 16 to compare the characteristics of monocots and dicots.

**Monocots**  Grasses, including corn, wheat, and rice, and plants such as lilies and tulips are monocots. The flowers of a monocot usually have either three petals or a multiple of three petals. Monocots usually have long, slender leaves with veins that run parallel to one another like train rails. The bundles of vascular tissue in monocot stems are usually scattered randomly throughout the stem.

**Dicots**  Dicots include plants such as roses and violets, as well as dandelions. Both oak and maple trees are dicots, as are food plants such as beans and apples. The flowers of dicots often have either four or five petals or multiples of these numbers. The leaves are usually wide, with veins that branch off from one another. Dicot stems usually have bundles of vascular tissue arranged in a circle.

✓ *Checkpoint How do the petals of monocots and dicots differ in number?*

## Angiosperms and the Living World

Angiosperms are an important source of food, clothing, and medicine for other organisms. Plant-eating animals, such as cows, elephants, and beetles, eat flowering plants such as grasses as well as the leaves of trees. People eat vegetables, fruits, and cereals, all of which are angiosperms.

People also produce clothing and other products from angiosperms. For example, the seeds of cotton plants, like the ones you see in Figure 17, are covered with cotton fibers. The stems of flax plants provide linen fibers. The sap of tropical rubber trees is used to make rubber for tires and other products. Furniture is often made from the wood of maple, cherry, and oak trees.

 **INTEGRATING HEALTH** Some angiosperms are used in the making of medicine. For example, aspirin was first made from a substance found in the leaves of willow trees. Digitalis, a heart medication, comes from the leaves of the foxglove plant. Cortisone is a medicine made from the roots of the Mexican yam. It is used to treat arthritis and other joint problems. These medicines have helped improve the health of many people.

**Figure 17** Cotton seeds, which develop in structures called bolls, are covered with fibers that are manufactured into cotton fabric.

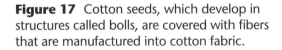
## Section 3 Review

1. What two characteristics do all angiosperms share? Explain the importance of those characteristics.
2. Give a brief description of how reproduction occurs in angiosperms.
3. List the parts of a typical flower. What is the function of each part?
4. **Thinking Critically Inferring** A certain plant has small, dull-colored flowers with no scent. Do you think the plant is pollinated by animals or by the wind? Explain.

**CHAPTER PROJECT 5**

**Check Your Progress**
Your plants should now have, or will soon have, flowers. Make a diagram of the flower's structure. When the flowers open, you'll have to pollinate them. This work is usually done by insects or birds. After pollination, watch how the flower changes. (*Hint:* Discuss with your teacher and classmates how to pollinate the flowers.)

# A Close Look at Flowers

**I**n this lab, you will examine a flower in order to understand how it works.

## Problem

What is the function of a flower, and what roles do its different parts play?

## Skills Focus

observing, measuring, inferring

## Materials

| | |
|---|---|
| paper towels | plastic dropper |
| hand lens | microscope |
| slide | large flower |
| coverslip | scalpel |
| tape | water |
| metric ruler | lens paper |

## Procedure

### Part 1 The Outer Parts of the Flower

1. Tape 4 sheets of paper towel on your work area. Obtain a flower from your teacher. While handling the flower gently, observe its shape and color. Use the ruler to measure it. Notice whether the petals have any spots or other markings. Does the flower have a scent? Record your observations with sketches and descriptions.

2. Observe the sepals. How many are there? How do they relate to the rest of the flower? (*Hint:* The sepals are often green, but not always.) Record your observations.

3. Use a scalpel to carefully cut off the sepals without damaging the structures beneath them. **CAUTION:** *Scalpels are sharp. Cut in a direction away from yourself and others.*

4. Observe the petals. How many are there? Are all the petals the same, or are they different? Record your observations.

### Part 2 The Male Part of the Flower

5. Carefully pull off the petals to examine the male part of the flower. Try not to damage the structures beneath the petals.

6. Observe the stamens. How many are there? How are they shaped? How tall are they? Record your observations.

7. Use a scalpel to carefully cut the stamens away from the rest of the flower without damaging the structures beneath them. Lay the stamens on the paper towel.

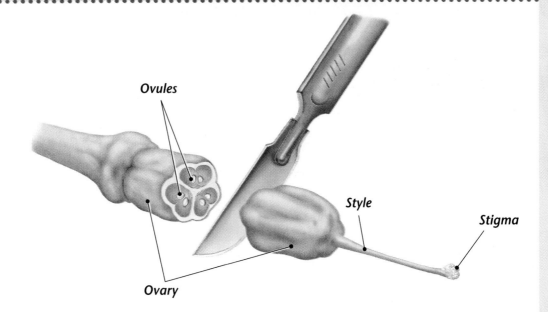

Ovules

Style

Stigma

Ovary

8. Obtain a clean slide and coverslip. Hold a stamen over the slide, and gently tap some pollen grains from the anther onto the slide. Add a drop of water to the pollen. Then place the coverslip over the water and pollen.

9. Observe the pollen under both the low-power objective and the high-power objective of a microscope. Draw and label a pollen grain.

### Part 3 The Female Part of the Flower

10. Use a scalpel to cut the pistil away from the rest of the flower. Measure the height of the pistil. Examine its shape. Observe the top of the pistil. Determine if that surface will stick to and lift a tiny piece of lens paper. Record your observations.

11. Lay the pistil on the paper towel. Holding it firmly at its base, use a scalpel to cut the pistil in half at its widest point, as shown in the diagram above. **CAUTION:** *Cut away from your fingers.* How many compartments do you see? How many ovules do you see? Record your observations.

## Analyze and Conclude

1. Based on your observations, describe how the petals, pistils, sepals, and stamens of a flower are arranged.

2. What is the main function of a flower? How are the sepals, petals, stamens, and pistil involved in that function?

3. How does a flower produce seeds?

4. Did your flower show any patterns in the number of sepals, petals, stamens, or other structures? If so, describe that pattern. Is your flower a monocot or a dicot?

5. **Apply** How do you think the flower you examined is pollinated? Use your observations, including the heights of the pistil and stamens, to support your answer.

## More to Explore

Some kinds of flowers do not have all the parts found in the flower in this lab. Obtain a different flower. Find out which parts this flower has, and which parts are missing. Get your teacher's approval before carrying out this investigation.

# SECTION 4 Plant Responses and Growth

## DISCOVER

### Can a Plant Respond to Touch?

1. Your teacher will give you two plants. Observe the first plant. Gently touch a leaf and observe what happens over the next three minutes. Record your observations.

2. Repeat Step 1 with the second plant. Record your observations.

3. Wash your hands with soap and water.

**Think It Over**
*Inferring* What advantage might a plant have if its leaves responded to touch?

---

### GUIDE FOR READING

◆ **What are three stimuli that produce plant responses?**

◆ **What functions do plant hormones control?**

*Reading Tip* As you read, use the headings to make an outline about plant responses and growth.

▼ **A floating bladderwort**

The bladderwort is a freshwater plant with small yellow flowers. Attached to its floating stems are open structures called bladders. When a water flea enters a bladder, the bladder snaps shut faster than you can blink. The plant then digests the trapped flea.

A bladderwort responds quickly—faster than many animals respond to a similar stimulus. You may be surprised to learn that some plants have lightning-quick responses. In fact, you might have thought that plants do not respond to stimuli at all. But plants do respond to some stimuli, although they usually do so more slowly than the bladderwort.

## Tropisms

Animals usually respond to stimuli by moving. Unlike animals, plants commonly respond by growing either toward or away from a stimulus. A plant's growth response toward or away from a stimulus is called a **tropism** (TROH pihz uhm). If a plant grows toward the stimulus, it is said to show a positive tropism. If a plant grows away from a stimulus, it shows a negative tropism. **Touch, light, and gravity are three important stimuli to which plants respond.**

**Touch** Some plants, such as bladderworts, show a response to touch called thigmotropism. The term *thigmo* comes from a Greek word that means "touch." The stems of many vines, such as grapes and morning glories, show a positive thigmotropism. As the vines grow, they coil around any object that they touch.

**Light** All plants exhibit a response to light called phototropism. The leaves, stems, and flowers of plants grow toward light, show-ing a positive phototropism. For example, sunflower plants exhibit a strong positive phototropism. As the sun's position changes during the day, sunflowers move on their stalks so that they are always facing the sun.

**Gravity** Plants also respond to gravity. This response is called gravitropism. Roots show positive gravitropism—they grow downward, with the pull of gravity. Stems, on the other hand, show negative gravitropism—they grow upward.

## Plant Hormones

Plants are able to respond to light, gravity, and touch because they produce hormones. A **hormone** produced by a plant is a chemical that affects how the plant grows and develops. **In addition to tropisms, plant hormones also control germination, the formation of flowers, stems, and leaves, the shedding of leaves, and the development and ripening of fruit.**

One important plant hormone is named **auxin** (AWX sin). Auxin speeds up the rate at which a plant's cells grow. Auxin controls a plant's response to light. When light shines on one side of a plant's stem, auxin moves to the shaded side of the stem. The cells on that side begin to grow faster. Eventually, the cells on the stem's shady side are longer than those on its sunny side. So the stem bends toward the light.

☑ *Checkpoint* *What role does the hormone auxin play in a plant?*

## Life Spans of Angiosperms

If you've ever planted a garden, you know that many flowering plants grow, flower, and die in a single year. Flowering plants that complete a life cycle within one growing season are called annuals. The word annual comes from the Latin word *annus,* which means "year." Most annuals have herbaceous stems. Annuals include many garden plants, such as marigolds, petunias, and pansies. Wheat, tomatoes, and cucumbers are also annuals.

Angiosperms that complete their life cycle in two years are called biennials (by EN ee ulz). The Latin prefix *bi* means "two."

**Figure 18** The face of this sunflower turns on its stalk throughout the day so that it always faces the sun. *Making Generalizations How does a positive phototropism help a plant survive?*

**Figure 19** A flowering plant is classified as an annual, biennial, or perennial depending on the length of its growing season. **A.** These morning glories are annuals. **B.** Foxglove, like this *Digitalis purpurea*, is a biennial. **C.** This peony, a perennial, will bloom year after year.

In the first year, biennials germinate and grow roots, very short stems, and leaves. During their second year, biennials grow new stems and leaves and then produce flowers and seeds. Once the flowers produce seeds, the plant dies. Parsley, celery, and foxglove are biennials.

Flowering plants that live for more than two years are called perennials. The Latin word *per* means "through." Perennials usually live through many years. Some perennials, such as peonies and asparagus, have herbaceous stems. The leaves and stems above the ground die each winter. New ones are produced each spring. Most perennials, however, have woody stems. Bristlecone pines, oak trees, and honeysuckle are examples of woody perennials.

## Section 4 Review

1. Name three stimuli to which plants respond.
2. What is a plant hormone? List four processes that a plant's hormones control.
3. Suppose you are growing a plant on a windowsill. After a few days, you notice that the plant's leaves and flowers are facing the window. Explain why this has occurred.
4. **Thinking Critically Applying Concepts** Is the grass that grows in most lawns an annual, a biennial, or a perennial? Explain.

### Science at Home

With a family member, soak some corn seeds or lima bean seeds in water overnight. Then push them gently into some soil in a paper cup until they are just covered. Keep the soil moist. When you see the stems break through the soil, place the cup in a sunny window. After a few days, explain to your family member why the plants responded the way they did.

# Which Way is Up?

In this lab, you will develop and test a hypothesis about how seedlings respond to gravity.

## Problem

How is the growth of a seed affected by gravity?

## Materials

4 corn seeds
paper towels
water
marking pencil

plastic petri dish
scissors
masking tape
clay

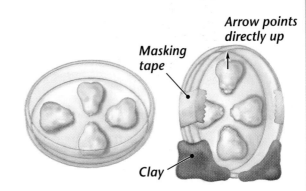

Arrow points directly up

Masking tape

Clay

## Procedure

1. Read over the entire procedure. Then, with your group, develop a hypothesis about the direction in which the seedlings will grow in response to gravity.
2. Arrange four seeds that have been soaked in water for 24 hours in a petri dish. The pointed ends of the seeds should face the center of the dish, as shown in the illustration.
3. Place a circle cut from a paper towel over the seeds. Moisten one or more paper towels with water so that they are wet but not dripping. Pack them in the dish to hold the seeds firmly in place. Cover the dish, and seal it with tape.
4. Lay the dish upside-down so the seeds show. Use a marking pencil to draw a small, outward-facing arrow over one of the seeds, as shown in the illustration. Turn the dish over and write your name and the date on it.
5. Use clay to stand up the petri dish so that the arrow points upward. Put the petri dish in a dark place.

6. Once a day for a week, remove the petri dish and check it. Do not open the dish. Observe and sketch the seeds. Note the seeds' direction of growth. Then return the dish, making sure that the arrow points upward.

## Analyze and Conclude

1. What new structures emerged as the seeds developed? How did the direction of growth compare from seed to seed?
2. Did your results confirm your hypothesis? If not, describe any differences between your hypothesis and your results.
3. Why was it necessary to grow these seeds in the dark?
4. **Think About It** What evidence or ideas did you consider when you wrote your hypothesis? Did any of your ideas change as a result of this experiment? Explain.

## Design an Experiment

How will your seedlings respond if you now allow them to grow in the light? Design an experiment to find out. Obtain your teacher's approval before carrying out your experiment.

# SECTION 5 Feeding the World

## DISCOVER ···································· ACTIVITY····

### Will There Be Enough to Eat?

1. Choose a numbered tag from the bag that your teacher provides. If you pick a tag with the number 1 on it, you're from a wealthy country. If you pick a tag with the number 2, you're from a middle-income country. If you pick a tag with the number 3, you're from a poor country.

2. Find classmates that have the same number on their tag. Sit down as a group.

3. Your teacher will serve your group a meal. The amount of food you receive will depend on the number on your tag.

4. As you eat, observe the people in your group and in the other groups. After you eat, record your observations. Also, record how you felt and what you were thinking during the meal.

**Think It Over**

*Predicting* Based on this activity, predict what effect an increase in the world's population would have on the world's food supply.

### GUIDE FOR READING

◆ What methods may help farmers produce more crops?

*Reading Tip* As you read, make a list of the technologies being used to increase Earth's food supply.

Today, about six billion people live on Earth. Some scientists predict that by the year 2050 the population will grow to ten billion people. Think about how much additional food will be needed to feed the growing population. How will farmers be able to grow enough food?

Fortunately, both scientists and farmers are already hard at work trying to find answers to this question. **In laboratories, scientists are developing plants that are more resistant to insects, disease, and drought. They are also developing plants that produce more food per plant. On farms, new, efficient, "high-tech" farming practices are being used.**

## Producing Better Plants

Wheat, corn, rice, and potatoes are the major sources of food for people on Earth today. To feed more people, then, the production, or yields, of these crops must be increased. This is not an easy task. One challenge facing farmers is that these crops grow only in certain climates. Another challenge is that the size and structure of these plants limit how much food they can produce.

Today scientists are using new technologies to address these challenges. Recall from Chapter 2 that scientists can manipulate the genetic material of certain bacteria to produce human insulin. The process that these scientists use is called genetic engineering. In **genetic engineering,** scientists alter an organism's genetic material to produce an organism with qualities that people find useful.

**Figure 20** In this high-tech greenhouse, scientists control the environmental conditions as they develop new types of plants. *Applying Concepts How might new plant types lead to increased crop yields in the future?*

Scientists are using genetic engineering to produce plants that can grow in a wider range of climates. They are also engineering plants to be more resistant to damage from insects. For example, scientists have inserted genetic material from a bacterium into corn and tomato plants. The new genetic material enables the plants to produce substances that kill insects. Caterpillars or other insects that bite into the leaves of these plants are killed. Today, many kinds of genetically engineered plants are grown on experimental farms. Some of these plants may produce the crops of the future.

☑ *Checkpoint* What are the four crops on which people depend?

## Improving the Efficiency of Farms

On the farms of the future, satellite images and computers will be just as important as tractors and harvesters. These new tools will allow farmers to practice "precision farming"—knowing just how much water and fertilizer different fields require. First, satellite images of the farmer's fields are taken. Then, a computer analyzes the images to determine the makeup of the soil in different fields on the farm. The computer uses the data to prepare a watering and fertilizing plan for each field. Precision farming benefits farmers because it saves time and money. It also increases crop yields by helping farmers maintain ideal conditions in all fields.

**Figure 21** The map on the computer screen of this tractor shows the makeup of the soil in a farm's fields. The map was obtained by satellite imaging.

 **INTEGRATING ENVIRONMENTAL SCIENCE** Precision farming also benefits the environment because farmers use only as much fertilizer as the soil needs. When less fertilizer is used, fewer nutrients wash off the land into lakes and rivers. As you read in Chapter 3, reducing the use of fertilizers is one way to prevent algal blooms from damaging bodies of water.

## Hydroponics

In some areas of the world, poor soil does not support the growth of crops. For example, on some islands in the Pacific Ocean, the soil contains large amounts of salt from the surrounding ocean. Food crops will not grow in the salty soil.

On these islands, people can use hydroponics to grow food crops. **Hydroponics** (hy druh PAHN iks) is a method by which plants are grown in solutions of nutrients instead of in soil. Usually, the plants are grown in containers in which their roots are anchored in gravel or sand. The nutrient-rich water is pumped through the gravel or sand. Unfortunately, hydroponics is a costly method of growing food crops. But, the process allows people to grow crops in areas with poor farmland to help feed a growing population.

 **Section 5 Review**

1. List three methods that farmers can use to increase crop yields.
2. Explain how genetic engineering may help farmers grow more food.
3. How does precision farming benefit farmers? How does it benefit the environment?
4. **Thinking Critically Applying Concepts** How are plants that are grown using hydroponics able to survive without soil?

*Check Your Progress* **CHAPTER PROJECT 5**

Your plants should be near the end of their growth cycle. Continue to observe them. Harvest the seeds carefully, observe them, and compare them with the original seeds. If you have time, plant a few of these new seeds to begin the life cycle again.

### SECTION 1 The Characteristics of Seed Plants

**Key Ideas**

◆ All seed plants have vascular tissue and produce seeds. All seed plants also have leaves, stems, and roots.

◆ A seed has three important parts: an embryo, stored food, and a seed coat.

◆ Photosynthesis occurs mainly in leaves. Stems support plants and transport materials between the roots and leaves. Roots anchor plants and absorb water and minerals.

**Key Terms**

| | | |
|---|---|---|
| phloem | cotyledon | transpiration |
| xylem | germination | cambium |
| seed | stomata | root cap |
| embryo | | |

### SECTION 2 Gymnosperms

**Key Ideas**

◆ All gymnosperms produce naked seeds. Many gymnosperms also have needlelike or scalelike leaves, and grow deep root systems.

◆ To reproduce, gymnosperms produce pollen in male cones and egg cells in female cones. Pollen falls onto a female cone. In time, a sperm cell and an egg cell join. The zygote develops into the embryo of the seed.

**Key Terms**

| | |
|---|---|
| gymnosperm | ovule |
| cone | pollination |
| pollen | |

### SECTION 3 Angiosperms

**Key Ideas**

◆ Two characteristics of angiosperms are that they produce flowers and fruits.

◆ To reproduce, the male parts of the flower produce pollen, while the female parts produce eggs. Pollen falls on the stigma. In time, the sperm cell and egg cell join in the ovule. The zygote develops into the seed's embryo.

**Key Terms**

| | | |
|---|---|---|
| angiosperm | sepal | fruit |
| ovary | stamen | monocot |
| flower | pistil | dicot |
| petal | | |

### SECTION 4 Plant Responses and Growth

**Key Ideas**

◆ A tropism is a plant's growth response toward or away from a stimulus. Plants respond to touch, light, and gravity.

◆ Plant hormones control tropisms and many other plant functions.

**Key Terms**

| | | |
|---|---|---|
| tropism | hormone | auxin |

### SECTION 5 Feeding the World

INTEGRATING TECHNOLOGY

**Key Ideas**

◆ Genetic engineering, precision farming, and hydroponics can help farmers produce more crops to feed the world's growing population.

**Key Terms**

| | |
|---|---|
| genetic engineering | hydroponics |

ACTIVITY

**USING THE INTERNET**

www.science-explorer.phschool.com

CHAPTER 5 REVIEW

## CHAPTER 5 REVIEW

## Reviewing Content

 For more review of key concepts, see the Interactive Student Tutorial CD-ROM.

### Multiple Choice
*Choose the letter of the best answer.*

1. The process by which a seed sprouts is called
   a. pollination.    b. fertilization.
   c. dispersal.      d. germination.
2. In woody stems, new xylem cells are produced by
   a. bark.           b. cambium.
   c. phloem.         d. pith.
3. Which of the following is the male part of the flower?
   a. pistil          b. ovule
   c. stamen          d. petal
4. What kind of tropism do roots display when they grow into the soil?
   a. positive gravitropism
   b. negative gravitropism
   c. positive phototropism
   d. negative thigmotropism
5. The process of growing crops in a nutrient solution is called
   a. genetic engineering.
   b. hydroponics.
   c. precision farming.
   d. satellite imaging.

### True or False
*If the statement is true, write true. If it is false, change the underlined word or words to make the statement true.*

6. <u>Stems</u> anchor plants and absorb water and minerals from the soil.
7. The needles of a pine tree are actually its <u>leaves</u>.
8. The seeds of <u>gymnosperms</u> are dispersed in fruits.
9. Plants that complete their life cycle in two years are called <u>perennials</u>.
10. The four basic food crops of the world are wheat, corn, rice, and <u>potatoes</u>.

## Checking Concepts

11. Describe four different ways that seeds can be dispersed.
12. Explain the role that stomata play in leaves.
13. What are annual rings? Explain how they form.
14. Describe the structure of a female cone.
15. What is the difference between pollination and fertilization?
16. What role do plant hormones play in phototropism?
17. How can the use of hydroponics help increase the amount of food that can be grown on Earth?
18. **Writing to Learn** Imagine that you are a seed inside a plump purple fruit that is floating in a stream. Describe your experiences on the journey you take to the place where you germinate.

## Thinking Visually

19. **Concept Map** Copy the concept map about seed plants onto a separate piece of paper. Then complete the map and add a title. (For more on concept maps, see the Skills Handbook.)

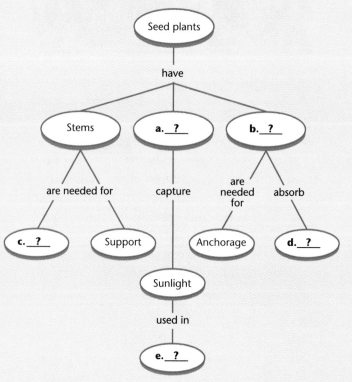

## Applying Skills

*A scientist measured the rate of transpiration in an ash tree over a 24-hour period. She also measured how much water the tree's roots took up during the same period. Use the data in the graph below to answer Questions 20–22.*

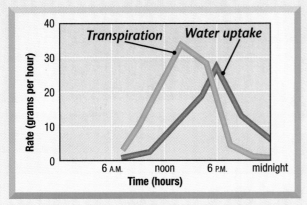

20. **Interpreting Data** At what time during the day is transpiration at its highest? At what time is water uptake at its highest?

21. **Inferring** Why do you think the transpiration rate increases and decreases as it does during the 24-hour period?

22. **Drawing Conclusions** Based on the graph, what is one possible conclusion you can reach about the pattern of water loss and gain in the ash tree?

## Thinking Critically

23. **Relating Cause and Effect** When a strip of bark is removed all the way around the trunk of a tree, the tree dies. Explain why.

24. **Applying Concepts** Explain why people who grow houseplants on windowsills should turn the plants every week or so.

25. **Predicting** Pesticides are designed to kill harmful insects. Sometimes, however, pesticides kill helpful insects as well. What effect could this have on angiosperms?

26. **Making Judgments** Suppose you were a scientist using genetic engineering to increase crop yields. What improvements would you try to introduce? How would they be beneficial?

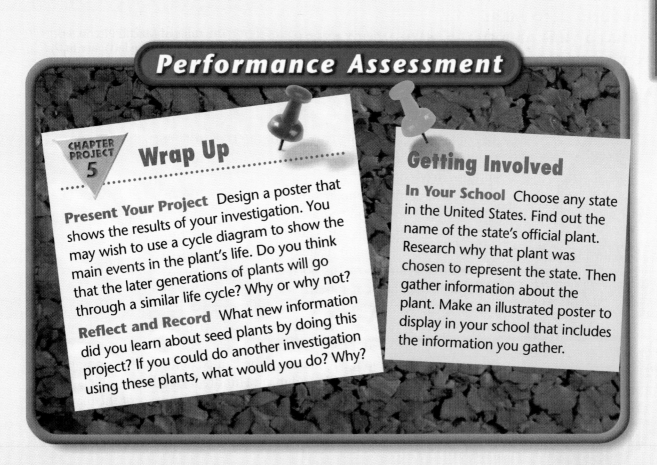

## Performance Assessment

### CHAPTER PROJECT 5 — Wrap Up

**Present Your Project** Design a poster that shows the results of your investigation. You may wish to use a cycle diagram to show the main events in the plant's life. Do you think that the later generations of plants will go through a similar life cycle? Why or why not?

**Reflect and Record** What new information did you learn about seed plants by doing this project? If you could do another investigation using these plants, what would you do? Why?

### Getting Involved

**In Your School** Choose any state in the United States. Find out the name of the state's official plant. Research why that plant was chosen to represent the state. Then gather information about the plant. Make an illustrated poster to display in your school that includes the information you gather.

# CORN
## THE AMAZING GRAIN

The ruins of Machu Picchu, an Incan city (above left), are in the Andes Mountains of Peru. In the drawing at right, an Incan farmer irrigates a field of maize.

## WHAT COMMON GRAIN IS—

* DRIED, THEN POPPED AND EATEN AT THE MOVIES?
* GROUND INTO MEAL?
* ROLLED THIN AND FILLED WITH VEGETABLES?
* EATEN IN FLAKES FOR BREAKFAST?

**P**eople have been eating corn in hundreds of different ways for thousands of years—since corn was first grown for food by ancient cultures in Mexico.

Because corn is useful, people have valued it throughout history. It tastes good, is nourishing, and stores well. Over time, knowledge of corn has spread among people and cultures. Christopher Columbus introduced corn to Europe. Columbus called it mahiz, meaning "a kind of grain." There have been corn myths, corn dances, corn palaces, shucking contests, corn medicines, and corn mattresses.

Today in many countries of the world, corn is a basic part of people's diet, whether in the form of kernels, meal, oil, syrup, or flour. The United States grows billions of bushels a year. But people eat only a tiny portion of this yield as corn. About 80 percent of the United States corn crop is fed to livestock to supply eggs, milk, and meat. Hundreds of other products— from chewing gum to fireworks—are also made from parts of the plant.

◀ This silver maize was crafted by the Incas.

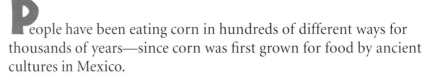

# Maize Through the Ages

Some people say, "Wherever corn went, civilization followed." Corn—or maize—was probably cultivated from a wild grass in Mexico around 8000 B.C. Early farmers planted seeds and harvested crops in planned spaces. They passed on their knowledge of corn to their children and to other farmers. Having plenty of corn is believed to be one reason the ancient agricultural empires of the Mayas and Incas developed and flourished.

In Central America the Mayan civilization was at its height between A.D. 300 and A.D. 800. In Mayan cities, the people built pyramid-shaped temples where they worshiped gods of the sun, rain, and corn. Maize was grown in fields around the cities. The timing of the stages for growing corn affected all Mayan activities. The life cycle of maize and its plant parts—leaves, silk, tassels, and kernels—became the basis for words in the Mayan language.

In South America, the Incan empire thrived between the 1400s and 1535. A powerful ruler of the Incas came to power in Peru in 1438. In less than a century, the Incas expanded their territory from a small area around Cuzco, Peru, to a vast empire. The Inca empire stretched through the Andes Mountains, from Chile to Ecuador. It was the last of Peru's thriving ancient civilizations. The Incan empire was destroyed by Spaniards who arrived in the 1530s in search of gold. In Cuzco, they found an eye-dazzling garden where corn stalks, leaves, husks, and cobs were crafted in silver and gold. To the Incas, corn was more precious than the metal the Spaniards sought.

Though the empires of the Mayas and Incas collapsed, corn-growing spread to other regions. Eventually, the plant was brought north to the Mississippi and Ohio river valleys and east to the Caribbean islands.

**The Mayan civilization in Central America and the Incan civilization in South America flourished before Europeans arrived.**

**Early Civilizations of Central and South America**

Atlantic Ocean

Yucatan Peninsula

Tikal

Caribbean Sea

Central America

Amazon River

Cuzco

South America

Andes Mountains

Pacific Ocean

KEY

Mayan Empire
A.D. 300–A.D. 900

Incan Empire
A.D. 1400s–A.D. 1535

0    1000 km

0    600 mi

## Social Studies Activity

Use a map of Central and South America today.

◆ Trace the approximate boundaries of the Mayan and Incan empires.

◆ Name the countries that are now located in these areas.

◆ Identify the geographical features within the empires.

◆ Find out about the climate. Why were these lands well suited to growing corn?

## From the Garden in the Sky

The word for corn in some Native American languages means "that which gives us life." How did humans discover corn? No one knows, but many cultures have myths and stories to explain how the plant came to be. To the Pawnee on the Nebraska plains, corn was Evening Star, the mother of all things. Evening Star gave corn from her garden in the sky. The Navajo in the southwestern United States tell a story of a turkey hen that flew in a straight line. As it traveled from the morning star, it shook an ear of corn from its feathers. The following folk tale comes from the Iroquois in Canada.

# The Corn Goddess

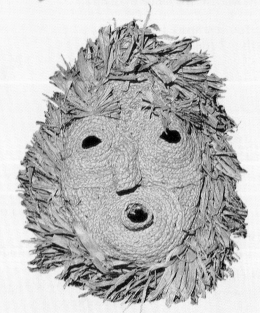

**Iroquois corn husk mask**

THE GREAT SPIRIT gave seeds of corn to a mysterious maiden who became the wife of a great hunter. The wife taught the hunter's people how to plant and harvest the corn, and how to grind it and bake it into bread. The people were pleased.

But the great hunter's brother disliked the bread and threw it to the ground. The wife was alarmed that he had dishonored the gift of the Great Spirit. That night she told her husband that she must leave his people.

Shortly before dawn, the people heard the sound of falling rain. But it was not rain. It was the sound of thousands of kernels dropping from the ears of corn. Soon all the stalks were empty. The men hunted but found little game. Before long the children cried because they were so hungry.

The great hunter was sad. He decided to leave and find his wife. She had told him, "If ever you want to find me, walk east. When you reach a lake, rest and listen for the cry of a child. Then you should plant an arrow in the ground, point it in the direction of the sound, and sleep. When you wake, the arrow will show you the way."

The great hunter went east to the big lake and lit a fire. Late that night he heard crying. He planted his arrow and lay down to sleep. At dawn, he walked as the arrow pointed. He walked all day, then stopped to rest at night. He lit another fire. Again he heard crying, placed his arrow, and slept. On the third night, his wife appeared.

He said his people were starving and he asked for her help. When winter passed, the great hunter returned to his people with corn from his wife. That year, the harvest was abundant. He rejoiced, but he missed his wife and left to find her again. He traveled to the lake and listened for crying, but he did not hear it. He traveled another day, and another, thinking he knew the direction to go. He searched day after day, listening for the cry. Perhaps he is still looking for her.

*Adapted from* The Corn Goddess and Other Tales from Indian Canada, *National Museum, Canada*

## Language Arts Activity

A folk tale is a story that is passed down from person to person. It may explain something in nature, as this story does, or teach a lesson. Find words and phrases that show that this tale was created a long time ago.

Write your own story about how corn came to be found in nature. Use a modern-day setting and characters in your story.

## Tassels to Silks

Corn must be planted by humans. Unlike many plants, a corn plant cannot disperse its own seeds: they stay inside the husk or modified leaves. For thousands of years, farmers have removed the husks and taken out the kernels to plant them. Today huge machines plant, irrigate, harvest, and shuck corn.

After a corn seed is planted, it begins to grow into a corn plant. An ear of corn begins with an arrangement of several hundred female flowers inside the husk. Each flower has a very long style, or silk, that grows outside the husk. The stigma at the end of the silk traps pollen grains. For pollination to occur, the corn silks must grow out of the husk during the time that the pollen is shed. So the timing of pollination is important in the growth of a corn plant.

Male flowers bloom on the plant's tassels and release pollen. One plant's tassels can shed millions of pollen grains in a period of 5 to 8 days. But it only takes one grain of pollen caught on a silk for fertilization to occur. Fertilization begins the process that results in kernels.

How long a corn plant takes to grow and how well it grows depends on the warmth, moisture, and quality of soil. Too much heat or too little water can damage the plant's flowers and result in poor crops. Depending on the climate, sweet corn takes about 125 days to mature from planting to harvesting.

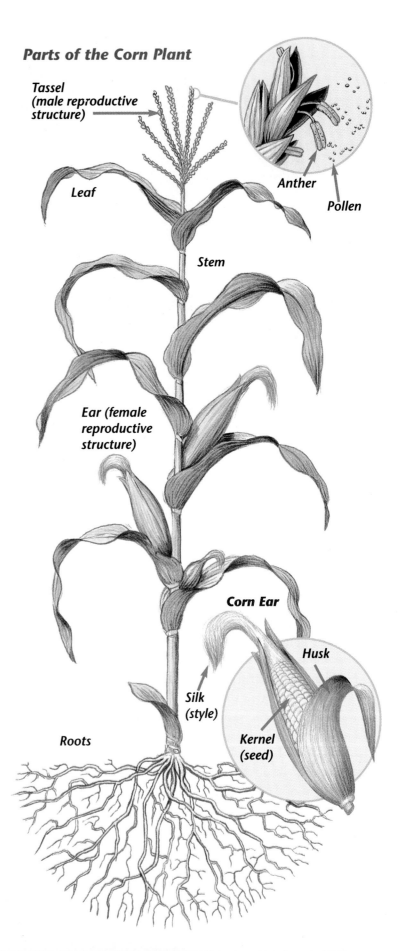

**Parts of the Corn Plant**

Tassel (male reproductive structure)

Leaf

Anther

Pollen

Stem

Ear (female reproductive structure)

Corn Ear

Husk

Silk (style)

Kernel (seed)

Roots

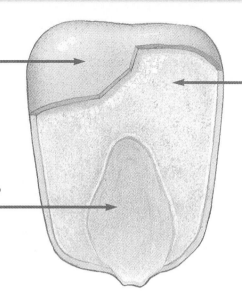

**Seed coat**
*protects the kernel*
Bran is made from
the seed coat

**Embryo**
*the part of the seed
that will develop into
a new corn plant*
Corn oil is made from
the embryo

**Stored food**
*inner starchy part that
feeds the embryo*
Many things are made
from the starchy part of
the corn kernel, including:
• *cornstarch*
• *corn sugar*
• *corn syrups*
• *ice cream*
• *animal feed*
• *glue*
• *fuel*

# A Kernel Goes a Long Way

Did you know that corn and corn products are used as fuel? Or that corn is found in some brands of baby food, crayons, soap, and tires? It's even found in ketchup, hot dogs, and toothpaste.

Today, only a small portion of the corn that is planted is sweet corn. Sweet corn is sold fresh or used to produce canned or frozen corn. But millions of bushels of field corn, which is less sweet, are trucked to refineries. There the kernels are turned into oil, starch, sugar, or fuel.

When ears of field corn arrive at a refinery, the corn is cleaned and soaked. Next, corn kernels are milled—crushed and ground. The milled substance is spun in giant tanks to separate out the embryos. Oil is extracted from the embryo of the kernel. The seed coat may be removed by sifting and can be dried to produce corn bran.

The remaining substance—the stored food—is ground into corn meal. One part of the ground meal is rich in proteins and is used for animal feed. The other part of the corn meal is the starch.

From cornstarch, corn sugars and syrups are processed. You eat these in breads, breakfast cereals, colas, ice cream, and salad dressings, to name only a few products. Cornstarch is also processed into glues and powders for the paper and textile industries, and into ethanol, a fuel.

**Corn is the main food for cattle and many other farm and ranch animals.**

## Science Activity

When you're at the supermarket, how do you decide which brand of a particular product to buy? What criteria do you use? Working with a partner, choose a corn product, such as tortillas, corn flakes, or popcorn to investigate.

◆ Collect several brands of the product to test.
◆ Decide what you will test for. For example, you might want to test which brand of popcorn produces more popped kernels.
◆ Before you begin, predict what your results will be.
◆ Design your own experiment. Write out the step-by-step procedure you will follow. Make sure that you keep all variables the same as you test each product.
◆ Make observations and collect data.
◆ Interpret the data and draw your conclusion. How did your results compare with your prediction?

# Mind-Boggling Corn Data

Every continent in the world except Antarctica produces some corn each year. The largest corn-producing country is the United States, growing 41 percent of the world's corn. The graph shows the leading corn-producing countries. China is next largest, growing 20 percent. The other countries in the world grow smaller amounts.

In the United States, corn is grown in nearly every state, producing over 9 billion bushels of corn a year. A bushel of corn contains about 72,800 kernels. Most of that corn is grown in a group of midwestern states known as the "Corn Belt." Iowa, Illinois, Nebraska, and Minnesota are the four major corn-growing states. Indiana, Missouri, Kansas, Ohio, South Dakota, Wisconsin, Michigan, and Kentucky are the other Corn Belt states.

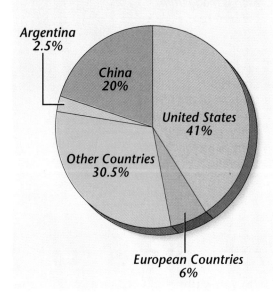

**World Corn Production**

Argentina 2.5%
China 20%
United States 41%
Other Countries 30.5%
European Countries 6%

**The Corn Belt of the United States**

KEY
- Major corn-producing states in the Corn Belt
- Other states in the Corn Belt
- States outside the Corn Belt

| United States Corn Production | Billions of Bushels |
|---|---|
| Major Corn Belt States (Iowa, Illinois, Nebraska, Minnesota) | 5.24 |
| Other Corn Belt States (Indiana, Missouri, Kansas, Ohio, South Dakota, Wisconsin, Michigan, and Kentucky) | 2.96 |
| States Outside the Corn Belt | 1.09 |
| Total for United States | 9.29 |

The Mitchell Corn Palace in South Dakota is decorated with about 3,000 bushels of corn. Corn repairs are made each year.

## Math Activity

Make a circle graph to show corn production in the United States. To create your graph, follow the steps in the Skills Handbook.

- Use the data in the table on the previous page to set up proportions to find the number of degrees in each slice. Then figure percents for Major Corn Belt States, Other Corn Belt States, and States Outside the Corn Belt. Round to the nearest tenth.
- Use a compass to draw a circle.
- Determine the size of each of the 3 slices.
- Measure out and mark off each slice in the circle.

What percent should you get when you add up these numbers?

## Tie It Together

### Plan a Corn Ball

Organize a corn carnival for your school. To advertise the carnival, create a huge popcorn ball with popped corn and glue made from a cornstarch and water mixture. (The largest popcorn ball on record weighed over a ton.) Here are some suggestions for activities.

- Display a variety of products made from corn.
- Bring in food made from corn.
- Set up a booth to explain how popcorn pops.
- Have a contest for visitors to guess the number of popcorn kernels in a jar.
- Set up a booth for telling corny jokes.
- Collect corn facts, pictures, and photographs that show corn in art or in history.
- Collect information on agriculture in the Mayan or Incan cultures.

# Think Like a Scientist

**A**lthough you may not know it, you think like a scientist every day. Whenever you ask a question and explore possible answers, you use many of the same skills that scientists do. Some of these skills are described on this page.

## Observing

When you use one or more of your five senses to gather information about the world, you are **observing.** Hearing a dog bark, counting twelve green seeds, and smelling smoke are all observations. To increase the power of their senses, scientists sometimes use microscopes, telescopes, or other instruments that help them make more detailed observations.

An observation must be factual and accurate—an exact report of what your senses detect. It is important to keep careful records of your observations in science class by writing or drawing in a notebook. The information collected through observations is called evidence, or data.

## Inferring

When you explain or interpret an observation, you are **inferring,** or making an inference. For example, if you hear your dog barking, you may infer that someone is at your front door. To make this inference, you combine the evidence—the barking dog—and your experience or knowledge—you know that your dog barks when strangers approach—to reach a logical conclusion.

Notice that an inference is not a fact; it is only one of many possible explanations for an observation. For example, your dog may be barking because it wants to go for a walk. An inference may turn out to be incorrect even if it is based on accurate observations and logical reasoning. The only way to find out if an inference is correct is to investigate further.

## Predicting

When you listen to the weather forecast, you hear many predictions about the next day's weather—what the temperature will be, whether it will rain, and how windy it will be. Weather forecasters use observations and knowledge of weather patterns to predict the weather. The skill of **predicting** involves making an inference about a future event based on current evidence or past experience.

Because a prediction is an inference, it may prove to be false. In science class, you can test some of your predictions by doing experiments. For example, suppose you predict that larger paper airplanes can fly farther than smaller airplanes. How could you test your prediction?

**ACTIVITY** Use the photograph to answer the questions below.

*Observing* Look closely at the photograph. List at least three observations.

*Inferring* Use your observations to make an inference about what has happened. What experience or knowledge did you use to make the inference?

*Predicting* Predict what will happen next. On what evidence or experience do you base your prediction?

# Classifying

Could you imagine searching for a book in the library if the books were shelved in no particular order? Your trip to the library would be an all-day event! Luckily, librarians group together books on similar topics or by the same author. Grouping together items that are alike in some way is called **classifying.** You can classify items in many ways: by size, by shape, by use, and by other important characteristics.

Like librarians, scientists use the skill of classifying to organize information and objects. When things are sorted into groups, the relationships among them become easier to understand.

**ACTIVITY**

Classify the objects in the photograph into two groups based on any characteristic you choose. Then use another characteristic to classify the objects into three groups.

# Making Models

Have you ever drawn a picture to help someone understand what you were saying? Such a drawing is one type of model. A model is a picture, diagram, computer image, or other representation of a complex object or process. **Making models** helps people understand things that they cannot observe directly.

Scientists often use models to represent things that are either very large or very small, such as the planets in the solar system, or the parts of a cell. Such models are physical models—drawings or three-dimensional structures that look like the real thing. Other models are mental models—mathematical equations or words that describe how something works.

**ACTIVITY**

This student is using a model to demonstrate what causes day and night on Earth. What do the flashlight and the tennis ball in the model represent?

# Communicating

Whenever you talk on the phone, write a letter, or listen to your teacher at school, you are communicating. **Communicating** is the process of sharing ideas and information with other people. Communicating effectively requires many skills, including writing, reading, speaking, listening, and making models.

Scientists communicate to share results, information, and opinions. Scientists often communicate about their work in journals, over the telephone, in letters, and on the Internet. They also attend scientific meetings where they share their ideas with one another in person.

**ACTIVITY**

On a sheet of paper, write out clear, detailed directions for tying your shoe. Then exchange directions with a partner. Follow your partner's directions exactly. How successful were you at tying your shoe? How could your partner have communicated more clearly?

# Making Measurements

**W**hen scientists make observations, it is not sufficient to say that something is "big" or "heavy." Instead, scientists use instruments to measure just how big or heavy an object is. By measuring, scientists can express their observations more precisely and communicate more information about what they observe.

## Measuring in SI

The standard system of measurement used by scientists around the world is known as the International System of Units, which is abbreviated as SI (in French, *Système International d'Unités*). SI units are easy to use because they are based on multiples of 10. Each unit is ten times larger than the next smallest unit and one tenth the size of the next largest unit. The table lists the prefixes used to name the most common SI units.

### Common SI Prefixes

| Prefix | Symbol | Meaning |
|--------|--------|---------|
| kilo-  | k  | 1,000 |
| hecto- | h  | 100 |
| deka-  | da | 10 |
| deci-  | d  | 0.1 (one tenth) |
| centi- | c  | 0.01 (one hundredth) |
| milli- | m  | 0.001 (one thousandth) |

**Length** To measure length, or the distance between two points, the unit of measure is the **meter (m)**. One meter is the approximate distance from the floor to a doorknob. Long distances, such as the distance between two cities, are measured in kilometers (km). Small lengths are measured in centimeters (cm) or millimeters (mm). Scientists use metric rulers and meter sticks to measure length.

### Common Conversions

1 km = 1,000 m
1 m  = 100 cm
1 m  = 1,000 mm
1 cm = 10 mm

The larger lines on the metric ruler in the picture show centimeter divisions, while the smaller, unnumbered lines show millimeter divisions. How many centimeters long is the shell? How many millimeters long is it?

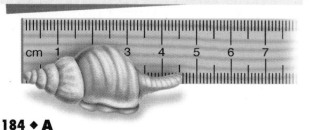

**Liquid Volume** To measure the volume of a liquid, or the amount of space it takes up, you will use a unit of measure known as the **liter (L)**. One liter is the approximate volume of a medium-sized carton of milk. Smaller volumes are measured in milliliters (mL). Scientists use graduated cylinders to measure liquid volume.

### Common Conversion

1 L = 1,000 mL

The graduated cylinder in the picture is marked in milliliter divisions. Notice that the water in the cylinder has a curved surface. This curved surface is called the *meniscus*. To measure the volume, you must read the level at the lowest point of the meniscus. What is the volume of water in this graduated cylinder?

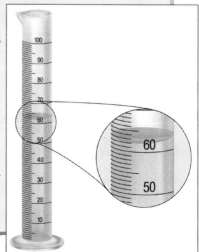

**Mass** To measure mass, or the amount of matter in an object, you will use a unit of measure known as the **gram (g)**. One gram is approximately the mass of a paper clip. Larger masses are measured in kilograms (kg). Scientists use a balance to find the mass of an object.

**Common Conversion**

1 kg = 1,000 g

The electronic balance displays the mass of an apple in kilograms. What is the mass of the apple? Suppose a recipe for applesauce called for one kilogram of apples. About how many apples would you need?

**ACTIVITY**

**Temperature**
To measure the temperature of a substance, you will use the **Celsius scale**. Temperature is measured in degrees Celsius (°C) using a Celsius thermometer. Water freezes at 0°C and boils at 100°C.

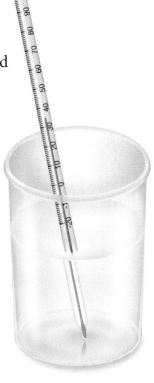

**ACTIVITY**

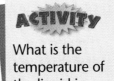
What is the temperature of the liquid in degrees Celsius?

SKILLS HANDBOOK

# Converting SI Units

To use the SI system, you must know how to convert between units. Converting from one unit to another involves the skill of **calculating**, or using mathematical operations. Converting between SI units is similar to converting between dollars and dimes because both systems are based on multiples of ten.

Suppose you want to convert a length of 80 centimeters to meters. Follow these steps to convert between units.

1. Begin by writing down the measurement you want to convert—in this example, 80 centimeters.
2. Write a conversion factor that represents the relationship between the two units you are converting. In this example, the relationship is *1 meter = 100 centimeters*. Write this conversion factor as a fraction, making sure to place the units you are converting from (centimeters, in this example) in the denominator.

3. Multiply the measurement you want to convert by the fraction. When you do this, the units in the first measurement will cancel out with the units in the denominator. Your answer will be in the units you are converting to (meters, in this example).

*Example*

80 centimeters = ____?____ meters

$$80 \text{ centimeters} \times \frac{1 \text{ meter}}{100 \text{ centimeters}} = \frac{80 \text{ meters}}{100}$$

$$= 0.8 \text{ meters}$$

Convert between the following units.
1. 600 millimeters = _?_ meters
2. 0.35 liters = _?_ milliliters
3. 1,050 grams = _?_ kilograms

**ACTIVITY**

# Conducting a Scientific Investigation

**I**n some ways, scientists are like detectives, piecing together clues to learn about a process or event. One way that scientists gather clues is by carrying out experiments. An experiment tests an idea in a careful, orderly manner. Although all experiments do not follow the same steps in the same order, many follow a pattern similar to the one described here.

## Posing Questions

Experiments begin by asking a scientific question. A scientific question is one that can be answered by gathering evidence. For example, the question "Which freezes faster—fresh water or salt water?" is a scientific question because you can carry out an investigation and gather information to answer the question.

## Developing a Hypothesis

The next step is to form a hypothesis. A **hypothesis** is a prediction about the outcome of the experiment. Like all predictions, hypotheses are based on your observations and previous knowledge or experience. But, unlike many predictions, a hypothesis must be something that can be tested. A properly worded hypothesis should take the form of an *If … then …* statement. For example, a hypothesis might be *"If I add salt to fresh water, then the water will take longer to freeze."* A hypothesis worded this way serves as a rough outline of the experiment you should perform.

# Designing an Experiment

Next you need to plan a way to test your hypothesis. Your plan should be written out as a step-by-step procedure and should describe the observations or measurements you will make.

Two important steps involved in designing an experiment are controlling variables and forming operational definitions.

**Controlling Variables** In a well-designed experiment, you need to keep all variables the same except for one. A **variable** is any factor that can change in an experiment. The factor that you change is called the **manipulated variable.** In this experiment, the manipulated variable is the amount of salt added to the water. Other factors, such as the amount of water or the starting temperature, are kept constant.

The factor that changes as a result of the manipulated variable is called the responding variable. The **responding variable** is what you measure or observe to obtain your results. In this experiment, the responding variable is how long the water takes to freeze.

An experiment in which all factors except one are kept constant is a **controlled experiment.** Most controlled experiments include a test called the control. In this experiment, Container 3 is the control. Because no salt is added to Container 3, you can compare the results from the other containers to it. Any difference in results must be due to the addition of salt alone.

**Forming Operational Definitions**
Another important aspect of a well-designed experiment is having clear operational definitions. An **operational definition** is a statement that describes how a particular variable is to be measured or how a term is to be defined. For example, in this experiment, how will you determine if the water has frozen? You might decide to insert a stick in each container at the start of the experiment. Your operational definition of "frozen" would be the time at which the stick can no longer move.

---

## EXPERIMENTAL PROCEDURE

1. Fill 3 containers with 300 milliliters of cold tap water.

2. Add 10 grams of salt to Container 1; stir. Add 20 grams of salt to Container 2; stir. Add no salt to Container 3.

3. Place the 3 containers in a freezer.

4. Check the containers every 15 minutes. Record your observations.

---

# Interpreting Data

The observations and measurements you make in an experiment are called data. At the end of an experiment, you need to analyze the data to look for any patterns or trends. Patterns often become clear if you organize your data in a data table or graph. Then think through what the data reveal. Do they support your hypothesis? Do they point out a flaw in your experiment? Do you need to collect more data?

# Drawing Conclusions

A conclusion is a statement that sums up what you have learned from an experiment. When you draw a conclusion, you need to decide whether the data you collected support your hypothesis or not. You may need to repeat an experiment several times before you can draw any conclusions from it. Conclusions often lead you to pose new questions and plan new experiments to answer them.

Is a ball's bounce affected by the height from which it is dropped? Using the steps just described, plan a controlled experiment to investigate this problem. **ACTIVITY**

# Thinking Critically

Has a friend ever asked for your advice about a problem? If so, you may have helped your friend think through the problem in a logical way. Without knowing it, you used critical-thinking skills to help your friend. Critical thinking involves the use of reasoning and logic to solve problems or make decisions. Some critical-thinking skills are described below.

## Comparing and Contrasting

When you examine two objects for similarities and differences, you are using the skill of **comparing and contrasting.** Comparing involves identifying similarities, or common characteristics. Contrasting involves identifying differences. Analyzing objects in this way can help you discover details that you might otherwise overlook.

**ACTIVITY** Compare and contrast the two animals in the photo. First list all the similarities that you see. Then list all the differences.

## Applying Concepts

When you use your knowledge about one situation to make sense of a similar situation, you are using the skill of **applying concepts.** Being able to transfer your knowledge from one situation to another shows that you truly understand a concept. You may use this skill in answering test questions that present different problems from the ones you've reviewed in class.

**ACTIVITY** You have just learned that water takes longer to freeze when other substances are mixed into it. Use this knowledge to explain why people need a substance called antifreeze in their car's radiator in the winter.

## Interpreting Illustrations

Diagrams, photographs, and maps are included in textbooks to help clarify what you read. These illustrations show processes, places, and ideas in a visual manner. The skill called **interpreting illustrations** can help you learn from these visual elements. To understand an illustration, take the time to study the illustration along with all the written information that accompanies it. Captions identify the key concepts shown in the illustration. Labels point out the important parts of a diagram or map, while keys identify the symbols used in a map.

Blood vessels

Reproductive organs

Hearts

Brain

Mouth

Bristles

Digestive tract

Nerve cord

Waste-removal organs

Intestine

▲ **Internal anatomy of an earthworm**

**ACTIVITY** Study the diagram above. Then write a short paragraph explaining what you have learned.

## Relating Cause and Effect

If one event causes another event to occur, the two events are said to have a cause-and-effect relationship. When you determine that such a relationship exists between two events, you use a skill called **relating cause and effect.** For example, if you notice an itchy, red bump on your skin, you might infer that a mosquito bit you. The mosquito bite is the cause, and the bump is the effect.

It is important to note that two events do not necessarily have a cause-and-effect relationship just because they occur together. Scientists carry out experiments or use past experience to determine whether a cause-and-effect relationship exists.

**ACTIVITY**
You are on a camping trip and your flashlight has stopped working. List some possible causes for the flashlight malfunction. How could you determine which cause-and-effect relationship has left you in the dark?

## Making Generalizations

When you draw a conclusion about an entire group based on information about only some of the group's members, you are using a skill called **making generalizations.** For a generalization to be valid, the sample you choose must be large enough and representative of the entire group. You might, for example, put this skill to work at a farm stand if you see a sign that says, "Sample some grapes before you buy." If you sample a few sweet grapes, you may conclude that all the grapes are sweet—and purchase a large bunch.

**ACTIVITY**
A team of scientists needs to determine whether the water in a large reservoir is safe to drink. How could they use the skill of making generalizations to help them? What should they do?

## Making Judgments

When you evaluate something to decide whether it is good or bad, or right or wrong, you are using a skill called **making judgments.** For example, you make judgments when you decide to eat healthful foods or to pick up litter in a park. Before you make a judgment, you need to think through the pros and cons of a situation, and identify the values or standards that you hold.

**ACTIVITY**
Should children and teens be required to wear helmets when bicycling? Explain why you feel the way you do.

## Problem Solving

When you use critical-thinking skills to resolve an issue or decide on a course of action, you are using a skill called **problem solving.** Some problems, such as how to convert a fraction into a decimal, are straightforward. Other problems, such as figuring out why your computer has stopped working, are complex. Some complex problems can be solved using the trial and error method—try out one solution first, and if that doesn't work, try another. Other useful problem-solving strategies include making models and brainstorming possible solutions with a partner.

# Organizing Information

As you read this textbook, how can you make sense of all the information it contains? Some useful tools to help you organize information are shown on this page. These tools are called *graphic organizers* because they give you a visual picture of a topic, showing at a glance how key concepts are related.

## Concept Maps

Concept maps are useful tools for organizing information on broad topics. A concept map begins with a general concept and shows how it can be broken down into more specific concepts. In that way, relationships between concepts become easier to understand.

A concept map is constructed by placing concept words (usually nouns) in ovals and connecting them with linking words. Often, the most general concept word is placed at the top, and the words become more specific as you move downward. Often the linking words, which are written on a line extending between two ovals, describe the relationship between the two concepts they connect. If you follow any string of concepts and linking words down the map, it should read like a sentence.

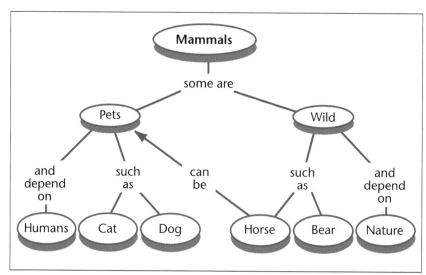

Some concept maps include linking words that connect a concept on one branch of the map to a concept on another branch. These linking words, called cross-linkages, show more complex interrelationships among concepts.

## Compare/Contrast Tables

Compare/contrast tables are useful tools for sorting out the similarities and differences between two or more items. A table provides an organized framework in which to compare items based on specific characteristics that you identify.

To create a compare/contrast table, list the items to be compared across the top of a table. Then list the characteristics that will form the basis of your comparison in the left-hand

| Characteristic | Baseball | Basketball |
|---|---|---|
| Number of Players | 9 | 5 |
| Playing Field | Baseball diamond | Basketball court |
| Equipment | Bat, baseball, mitts | Basket, basketball |

column. Complete the table by filling in information about each characteristic, first for one item and then for the other.

## Venn Diagrams

Another way to show similarities and differences between items is with a Venn diagram. A Venn diagram consists of two or more circles that partially overlap. Each circle represents a particular concept or idea. Common characteristics, or similarities, are written within the area of overlap between the two circles. Unique characteristics, or differences, are written in the parts of the circles outside the area of overlap.

To create a Venn diagram, draw two over-lapping circles. Label the circles with the names of the items being compared. Write the

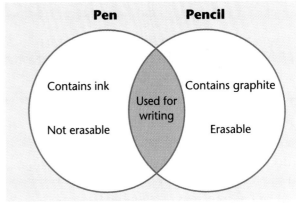

unique characteristics in each circle outside the area of overlap. Then write the shared characteristics within the area of overlap.

## Flowcharts

A flowchart can help you understand the order in which certain events have occurred or should occur. Flowcharts are useful for outlining the stages in a process or the steps in a procedure.

To make a flowchart, write a brief description of each event in a box. Place the first event at the top of the page, followed by the second event, the third event, and so on. Then draw an arrow to connect each event to the one that occurs next.

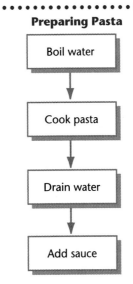

**Preparing Pasta**

## Cycle Diagrams

A cycle diagram can be used to show a sequence of events that is continuous, or cyclical. A continuous sequence does not have an end because, when the final event is over, the first event begins again. Like a flowchart, a cycle diagram can help you understand the order of events.

To create a cycle diagram, write a brief description of each event in a box. Place one event at the top of the page in the center. Then, moving in a clockwise direction around an imaginary circle, write each event in its proper sequence. Draw arrows that connect each event to the one that occurs next, forming a continuous circle.

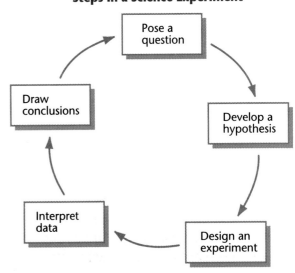

**Steps in a Science Experiment**

# Creating Data Tables and Graphs

**H**ow can you make sense of the data in a science experiment? The first step is to organize the data to help you understand them. Data tables and graphs are helpful tools for organizing data.

## Data Tables

You have gathered your materials and set up your experiment. But before you start, you need to plan a way to record what happens during the experiment. By creating a data table, you can record your observations and measurements in an orderly way.

Suppose, for example, that a scientist conducted an experiment to find out how many Calories people of different body masses burn while doing various activities. The data table shows the results.

Notice in this data table that the manipulated variable (body mass) is the heading of one column. The responding variable (for Experiment 1, the number of Calories burned while bicycling) is the heading of the next column. Additional columns were added for related experiments.

| CALORIES BURNED IN 30 MINUTES OF ACTIVITY | | | |
|---|---|---|---|
| Body Mass | Experiment 1 Bicycling | Experiment 2 Playing Basketball | Experiment 3 Watching Television |
| 30 kg | 60 Calories | 120 Calories | 21 Calories |
| 40 kg | 77 Calories | 164 Calories | 27 Calories |
| 50 kg | 95 Calories | 206 Calories | 33 Calories |
| 60 kg | 114 Calories | 248 Calories | 38 Calories |

## Bar Graphs

To compare how many Calories a person burns doing various activities, you could create a bar graph. A bar graph is used to display data in a number of separate, or distinct, categories. In this example, bicycling, playing basketball, and watching television are three separate categories.

To create a bar graph, follow these steps.

1. On graph paper, draw a horizontal, or *x*-, axis and a vertical, or *y*-, axis.
2. Write the names of the categories to be graphed along the horizontal axis. Include an overall label for the axis as well.
3. Label the vertical axis with the name of the responding variable. Include units of measurement. Then create a scale along the axis by marking off equally spaced numbers that cover the range of the data collected.
4. For each category, draw a solid bar using the scale on the vertical axis to determine the

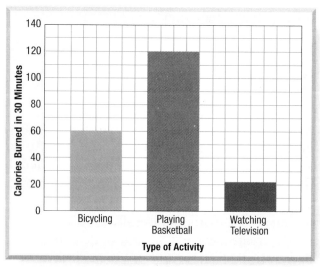

**Calories Burned by a 30-kilogram Person in Various Activities**

appropriate height. For example, for bicycling, draw the bar as high as the 60 mark on the vertical axis. Make all the bars the same width and leave equal spaces between them.
5. Add a title that describes the graph.

# Line Graphs

To see whether a relationship exists between body mass and the number of Calories burned while bicycling, you could create a line graph. A line graph is used to display data that show how one variable (the responding variable) changes in response to another variable (the manipulated variable). You can use a line graph when your manipulated variable is *continuous*, that is, when there are other points between the ones that you tested. In this example, body mass is a continuous variable because there are other body masses between 30 and 40 kilograms (for example, 31 kilograms). Time is another example of a continuous variable.

Line graphs are powerful tools because they allow you to estimate values for conditions that you did not test in the experiment. For example, you can use the line graph to estimate that a 35-kilogram person would burn 68 Calories while bicycling.

To create a line graph, follow these steps.

1. On graph paper, draw a horizontal, or *x*-, axis and a vertical, or *y*-, axis.
2. Label the horizontal axis with the name of the manipulated variable. Label the vertical axis with the name of the responding variable. Include units of measurement.
3. Create a scale on each axis by marking off equally spaced numbers that cover the range of the data collected.
4. Plot a point on the graph for each piece of data. In the line graph above, the dotted lines show how to plot the first data point (30 kilograms and 60 Calories). Draw an imaginary vertical line extending up from the horizontal axis at the 30-kilogram mark. Then draw an imaginary horizontal line extending across from the vertical axis at the 60-Calorie mark. Plot the point where the two lines intersect.

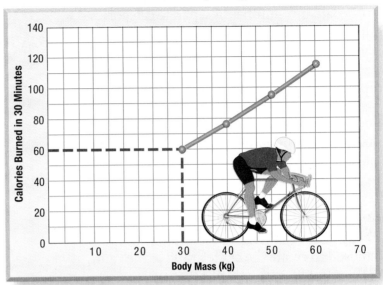

**Effect of Body Mass on Calories Burned While Bicycling**

5. Connect the plotted points with a solid line. (In some cases, it may be more appropriate to draw a line that shows the general trend of the plotted points. In those cases, some of the points may fall above or below the line.)
6. Add a title that identifies the variables or relationship in the graph.

> Create line graphs to display the data from Experiment 2 and Experiment 3 in the data table. **ACTIVITY**

> You read in the newspaper that a total of 4 centimeters of rain fell in your area in June, 2.5 centimeters fell in July, and 1.5 centimeters fell in August. What type of graph would you use to display these data? Use graph paper to create the graph. **ACTIVITY**

# Circle Graphs

Like bar graphs, circle graphs can be used to display data in a number of separate categories. Unlike bar graphs, however, circle graphs can only be used when you have data for *all* the categories that make up a given topic. A circle graph is sometimes called a pie chart because it resembles a pie cut into slices. The pie represents the entire topic, while the slices represent the individual categories. The size of a slice indicates what percentage of the whole a particular category makes up.

The data table below shows the results of a survey in which 24 teenagers were asked to identify their favorite sport. The data were then used to create the circle graph at the right.

**Sports That Teens Prefer**

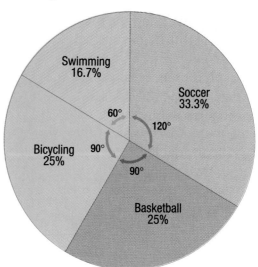

### FAVORITE SPORTS

| Sport | Number of Students |
|---|---|
| Soccer | 8 |
| Basketball | 6 |
| Bicycling | 6 |
| Swimming | 4 |

To create a circle graph, follow these steps.

1. Use a compass to draw a circle. Mark the center of the circle with a point. Then draw a line from the center point to the top of the circle.

2. Determine the size of each "slice" by setting up a proportion where $x$ equals the number of degrees in a slice. (NOTE: A circle contains 360 degrees.) For example, to find the number of degrees in the "soccer" slice, set up the following proportion:

$$\frac{\text{students who prefer soccer}}{\text{total number of students}} = \frac{x}{\text{total number of degrees in a circle}}$$

$$\frac{8}{24} = \frac{x}{360}$$

Cross-multiply and solve for $x$.

$$24x = 8 \times 360$$
$$x = 120$$

The "soccer" slice should contain 120 degrees.

3. Use a protractor to measure the angle of the first slice, using the line you drew to the top of the circle as the 0° line. Draw a line from the center of the circle to the edge for the angle you measured.

4. Continue around the circle by measuring the size of each slice with the protractor. Start measuring from the edge of the previous slice so the wedges do not overlap. When you are done, the entire circle should be filled in.

5. Determine the percentage of the whole circle that each slice represents. To do this, divide the number of degrees in a slice by the total number of degrees in a circle (360), and multiply by 100%. For the "soccer" slice, you can find the percentage as follows:

$$\frac{120}{360} \times 100\% = 33.3\%$$

6. Use a different color to shade in each slice. Label each slice with the name of the category and with the percentage of the whole it represents.

7. Add a title to the circle graph.

**ACTIVITY**

In a class of 28 students, 12 students take the bus to school, 10 students walk, and 6 students ride their bicycles. Create a circle graph to display these data.

# Laboratory Safety

## Safety Symbols

*These symbols alert you to possible dangers in the laboratory and remind you to work carefully.*

**Safety Goggles** Always wear safety goggles to protect your eyes in any activity involving chemicals, flames or heating, or the possibility of broken glassware.

**Lab Apron** Wear a laboratory apron to protect your skin and clothing from damage.

**Breakage** You are working with materials that may be breakable, such as glass containers, glass tubing, thermometers, or funnels. Handle breakable materials with care. Do not touch broken glassware.

**Heat-resistant Gloves** Use an oven mitt or other hand protection when handling hot materials. Hot plates, hot glassware, or hot water can cause burns. Do not touch hot objects with your bare hands.

**Heating** Use a clamp or tongs to pick up hot glassware. Do not touch hot objects with your bare hands.

**Sharp Object** Pointed-tip scissors, scalpels, knives, needles, pins, or tacks are sharp. They can cut or puncture your skin. Always direct a sharp edge or point away from yourself and others. Use sharp instruments only as instructed.

**Electric Shock** Avoid the possibility of electric shock. Never use electrical equipment around water, or when the equipment is wet or your hands are wet. Be sure cords are untangled and cannot trip anyone. Disconnect the equipment when it is not in use.

**Corrosive Chemical** You are working with an acid or another corrosive chemical. Avoid getting it on your skin or clothing, or in your eyes. Do not inhale the vapors. Wash your hands when you are finished with the activity.

**Poison** Do not let any poisonous chemical come in contact with your skin, and do not inhale its vapors. Wash your hands when you are finished with the activity.

**Physical Safety** When an experiment involves physical activity, take precautions to avoid injuring yourself or others. Follow instructions from your teacher. Alert your teacher if there is any reason you should not participate in the activity.

**Animal Safety** Treat live animals with care to avoid harming the animals or yourself. Working with animal parts or preserved animals also may require caution. Wash your hands when you are finished with the activity.

**Plant Safety** Handle plants in the laboratory or during field work only as directed by your teacher. If you are allergic to certain plants, tell your teacher before doing an activity in which those plants are used. Avoid touching harmful plants such as poison ivy, poison oak, or poison sumac, or plants with thorns. Wash your hands when you are finished with the activity.

**Flames** You may be working with flames from a lab burner, candle, or matches. Tie back loose hair and clothing. Follow instructions from your teacher about lighting and extinguishing flames.

**No Flames** Flammable materials may be present. Make sure there are no flames, sparks, or other exposed heat sources present.

**Fumes** When poisonous or unpleasant vapors may be involved, work in a ventilated area. Avoid inhaling vapors directly. Only test an odor when directed to do so by your teacher, and use a wafting motion to direct the vapor toward your nose.

**Disposal** Chemicals and other laboratory materials used in the activity must be disposed of safely. Follow the instructions from your teacher.

**Hand Washing** Wash your hands thoroughly when finished with the activity. Use antibacterial soap and warm water. Lather both sides of your hands and between your fingers. Rinse well.

**General Safety Awareness** You may see this symbol when none of the symbols described earlier appears. In this case, follow the specific instructions provided. You may also see this symbol when you are asked to develop your own procedure in a lab. Have your teacher approve your plan before you go further.

# Science Safety Rules

*To prepare yourself to work safely in the laboratory, read over the following safety rules. Then read them a second time. Make sure you understand and follow each rule. Ask your teacher to explain any rules you do not understand.*

## Dress Code

1. To protect yourself from injuring your eyes, wear safety goggles whenever you work with chemicals, burners, glassware, or any substance that might get into your eyes. If you wear contact lenses, notify your teacher.
2. Wear a lab apron or coat whenever you work with corrosive chemicals or substances that can stain.
3. Tie back long hair to keep it away from any chemicals, flames, or equipment.
4. Remove or tie back any article of clothing or jewelry that can hang down and touch chemicals, flames, or equipment. Roll up or secure long sleeves.
5. Never wear open shoes or sandals.

## General Precautions

6. Read all directions for an experiment several times before beginning the activity. Carefully follow all written and oral instructions. If you are in doubt about any part of the experiment, ask your teacher for assistance.
7. Never perform activities that are not assigned or authorized by your teacher. Obtain permission before "experimenting" on your own. Never handle any equipment unless you have specific permission.
8. Never perform lab activities without direct supervision.
9. Never eat or drink in the laboratory.
10. Keep work areas clean and tidy at all times. Bring only notebooks and lab manuals or written lab procedures to the work area. All other items, such as purses and backpacks, should be left in a designated area.
11. Do not engage in horseplay.

## First Aid

12. Always report all accidents or injuries to your teacher, no matter how minor. Notify your teacher immediately about any fires.
13. Learn what to do in case of specific accidents, such as getting acid in your eyes or on your skin. (Rinse acids from your body with lots of water.)
14. Be aware of the location of the first-aid kit, but do not use it unless instructed by your teacher. In case of injury, your teacher should administer first aid. Your teacher may also send you to the school nurse or call a physician.
15. Know the location of emergency equipment, such as the fire extinguisher and fire blanket, and know how to use it.
16. Know the location of the nearest telephone and whom to contact in an emergency.

## Heating and Fire Safety

17. Never use a heat source, such as a candle, burner, or hot plate, without wearing safety goggles.
18. Never heat anything unless instructed to do so. A chemical that is harmless when cool may be dangerous when heated.
19. Keep all combustible materials away from flames. Never use a flame or spark near a combustible chemical.
20. Never reach across a flame.
21. Before using a laboratory burner, make sure you know proper procedures for lighting and adjusting the burner, as demonstrated by your teacher. Do not touch the burner. It may be hot. And never leave a lighted burner unattended!
22. Chemicals can splash or boil out of a heated test tube. When heating a substance in a test tube, make sure that the mouth of the tube is not pointed at you or anyone else.
23. Never heat a liquid in a closed container. The expanding gases produced may blow the container apart.
24. Before picking up a container that has been heated, hold the back of your hand near it. If you can feel heat on the back of your hand, the container is too hot to handle. Use an oven mitt to pick up a container that has been heated.

## Using Chemicals Safely

25. Never mix chemicals "for the fun of it." You might produce a dangerous, possibly explosive substance.

26. Never put your face near the mouth of a container that holds chemicals. Never touch, taste, or smell a chemical unless you are instructed by your teacher to do so. Many chemicals are poisonous.

27. Use only those chemicals needed in the activity. Read and double-check labels on supply bottles before removing any chemicals. Take only as much as you need. Keep all containers closed when chemicals are not being used.

28. Dispose of all chemicals as instructed by your teacher. To avoid contamination, never return chemicals to their original containers. Never simply pour chemicals or other substances into the sink or trash containers.

29. Be extra careful when working with acids or bases. Pour all chemicals over the sink or a container, not over your work surface.

30. If you are instructed to test for odors, use a wafting motion to direct the odors to your nose. Do not inhale the fumes directly from the container.

31. When mixing an acid and water, always pour the water into the container first and then add the acid to the water. Never pour water into an acid.

32. Take extreme care not to spill any material in the laboratory. Wash chemical spills and splashes immediately with plenty of water. Immediately begin rinsing with water any acids that get on your skin or clothing, and notify your teacher of any acid spill at the same time.

## Using Glassware Safely

33. Never force glass tubing or thermometers into a rubber stopper or rubber tubing. Have your teacher insert the glass tubing or thermometer if required for an activity.

34. If you are using a laboratory burner, use a wire screen to protect glassware from any flame. Never heat glassware that is not thoroughly dry on the outside.

35. Keep in mind that hot glassware looks cool. Never pick up glassware without first checking to see if it is hot. Use an oven mitt. See rule 24.

36. Never use broken or chipped glassware. If glassware breaks, notify your teacher and dispose of the glassware in the proper broken-glassware container. Never handle broken glass with your bare hands.

37. Never eat or drink from lab glassware.

38. Thoroughly clean glassware before putting it away.

## Using Sharp Instruments

39. Handle scalpels or other sharp instruments with extreme care. Never cut material toward you; cut away from you.

40. Immediately notify your teacher if you cut your skin when working in the laboratory.

## Animal and Plant Safety

41. Never perform experiments that cause pain, discomfort, or harm to mammals, birds, reptiles, fishes, or amphibians. This rule applies at home as well as in the classroom.

42. Animals should be handled only if absolutely necessary. Your teacher will instruct you as to how to handle each animal species brought into the classroom.

43. If you know that you are allergic to certain plants, molds, or animals, tell your teacher before doing an activity in which these are used.

44. During field work, protect your skin by wearing long pants, long sleeves, socks, and closed shoes. Know how to recognize the poisonous plants and fungi in your area, as well as plants with thorns, and avoid contact with them.

45. Never eat any part of an unidentified plant or fungus.

46. Wash your hands thoroughly after handling animals or the cage containing animals. Wash your hands when you are finished with any activity involving animal parts, plants, or soil.

## End-of-Experiment Rules

47. After an experiment has been completed, clean up your work area and return all equipment to its proper place.

48. Dispose of waste materials as instructed by your teacher.

49. Wash your hands after every experiment.

50. Always turn off all burners or hot plates when they are not in use. Unplug hot plates and other electrical equipment. If you used a burner, check that the gas-line valve to the burner is off as well.

# Using the Microscope

The microscope is an essential tool in the study of life science. It allows you to see things that are too small to be seen with the unaided eye.

You will probably use a compound microscope like the one you see here. The compound microscope has more than one lens that magnifies the object you view.

Typically, a compound microscope has one lens in the eyepiece, the part you look through. The eyepiece lens usually magnifies 10 ×. Any object you view through this lens would appear 10 times larger than it is.

The compound microscope may contain one or two other lenses called objective lenses. If there are two objective lenses, they are called the low-power and high-power objective lenses. The low-power objective lens usually magnifies 10 ×. The high-power objective lens usually magnifies 40 ×.

To calculate the total magnification with which you are viewing an object, multiply the magnification of the eyepiece lens by the magnification of the objective lens you are using. For example, the eyepiece's magnification of 10 × multiplied by the low-power objective's magnification of 10 × equals a total magnification of 100 ×.

Use the photo of the compound microscope to become familiar with the parts of the microscope and their functions.

## The Parts of the Compound Microscope

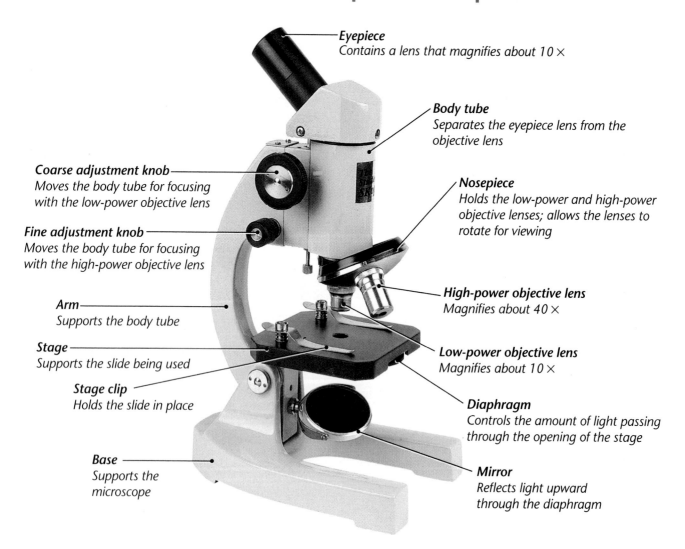

**Eyepiece**
Contains a lens that magnifies about 10 ×

**Body tube**
Separates the eyepiece lens from the objective lens

**Coarse adjustment knob**
Moves the body tube for focusing with the low-power objective lens

**Nosepiece**
Holds the low-power and high-power objective lenses; allows the lenses to rotate for viewing

**Fine adjustment knob**
Moves the body tube for focusing with the high-power objective lens

**High-power objective lens**
Magnifies about 40 ×

**Arm**
Supports the body tube

**Stage**
Supports the slide being used

**Low-power objective lens**
Magnifies about 10 ×

**Stage clip**
Holds the slide in place

**Diaphragm**
Controls the amount of light passing through the opening of the stage

**Base**
Supports the microscope

**Mirror**
Reflects light upward through the diaphragm

## Using the Microscope

*Use the following procedures when you are working with a microscope.*

1. To carry the microscope grasp the microscope's arm with one hand. Place your other hand under the base.

2. Place the microscope on a table with the arm toward you.

3. Turn the coarse adjustment knob to raise the body tube.

4. Revolve the nosepiece until the low-power objective lens clicks into place.

5. Adjust the diaphragm. While looking through the eyepiece, also adjust the mirror until you see a bright white circle of light. **CAUTION:** *Never use direct sunlight as a light source.*

6. Place a slide on the stage. Center the specimen over the opening on the stage. Use the stage clips to hold the slide in place. **CAUTION:** *Glass slides are fragile.*

7. Look at the stage from the side. Carefully turn the coarse adjustment knob to lower the body tube until the low-power objective almost touches the slide.

8. Looking through the eyepiece, very slowly turn the coarse adjustment knob until the specimen comes into focus.

9. To switch to the high-power objective lens, look at the microscope from the side. Carefully revolve the nosepiece until the high-power objective lens clicks into place. Make sure the lens does not hit the slide.

10. Looking through the eyepiece, turn the fine adjustment knob until the specimen comes into focus.

## Making a Wet-Mount Slide

*Use the following procedures to make a wet-mount slide of a specimen.*

1. Obtain a clean microscope slide and a coverslip. **CAUTION:** *Glass slides and coverslips are fragile.*

2. Place the specimen on the slide. The specimen must be thin enough for light to pass through it.

3. Using a plastic dropper, place a drop of water on the specimen.

4. Gently place one edge of the coverslip against the slide so that it touches the edge of the water drop at a 45° angle. Slowly lower the coverslip over the specimen. If air bubbles are trapped beneath the coverslip, tap the coverslip gently with the eraser end of a pencil.

5. Remove any excess water at the edge of the coverslip with a paper towel.

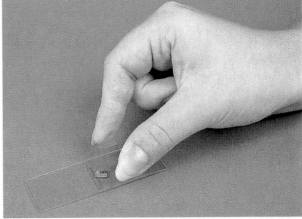

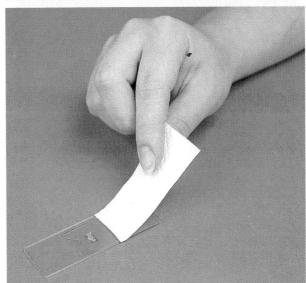

# Glossary

## A

**accessory pigment** A yellow, orange, or red pigment found in plant cells. (p. 121)

**alga** A plantlike protist. (p. 86)

**algal bloom** The rapid growth of a population of algae. (p. 90)

**angiosperm** A plant that produces seeds that are enclosed in a protective structure. (p. 156)

**antibiotic** A chemical that can kill bacteria without harming a person's cells. (p. 72)

**asexual reproduction** The reproductive process that involves only one parent and produces offspring that are identical to the parent. (p. 59)

**autotroph** An organism that makes its own food. (p. 21)

**auxin** The plant hormone that speeds up the rate of growth of plant cells. (p. 165)

## B

**bacteriophage** A virus that infects bacteria. (p. 50)

**binary fission** A form of asexual reproduction in which one cell divides to form two identical cells. (p. 59)

**binomial nomenclature** The naming system for organisms in which each organism is given a two-part name—a genus name and a species name. (p. 30)

**bog** A wetland where sphagnum moss grows on top of acidic water. (p. 127)

**budding** A form of asexual reproduction of yeast in which a new yeast cell grows out of the body of a parent. (p. 98)

## C

**cambium** The layer of cells in a plant that produces new phloem and xylem cells. (p. 147)

**cell** The basic unit of structure and function in an organism. (p. 17)

**cell wall** The boundary that surrounds the cell membrane in some cells. (p. 111)

**cellulose** A chemical that makes the cell walls of plants rigid and strong. (p. 111)

**chlorophyll** A green pigment found in the chloro- plasts of plants as well as in algae and some bacteria. (p. 112)

**chloroplast** The structure of plant cells in which food is made. (p. 111)

**cilia** The hairlike projections on the outside of cells that move in a wavelike manner. (p. 83)

**classification** The process of grouping things based on their similarities. (p. 28)

**cone** The reproductive structure of a gymnosperm. (p. 152)

**conjugation** The process in which a unicellular organism transfers some of its genetic material to another unicellular organism. (p. 60)

**contractile vacuole** The cell structure that collects extra water from the cytoplasm and then expels it from the cell. (p. 82)

**controlled experiment** An experiment in which all factors are identical except one. (p. 19)

**cotyledon** A seed leaf that stores food. (p. 142)

**cuticle** The waxy, waterproof layer that covers the leaves and stems of some plants. (p. 113)

**cytoplasm** The region of a cell located inside the cell membrane (in prokaryotes) or between the cell membrane and nucleus (in eukaryotes); contains a gel-like material and cell organelles. (p. 57)

## D

**decomposer** An organism that breaks down large chemicals from dead organisms into small chemicals and returns important materials to the soil and water. (p. 63)

**development** The process of change that occurs during an organism's life to produce a more complex organism. (p. 18)

**dicot** An angiosperm that has two seed leaves. (p. 157)

## E

**embryo** The young plant that develops from a zygote. (p. 142)

**endospore** A small, rounded, thick-walled, resting cell that forms inside a bacterial cell. (p. 61)

**eukaryote** An organism with cells that contain nuclei and other cell structures. (p. 41)

**eutrophication** The buildup over time of nutrients in freshwater lakes and ponds that leads to an increase in the growth of algae. (p. 92)

**evolution** The process by which species gradually change over time. (p. 34)

## F

**fertilization** The joining of a sperm cell and an egg cell. (p. 116)

**flagellum** A long, whiplike structure that extends out through the cell membrane and cell wall. (p. 58)

**flower** The reproductive structure of an angiosperm. (p. 157)

**fossil** The trace of an ancient organism that has been preserved in rock or other substance. (p. 27)

**frond** The leaf of a fern plant. (p. 132)

**fruit** The ripened ovary and other structures that enclose one or more seeds of an angiosperm. (p. 159)

**fruiting body** The reproductive hypha of a fungus. (p. 98)

## G

**gamete** A sperm cell or an egg cell. (p. 117)

**gametophyte** The stage in the life cycle of a plant in which the plant produces gametes, or sex cells. (p. 117)

**genetic engineering** The process of altering an organism's genetic material to produce an organism with qualities that people find useful. (p. 169)

**genus** A classification grouping that consists of a number of similar, closely related species. (p. 30)

**germination** The early growth stage of the embryo plant in a seed. (p. 144)

**gymnosperm** A plant that produces seeds that are not enclosed by a protective covering. (p. 150)

## H

**heterotroph** An organism that cannot make its own food. (p. 22)

**homeostasis** The maintenance of stable internal conditions despite changes in the surroundings. (p. 23)

**hormone** A chemical that affects growth and development. (p. 165)

**host** An organism that provides a source of energy or a suitable environment for a virus or for another organism to live. (p. 49)

**hydroponics** The method of growing plants in a solution of nutrients instead of in soil. (p. 170)

**hypha** One of many branching, threadlike tubes that make up the body of a fungus. (p. 96)

**hypothesis** A prediction about the outcome of an experiment. (p. 186)

## I

**infectious disease** An illness that can pass from one organism to another. (p. 68)

## L

**lichen** The combination of a fungus and either an alga or an autotrophic bacteria that live together in a mutualistic relationship. (p. 104)

## M

**manipulated variable** The one factor that a scientist changes during an experiment. (p. 187)

**monocot** An angiosperm that has only one seed leaf. (p. 157)

**multicellular** A type of organism that is made up of many cells. (p. 17)

**mutualism** A type of symbiosis in which both partners benefit from living together. (p. 84)

## N

**nonvascular plant** A low-growing plant that lacks vascular tissue. (p. 125)

**nucleus** The dense area in a eukaryotic cell that contains nucleic acids, the chemical instructions that direct the cell's activities. (p. 41)

## O

**operational definition** A statement that describes how a particular variable is to be measured or how a term is to be defined. (p. 187)

**organism** A living thing. (p. 16)

**ovary** A protective structure in plants that encloses the developing seeds. (p. 157)

**ovule** A plant structure in seed plants that contains an egg cell. (p. 153)

## P

**parasite** An organism that lives on or in a host and causes harm to the host. (p. 49)

**peat** The blackish-brown material consisting of compressed layers of dead sphagnum mosses that grow in bogs. (p. 127)

**petal** The colorful, leaflike structures of a flower. (p. 157)

**phloem** The vascular tissue through which food moves in some plants. (p. 141)

**photosynthesis** The process by which plants and some other organisms capture light energy and use it to make food from carbon dioxide and water. (p. 111)

**pigment** A chemical that produces color. (p. 87)

**pistil** The female reproductive parts of a flower. (p. 158)

**pollen** Tiny particles produced by plants that contain the microscopic cells that later become sperm cells. (p. 152)

**pollination** The transfer of pollen from male reproductive structures to female reproductive structures in plants. (p. 153)

**prokaryote** An organism whose cells lack a nucleus and some other cell structures. (p. 41)

**protozoan** An animal-like protist. (p. 81)

**pseudopod** A "false foot" or temporary bulge of the cell membrane used for feeding and movement in some protozoans. (p. 81)

**red tide** An algal bloom that occurs in salt water. (p. 91)

**reproduce** The production of offspring that are similar to the parents. (p. 19)

**respiration** The process of breaking down food to release its energy. (p. 60)

**responding variable** The factor that changes as a result of changes to the manipulated variable in an experiment. (p. 187)

**response** An action or change in behavior that occurs as a result of a stimulus. (p. 19)

**rhizoid** The thin, rootlike structure that anchors a moss and absorbs water and nutrients for the plant. (p. 126)

**ribosome** A tiny structure located in the cytoplasm of a cell where proteins are made. (p. 57)

**root cap** A structure that covers the tip of a root, protecting the root from injury. (p. 149)

**seed** The plant structure that contains a young plant inside a protective covering. (p. 142)

**sepal** A leaflike structure that encloses the bud of a flower. (p. 158)

**sexual reproduction** The reproductive process that involves two parents who combine their genetic material to produce a new organism, which differs from both parents. (p. 60)

**species** A group of similar organisms that can mate and produce fertile offspring in nature. (p. 30)

**spontaneous generation** The mistaken idea that living things arise from nonliving sources (p. 19)

**spore** A tiny cell that is able to grow into a new organism. (p. 85)

**sporophyte** The stage in the life cycle of a plant in which the plant produces spores for reproduction. (p. 117)

**stamen** The male reproductive parts of a flower. (p. 158)

**stimulus** A change in an organism's surroundings that causes the organism to react. (p. 18)

**stomata** The small openings on the undersides of most leaves through which oxygen and carbon dioxide can move. (p. 144)

**symbiosis** A close relationship between two organisms in which at least one of the organisms benefits. (p. 84)

**taxonomic key** A series of paired statements that describe the physical characteristics of different organisms. (p. 36)

**taxonomy** The scientific study of how living things are classified. (p. 29)

**tissue** A group of similar cells that perform a specific function in an organism. (p. 112)

**toxin** A poison that can harm an organism. (p. 70)

**transpiration** The process by which water is lost through a plant's leaves. (p. 146)

**tropism** The growth response of a plant toward or away from a stimulus. (p. 164)

**unicellular** A type of organism that is made up of a single cell. (p. 17)

**vaccine** A substance that stimulates the body to produce chemicals that destroy viruses, bacteria, or other disease-causing organisms. (p. 73)

**vacuole** A large sac-like storage area in a cell. (p. 112)

**variable** Any factor that can change in an experiment. (p. 19)

**vascular plant** A plant that has vascular tissue. (p. 131)

**vascular tissue** The internal transporting tissue in some plants that is made up of tubelike structures. (p. 116)

**virus** A small, nonliving particle that invades and then reproduces inside a living cell. (p. 48)

**xylem** The vascular tissue through which water and nutrients move in some plants. (p. 141)

**zygote** A fertilized egg. (p. 116)

# Index

accessory pigments 121
active viruses 51–52
adaptations of plants 113, 114–115
AIDS (acquired immunodeficiency syndrome) 54, 71
air pollution, lichens as indicators of 104
*Alexandrium tamarense* 90
alfalfa mosaic disease 54
algae 86–89, 112, 113
  brown 89
  defined 86
  green 88, 92, 112
  lichens formed by fungus and 104
  red 81, 89
algal blooms 90–94
  eutrophication and 92, 94
  freshwater 92
  saltwater 91
algins 89
amebas 82–83
ancient cultures, food preservation in 62–63
*Anemone patens* 114
angiosperms 156–163
  defined 156–157
  flowers, structure of 157–158, 162–163
  life cycle of 159
  life spans of 165–166
  reproduction in 157, 158, 159
  types of 160
  uses of 161
Animalia (kingdom) 33, 42
animal-like protists 81–85
animals 42
  disease spread by bites of 69
  living space of 23
  pollination of angiosperms and 158
  seed dispersed by 143
annual rings of trees 147–148
annuals 165
*Anopheles* mosquitoes 85
anther 157
antibiotic resistance 72–73, 74
antibiotics 72, 74, 99
  limiting non-medical uses of 74
  penicillin 72, 74, 103
antitoxin 70
applying concepts, skill of 188
archaebacteria 40–41, 58, 61
Aristotle 29, 30, 32
asexual reproduction
  in bacteria 59
  defined 59
  in fungi 98
  in paramecium 83
aspirin, source of 161
athlete's foot 97, 102
atmosphere of Earth, early 25–26
autotrophic bacteria 59, 60
autotrophs 21, 22, 41, 111 See also **algae**
auxin 165
Aves (class) 32, 33

bacteria 19, 26, 56–65, 72
  autotrophic 59, 60

bacterial cells 56–58
  decomposers 63–64
  defined 57
  heterotrophic 60
  infectious disease and 68–74
  kingdoms of 58–59
  lichens formed by fungus and 104
  living world and 61–65
  reproduction in 59–60
  salmonella 10, 11–13, 70
  survival needs of 60–61
bacterial diseases 72–73
bacteriophage 49, 50
baobab trees 146
bark 147
barnacles, homeostasis in 23
biennials 165–166
binary fission 59, 60, 83
binomial nomenclature 30–31
biologists 29
bird's nest fungi 99
bites, animal 69
bladderwort 164
body temperature 23
bog 127
*Borrelia burgdorferi* 57
botulism 70
bracket fungi 96
bread molds 24, 98
bristlecone pine tree 114, 152
brown algae 89
*Bubo* (Genus) 33
*Bubo virginianus* (species) 33
budding 98

cactus finch 34
calculating, skill of 185
Calvin, Melvin 123
cambium 147
carbohydrate 17
  produced during photosynthesis 123
carbon dioxide 22, 25
  photosynthesis and 124, 145
carrageenan 89
cell(s)
  bacterial 56–58
  chemicals in 17
  defined 17
  energy use of 18
  first 27
  of fungi, structure of 96
  nucleus of 41
  of plants 111–112
cell membrane 57, 81
  in ameba 82
  of bacterial cell 58
cellular organization 17
cellulose 111
cell wall 111
  of bacterium 57
Centers for Disease Control and Prevention (CDC) 10
cheesemaking 62
chemicals of life 17, 26
chicken pox 46–47, 71

childhood diseases 47
*Chlamydomonas* 41
chlorophyll 112, 121, 122, 123, 144
chloroplasts 111, 122, 144
Chordata (phylum) 33
cilia, protozoans with 83
ciliates 83
classes 32
classification 28–37
  defined 28
  early systems of 29–31
  evolution and 34
  of fungi 99
  kingdoms 32, 40–42
  levels of 32–33
  reasons for 28–29
  of today 34–36
  using system of 36–37
classifying, skill of 183
clear cutting 155
climate changes, red tides and 91
*Clostridium botulinum* 70
*Clostridium tetani* 70
club fungi 99
club mosses 133
coal deposits 131
cocoa plants 63
cold sore virus 53, 69
cold viruses 49
colonies of algae 87
colors 120, 121
Columbus, Christopher 174
communicating, skill of 183
compare/contrast tables 190
comparing and contrasting, skill of 188
concept maps 190
cones 152–153, 154
conifers 152
conjugation 60
contact, spread of infectious disease by 69
contaminated object, contact with 69
contractile vacuole 82, 83
controlled experiment 19, 20–21, 187
controlling variables, skill of 187
coral fungus 14–15
corn 174–181
  production data on 180–181
  structure of 178
  uses of 179
Corn Belt 180
corn goddess folk tale, 176–177
corn meal 179
corn smut 102
cornstarch 179
cortisone, source of 161
cotton plants 161
cotyledons 142, 160
cricket-killing fungus 95, 99
critical thinking skills 188–189
*Culex nigripalpus* 69
cultures 13
curds and whey 62
cuticle 113
  of leaf 145
cycads 151

cycle diagrams 191
cystic fibrosis 54
cytoplasm 81–82
    in ameba 82
    of bacterial cell 58
    defined 57
    of paramecium 83

dandelions 140
Darwin, Charles 34
data tables 192
date palms 115
decomposers
    bacteria as 63–64
    fungi as 102
designing experiments, skill of 187
developing hypotheses, skill of 186
development 18
diabetes 65
diatomaceous earth 88
diatoms 80, 86, 88
dicots 160
digitalis, source of 161
dinoflagellates 88, 90
diphtheria 70
direct contact, spread of disease by 69
disease-causing fungi 102–103
disease-fighting fungi 103
diseases
    childhood 47
    fungal plant diseases 102
    infectious 10, 11–13, 68–74
    viruses causing 54, 68–74
disinfectants 66–67
distemper 54
downy mildews 85
drawing conclusions, skill of 187
droughts 148
Dutch elm disease 97

Earth, early atmosphere of 25–26
Ebola virus 49
egg cells 117
embryo 142, 144
    corn 79
encephalitis 69
endospore 61
energy
    for bacteria 60
    cellular use of 18
    in form of light 120–121
    light as form of 122
    need for 21–22
Engelmann, T.W. 120, 123
environmental cleanup, bacterial for 64
environmental recycling 63–64
    fungi and 102
environmental sources of infectious
    disease 70
Epstein–Barr virus 49
*Escherichia coli* 57, 59
ethanol 179
eubacteria 41, 59
    recycling by 63–64
euglena 87

euglenoids 87
eukaryotes 41, 80, 96, 111 See also **fungus,**
    **fungi; plants; protists**
    multicellular 42
eutrophication 92, 94
evergreen plants 152
evolution, classification and 34
evolutionary history of species 35–36
experiment See also **scientific**
    **investigations**
    controlled 19, 20–21, 187
experimental farms 169

"fairy ring" 103
fall leaves, color of 121
families 32
farming of seed plants 168–170
    improving efficiency of farms 169–170
*Felis* genus 30, 31
female cones 152, 153, 154
ferns 114, 130–133
    ancient 130–131
    fossil 112, 132
    importance of 133
    reproduction in 133
fertilization
    in angiosperms 158, 159
    in corn 178
    defined 116
    in gymnosperms 153, 154
fertilizers
    eutrophication and 92, 93
    precision farming and 170
fibrous root systems 148
fiddleheads 133
field corn 179
field guides 36
filament 157
finches of Galapagos Islands 34
flagellum, flagella 58
    protozoans with 84
flax plants 161
Fleming, Alexander 103
flowcharts 191
flowers 157, 159
    of dicots 160
    of monocot 160
    structure of 157–158, 162–163
flu virus 69
folk tales 103
    defined 177
    Native American corn 176–177
food
    bacteria and production of 62–63
    fungi and 102
    from plants 124, 148, 168–170
    preserving 62–63
    roots as storage area for 148
food, methods of obtaining
    in bacteria 60
    in fungi 97
food poisoning 70, 71
food vacuole 82, 83
forests, cutting methods in 155
foraminiferans 81

forming operational definitions 187
fossils 27
    evolutionary history from 35
    of gymnosperms 151
    plant 112, 132
foxglove plant 161, 166
freshwater algal blooms 92
Friedman, Cindy 10–13
frond 132, 133
fruiting bodies 98, 103
fruits 156–157, 158, 159
fuel
    bacteria and production of 61
    coal deposits 131
    ethanol, from corn 179
fungus, fungi 14–15, 42, 95–104
    cell structure of 96
    classification of 99
    defined 95–96
    disease-causing 102–103
    disease-fighting 103
    food, obtaining 97
    kingdom of 42, 95
    living world and 102–104
    reproduction in 97–98
funguslike protists 85–86

Galapagos Islands, finches of 34
gametes 117
gametophytes 117, 132, 141
    fern 133
    moss 126
gases in Earth's atmosphere 25
gene therapy 54
genetic engineering 169
genetic material, conjugation in bacteria
    and new 60
genus 30, 31, 32
geologists 29
germination 144
giant kelps 81, 89
giant sequoia trees 150, 152
*Giardia* 84
ginkgo 151
*Ginkgo biloba* 151
gnetophytes 151
graphs 192–194
gravitropism 165
gravity, plant response to 165, 167
green algae 88, 92, 112
growth 18
gymnosperms 150–155
    defined 150
    life cycle of 154
    methods of growing 155
    reproduction in 152–153, 154
    types of 151–152
    uses of 155

handwashing, importance of 12, 13
health, bacteria and 64–65
heartwood 147
herbaceous stems 146, 147
heterotrophic bacteria 60

heterotrophs 22, 27, 41, 42, 96 See also
    **fungus, fungi; funguslike protists**
    animal-like protists 81–85
    defined 22
**hidden viruses** 52–53
**hiker's disease** 84
**HIV** (human immunodeficiency virus) 51
**Hoh rain forest** 110
**homeostasis** 23
**hormones,** plant 165
**hornworts** 128
**horsetails** 133
    fossil 112
**host** 49
**house cats** (*Felis domesticus*) 30, 31
**human body,** water in 22
**human immunodeficiency virus** (HIV) 51
**humpback whales** 90
**hydroponics** 170
**hyphae** 96, 97, 103
    reproductive 97–98
**hypothesis** 186

**Iditarod Trail** 70
**imperfect fungi** 99
**Incan Empire** 175
**indirect contact,** spread of disease by 69
**infectious diseases** 10, 11–13, 68–74
    antibiotics and 72, 74
    common 70–71
    defined 68
    preventing 73
    spread of 68–70, 72–74
    treating 72–73
**infectious mononucleosis** 49
**inferring,** skill of 182
**influenza** (flu) 71
**Ingenhousz, Jan** 122
**insulin-making bacteria** 65
**interpreting data,** skill of 187
**interpreting illustrations,** skill of 188
**Irish potato famine** (1845 and 1846) 85
**Iroquois corn folk tale** 176–177

**kingdoms** 32, 40–42
    animals 33, 42
    archaebacteria 40–41, 58, 61
    eubacteria 41, 59
    fungi 42
    plant 42, 110–117
    protist 41, 80–89
**Komodo dragon** 12, 13
**kudzu** 159

**laboratory safety** 195–197
*Lactobacillus san francisco* 63
**land,** plants on 113–116
**large-billed ground finch** 34
**leaves**
    of dicots 160
    fall, color of 121
    of monocot 160
    photosynthesis and 144–145
    of seed plants 144–146
    structure of 144

**Leeuwenhoek, Anton van** 56–57
**lichens** 104
**life** 16–27
    building blocks of 26
    characteristics of living things 16–19
    chemicals of 17, 26
    needs of living things 20–23
    origin of 25–27
    reproduction and 19–20
**life cycle**
    of angiosperms 159
    complex 117
    of gymnosperms 154
**light**
    as form of energy 122
    nature of 120–121
    photosynthesis and 120–124
    plants and 121–122, 164–165
**Linnaeus, Carolus** 30–31, 32, 34
**lipids** 17
**liverworts** 128
**living space,** need for 23
**lockjaw** (tetanus) 70, 71
**lodgepole pines** 141
**Lyme disease** 57, 69, 71

**maize** (corn) 174–181
    history of 175
    Native American folk tale of 176–177
**making generalizations,** skill of 189
**making judgments,** skill of 189
**making models,** skill of 183
**malaria** 84–85
**male cones** 152, 153, 154
**mangrove trees** 115
**Mayan civilization** 175
**measles** 71
**measuring,** skill of 184
**meat preservation** 62
**medicine**
    angiosperms as source of 161
    bacteria and 64–65
**Mephitidae** (family) 36
**methane** 25, 61
**microscopes** 17, 56
**mildew** 42
    downy 85
**Miller, Stanley** 26, 27
**Mitchell Corn Palace** (South Dakota) 181
**molds** 42, 99, 102
    bread 24, 98
    *Penicillium* 97, 99, 103
    slime 16, 41, 81, 86
    water 85
**monocots** 160
**mononucleosis,** infectious 49, 69
**morning glories** 166
**mosquito bites,** disease spread by 69
**mosses** 109, 126–127, 129
    importance of 127
    structure of 126
**mountain lions** (*Felis concolor*) 30
**multicellular organisms** 17, 87
    eukaryotes 42
    plants 112

**mushrooms** 42, 79, 96, 98, 99, 102
    "fairy ring" of 103
**Mustelidae** (family) 36
**mutualism** 84

**nanometers** (nm) 50
**Native American corn folk tale** 176–177
**natural gas** 61
**Navajo corn folk tale** 176
**nectar** 158
**needs of living things** 20–23
    of bacteria 60–61
**nerve cells** 17
**New Zealand pygmy pines** 152
**nitrogen** 25
    bacterial conversion for plants 64
**nomenclature,** binomial 30–31
**nonvascular plants** 125–128
**nucleic acids** 17, 41
**nucleus**
    in ameba 82
    defined 41
    of paramecium 83
**nutrients**
    eutrophication and excess 92, 94
    plant adaptations for obtaining 113
    red tides and excess 91

**oak tree,** roots of 148
**observations,** classifications based on 29, 30
**observing,** skill of 182
**ocean temperature,** red tides and 91
**ocelots** (*Felis pardalis*) 30, 31
*Ochrobactrum anthropi* 64
**O'Keeffe, Georgia** 158
**Olympic Mountains in Washington State** 110
**operational definitions** 187
**oral groove of paramecium** 83
**orders** 32
**organisms**
    characteristics of 16–19
    classifying 28–37
    early life forms 26, 27
    fossils of bacteria–like 27
    multicellular 17, 42, 87, 112
    needs of 20–23
    "pioneer," 104
    unicellular 17, 26, 40, 86–87
**organpipe cacti** 141
**origin of life** 25–27
**ovary** 157, 158
**over-the-counter medications** 72
**ovule** 153, 154, 158, 159
**owl,** classifying 32–33
**oxygen** 25
    algae and production of 86
    autotrophic bacteria and 59
    photosynthesis and 122, 145

**papilloma viruses** 49
**paramecium** 82, 83, 84
**parasites** 49 See also **viruses**
    sporozoans 84–85

**Pasque flower** 114
**Pasteur, Louis** 20, 21, 26
**Pawnee corn folk tale** 176
**peat** 127
**peat moss** 125, 127
**pellicle of paramecium** 83
**penicillin** 72, 74, 103
*Penicillium* mold 97, 99, 103
*Penicillium roqueforti* 102
**peonies** 166
**perennials** 166
**petals** 157
**phloem** 141, 144, 145, 147, 149
**photosynthesis** 111, 118–124, 144–145
　chemistry of 123
　defined 111
　discovery of 122–123
　experiment on 118–119
　light and 120–124
**phototropism** 164–165
**phyla** 32
**pigments**
　in algae 87
　plant 121
**pine trees** 154
*Pinus taeda* 31
**"pioneer" organisms** 104
　pioneer plants 127
**pistils** 158
**plant diseases,** fungal 102
**plant hormones** 165
**plantlike protists** 86–89
**plant pigments** 121
**plants** 42, 108–137
　adaptations of 113, 114–115
　cells of 111–112
　complex life cycles 117
　defined 111
　diseases caused by viruses in 54
　ferns and their relatives 114, 130–134
　fixed living space of 23
　fungus-plant root associations 103
　on land 113–116
　light and 121–122, 164–165
　liverworts and hornworts 128
　mosses 109, 126–127, 129
　nonvascular 125–128
　origins of 112
　photosynthesis 111, 119–124, 144–145
　plant kingdom 42, 110–117
　producing better 169
　reproduction in 116
*Plasmodium* 84–85
**poliomyelitis** (polio) 71
**pollen** 152, 153, 154, 158, 159
**pollination** 153
　of angiosperms 157, 158, 159
　of corn 178
　of gymnosperm 154
**pollution**
　air, lichens as indicators of 104
　eutrophication and 94
**Ponderosa pine** 152
**posing questions,** skill of 186
**precision farming** 169–170

**predicting,** skill of 182
**Priestley, Joseph** 122
**prism** 120
**problem solving,** skill of 189
**prokaryotes** 41, 57 See also *bacteria*
**proteins** 17
　in coat of virus 51
**protists** 41, 80–89
　animal-like 81–85
　defined 80–81
　funguslike 85–86
　plantlike 86–89
**protozoans** 81–84
　with cilia 83
　with flagella 84
　with pseudopods 81–83
**pseudopods** 81–83
**puffballs** 98, 99

**rabies virus** 49, 54, 69, 71
**rafflesia** 115
**rainfall,** annual rings and information on 148
**rain forest** 110
**recycling,** environmental 63–64, 102
**red algae** 81, 89
**Redi, Francesco** 19, 26
**red tides** 91
**relating cause and effect,** skill of 189
**reproduction** 19–20
　in angiosperms 157, 158, 159
　asexual 59
　in bacteria 59–60
　in corn 178
　defined 19
　in ferns 133
　in fungi 97–98
　in gymnosperms 152–153, 154
　of nonvascular plants 126
　in plants 116
　sexual 60, 98, 116
　spores for 132
**resistance**
　antibiotic 72–73, 74
　engineering plants for 169
**respiration** 60
**responding variable** 187
**response to surroundings** 18–19
**rhizoids** 126
*Rhizopus nigrens* 99
**ribosomes** 57, 58
**rice dwarf virus** 54
**rings of trees,** annual 147–148
**ringworm** 102
**rockweed** 89
**rodlike bacterial cells** 57
**root cap** 149
**root hairs** 149
**roots**
　fern 132
　of seed plants 148–149
**rubber trees** 161

**sac fungi** 99
**Sachs, Julius** 123

**safety in the laboratory** 195–197
**salmonella bacteria** 10, 11–13, 70
**saltwater algal blooms** 91
**sapwood** 147
**sarcodines** 81, 82–83
**scientific investigations** 186–187
**scientific method** See **scientific investigations**
**seaweeds** 41, 86, 89
**seed coat** 142, 179
**seed dispersal** 143
　in angiosperms 158
　in gymnosperms 153
**seedless vascular plants** 130–134
　characteristics of 131–132
　club mosses and horsetails 134
　ferns 114, 130–133
**seed plants** 138–173
　angiosperms 156–163
　defined 140–141
　farming 168–170
　germination in 144
　gymnosperms 150–155
　leaves of 144–146
　plant responses and growth 164–167
　roots of 148–149
　seed dispersal 143, 153, 158
　seeds 142, 153
　stems of 146–148
　vascular tissue of 141
**seedpods,** dispersal by bursting of 143
**seeds** 142
　development of 153
**sepals** 157
**septic systems,** eutrophication and leaking 92
**sexual reproduction** 60
　in bacteria 60
　in fungi 98
　in plants 116
**SI units of measurement** 184–185
**skills,** science process 182–194
**skunks** 36
**slime mold** 16, 41, 81, 85, 86
**sourdough bread** 63
**soybeans** 63
**species** 31, 32
　defined 30
　evolutionary history of 35–36
**sperm cells** 117
　of nonvascular plants 126
**sphagnum moss** 127
**spherical bacterial cells** 57
**spiral shaped bacterial cells** 57
**spoiled food,** prevention of 62–63
**spontaneous generation** 19–20, 21
**spores** 97–98, 99, 117
　defined 85
　fern 133
　for reproduction 132
**sporophytes** 117, 141
　of hornworts 128
　of liverworts 128
　of moss 126
**sporozoans** 84–85

staghorn fern 114
stamens 157
*Staphylococcus aureus* 57
stem of seed plants 146–148
    of dicot 160
    of monocot 160
    structure of 146–147
stigma 158, 159
stimulus 18
stomata 144, 145, 146
strep throat 71, 72
*Streptococci* 41
Strigiformes (order) 32, 33
Strygidae (family) 33
style 158
sunflowers 165
sweet corn 179
symbiosis 84

taproot system 148
taxonomic key 36–37
taxonomy 29, 36 See also **classification**
temperature
    body 23
    measuring 185
    red tides and ocean 91
termites, zooflagellates in intestines of 84
tetanus (lockjaw) 70, 71, 73
thigmotropism 164
threadlike fungi 99
tick bites, disease spread by 69
tissues 112
tobacco mosaic virus 49
touch, plant response to 164
toxins 70
    algal blooms and 90, 91
transpiration 146
transporting tissue in plants 116

trees 150 See also **seed plants**
    annual rings of 147–148
tropisms 164–165
tuberculosis (TB) 71
    antibiotic resistance and 72–73
tulip mosaic virus 54

unicellular organism 17, 26, 40, 86–87
United States Centennial Exhibition
    (1876) 159
units of measurement 184–185
Urey, Harold 26, 27

vaccines 73
vacuole 112
    contractile 82, 83
    food 82, 83
Van Helmont, Jean-Baptiste 122
variables 19, 187
vascular plants, seedless 130–134
vascular tissue 116, 141
    of dicots 160
    of monocot stems 160
    of root 149
    of seedless vascular plants 131
vegetables, preserving 62
Venn diagrams 191
Venus fly trap 115
viral diseases 72
viruses 46–55
    active 51–52
    defined 48–49
    hidden 52–53
    infectious disease and 49, 68–74
    living world and 54
    multiplication of 51–53
    naming 49
    shapes of 50
    size of 50, 55
    structure of 50–51

visible spectrum 120, 121
volume, measuring 184
*Volvox* 22
warbler finch 34
wastewater, eutrophication and 94
water
    in cells 17
    need for 22
    photosynthesis and 124
    plant adaptations for obtaining and
        reducing loss of 113
    as raw material of photosynthesis 122
    seeds dispersed by 143
water lily 114
water loss of leaf, controlling 146
water molds 85
water vapor 25
weasels 36
weather conditions, annual rings and
    information on 148
Weiss Lake 94
wheat plants 141
wheat rust 102
willow trees 161
wind, seed dispersal by 143, 153
woody perennials 166
woody stems 147

xylem 141, 144, 145, 147, 149
    annual rings of 147–148

yam, Mexican 161
yeasts 96, 98, 100–101, 102

zooflagellates 84
zygote 116, 117, 142, 154

# Acknowledgments

## Illustration

**Patrice Rossi Calkin:** 35, 52, 53, 82, 83
**Warren Cutler:** 39
**David Fuller:** 175
**GeoSystems Global Corporation:** 70, 180(b)
**Keith Kasnot:** 87
**Martucci Design:** 77, 107, 173, 180(t), 192(b), 193, 194,
**Morgan Cain & Associates:** 17, 20-21, 45, 50(t,b), 51(b), 98, 111, 122, 145, 184 (l,r), 185 (l,r)
**Matt Myerchak:** 44, 76, 106, 172, 190, 191
**Ortelius Design Inc.:** 62, 63, 94
**Stephanie Pershing:** 26-27
**Tim Spransy:** 176-177
**Walter Stuart:** 96, 126, 132, 178, 179
**Cynthia Turner:** 117, 142, 154, 159
**J/B Woolsey Associates:** 18, 29, 33, 37, 51(t), 89, 97, 124, 149, 157, 163, 167, 188

## Photography

**Photo Research** Paula Wehde
**Cover image** - Perry D. Slocum/Animals Animals/Earth Scenes

### Nature of Science
**Page 10,** Courtesy of Cindy Friedman; **11,** Michael Dick/Animals Animals; **13l,** Courtesy of Cindy Friedman; **13r,** USDA/S.S./Photo Researchers.

### Chapter 1
**Pages 14-15,** Joe McDonald/DRK Photo; **16t,** Russ Lappa; **16b,** Beatty/Visuals Unlimited; **17,** John Pontier/Animals Animals **19,** Michael Quinton/Minden Pictures; **20,** The Granger Collection, NY; **21,** The Granger Collection, NY; **22l,** James Dell/Science Source/Photo Researchers; **22r,** Zig Leszcynski/Animals Animals; **23,** Jim Brandenburg/Minden Pictures; **25,** Russ Lappa; **27,** Biological Photo Service; **28t,** Russ Lappa; **28b,** Inga Spence/The Picture Cube; **30,** Gerard Lacz/Animals Animals; **31t,** J. Serrao/Visuals Unlimited; **31bl,** Tom Brakefield/DRK Photo; **31br,** Ron Kimball **32-33,** Thomas Kitchin/Tom Stack & Associates; **34 all,** Tui de Roy/Minden Pictures; **36t,** Phil A. Dotson/Photo Researchers; **36b,** Richard Day/Animals Animals; **38,** Mike Ederegger/DRK Photo; **39tl,** Fernandez & Peck/Adventure Photo & Film; **39 all others,** Frans Lanting/Minden Pictures; **40,** Alan L. Detrick/Photo Researchers; **41t,** David M. Phillips/Photo Researchers; **41b,** Microfield Scientific Ltd/Science Photo Library/Photo Researchers; **42,** Ray Coleman/Photo Researchers; **43r,** Frans Lanting/Minden Pictures.

### Chapter 2
**Pages 46-47,** Institut Pasteur/CNRI/Phototake; **48t,** Russ Lappa; **48bl,** Dr. Linda Stannard, UCT/Science Photo Library/Photo Researchers; **48bm,** Lee D. Simon/Science Source/Photo Researchers **48-49,** Dr. Brad Fute/Peter Arnold; **49m,** Tektoff-RM/CNRI/Science Photo Library/Photo Researchers; **49r,** CDC/Science Source/Photo Researchers; **53,** Lee D. Simon/Science Source/Photo Researchers; **54,** Henryk T. Kaiser/Photo Network Tustin; **55,** Custom Medical Stock; **56t,** Richard Haynes; **56b,** Science Photo Library/Photo Researchers; **57l,** Scott Camazine/Photo Researchers; **57m,** David M. Phillips/Visuals Unlimited; **57r,** Oliver Meckes/Photo Researchers; **58,** Dr. Tony Brain/Science Photo Library/Photo Researchers; **59,** Dr. K. S Kim/Peter Arnold; **60,** Dr. Dennis Kunkel/PhotoTake; **61,** Alfred Pasieka/Peter Arnold; **62t,** PhotoDisc; **62b,** Sally Ann Ullmann/FoodPix; **63t,** John Marshall/TSI; **63b,** FoodPix; **64t,** E. Webben/Visuals Unlimited; **64b,** Ben Osborne; **64 inset,** Michael Abbey/Photo Researchers; **65,** Hank Morgan; **67,** Richard Haynes; **69t,** James Darell/TSI; **69b,** David M. Dennis/Tom Stack & Associates; **70,** Kevin Horan/TSI; **72,** American Lung Association of Wisconsin; **73,** B. Daemmrich/The Image Works; **74,** Johnathan Selig/Photo 20-20; **75t,** Biozentrum, University of Basel/Science Photo Library/Photo Researchers; **75b,** Alfred Pasieka/Peter Arnold.

### Chapter 3
**Pages 78-79,** David M. Dennis/Tom Stack & Associates; **80t,** Science VU/Visuals Unlimited; **80b,** Jan Hinsch/Science Photo Library/Photo Researchers; **81l,** O.S.F./Animals Animals; **81tr,** A. Le Toquin/Photo Researchers; **81br,** Gregory G. Dimijian/Photo Researchers; **82,** Astrid & Hanns-Frieder Michler/Science Photo Library/Photo Researchers; **83,** Eric Grave/Science Source/Photo Researchers; **84l,** Jerome Paulin/Visuals Unlimited; **84r,** Michael P. Gadomski/Photo Researchers; **85t,** Oliver Meckes/Photo Researchers; **85b,** Dwight R. Kuhn; **86 both,** David M. Dennis/Tom Stack & Associates; **87l,** Sinclair Stammers Oxford Scientific Films;

**87r,** Russ Lappa; **88t,** David M. Phillips/Visuals Unlimited; **88bl,** D. P. Wilson/Eric & Daid Hosking/Photo Researchers; **88br,** Andrew Syred/Science Photo Library/Photo Researchers; **90t,** Richard Haynes; **90b,** Doug Perrine/Hawaii Whale Research Foundation - NMFS permit#882/Innerspace Visions; **91,** Sanford Berry/Visuals Unlimited; **92,** Kenneth H. Thomas/Photo Researchers; **94,** Robert P. Falls; **95t,** Russ Lappa; **95b,** Michael Fogden/Animals Animals; **96,** Fred Unverhau/Animals Animals/Earth Scenes; **97,** Nobel Proctor/Science Source/Photo Researchers; **98,** David Scharf/Peter Arnold; **99tl,** E.R. Degginger/Photo Researchers; **99tr,** Rod Planck/Tom Stack & Associates; **99bl,** Michael Fogden/Animals Animals/Earth Scenes; **99br,** Andrew McClenagham/Sicence Photo Library/Photo Researchers; **101,** Richard Haynes; **102,** David M. Dennis/Tom Stack & Associates; **103,** Rob Simpson/Visuals Unlimited; **104l,** Rod Planck/Tom Stack & Associates; **104r,** Frans Lanting/Minden Pictures; **105l,** Gregory G. Dimijian/Photo Researchers; **105r,** Michael Fogden/Animals Animals/Earth Scenes.

### Chapter 4
**Pages 108-109,** J. Lotter Gurling/Tom Stack & Associates; **110,** Joanne Lotter/Tom Stack & Associates; **111, 112,** Runk/Schoenberger/Grant Heilman Photography; **113,** Kjell B. Sandved/Photo Researchers; **114tl,** Richard J. Green/Photo Researchers; **114tr,** Brenda Tharp/Photo Researchers; **114m,** R. Van Nostrand/Photo Researchers; **114b,** Joe McDonald/Visuals Unlimited; **115tl,** Prenzel/Animals Animals/Earth Scenes; **115tr,** Frans Lanting/Minden Pictures; **115m,** Andrew J. Martinez/Photo Researchers; **115b,** Runk/Schoenberger/Grant Heilman Photography; **116,** Doug Wechsler/Animals Animals/Earth Scenes; **118,** Richard Haynes; **119,** Images International/Erwin C. Bud Nielsen/Visuals Unlimited; **120t,** Richard Haynes; **120b,** Runk/Schoenberger/Grant Heilman Photography; **121,** Carr Clifton/Minden Pictures; **122,** Runk/Schoenberger/Grant Heilman Photography; **123tl,** Interfoto-Pressebild-Agentur; **123b,** Georg Gerster/Photo Researchers; **125t,** Russ Lappa; **125b,** Christi Carter/Grant Heilman Photography; **126,** Runk/Schoenberger/Grant Heilman Photography; **127t,** Silkeborg Museum; **127b,** Farrell Grehan/Photo Researchers; **128l,** Runk/Schoenberger/Grant Heilman Photography; **128r** William E. Ferguson; **129, 130t,** Richard Haynes; **132,** Rod Planck/Tom Stack & Associates; **133t,** Milton Rand/Tom Stack & Associates; **133b,** Joanne Lotter/Tom Stack & Associates; **134l,** Runk/Schoenberger/Grant Heilman Photography; **134r,** Frans Lanting/Minden Pictures; **135,** Rod Planck/Tom Stack & Associates.

### Chapter 5
**Pages 138-139,** E.R. Degginger; **140t,** Russ Lappa; **140b,** E. R. Degginger/Animals Animals/Earth Scenes; **141l,** Thomas Kitchin/Tom Stack & Associates; **141m&r,** Carr Clifton/Tom Stack & Associates; **143tl,** D. Cavagnaro/Visuals Unlimited; **143tr,** Frans Lanting/Minden Pictures; **143bl,** E. R. Degginger; **143br,** William Harlow/Photo Researchers; **144 both,** Runk/Schoenberger/Grant Heilman Photography; **146,** Dani/Jeske/Animals Animals/Earth Scenes; **148t,** Runk/Schoenberger/Grant Heilman Photography; **148b both,** Robert Calentine/Visuals Unlimited; **150t,** Richard Haynes; **150b,** Bruce M. Herman/Photo Researchers; **151tl,** Ken Brate/Photo Researchers; **151tr,** Jim Strawser/Grant Heilman Photography; **151b,** Michael Fogden/Animals Animals/Earth Scenes; **152l,** Runk/Schoenberger/Grant Heilman Photography; **152r,** Breck P. Kent/Animals Animals/Earth Scenes; **153,** Breck P. Kent; **155,** C.J. Allen/Stock Boston; **156t,** Russ Lappa; **156b,** Jim Strawser/Grant Heilman Photography; **157,** E. R. Degginger; **158,** Private Collections/Art Resource; **161,** Alan Pitcairn/Grant Heilman Photography; **162,** Richard Haynes; **164,** William J. Weber/Visuals Unlimited; **165,** Porterfield-Chickering/Photo Researchers; **166tl,** E. R. Degginger; **166tr,** Mark E. Gibson/The Stock Market; **166b,** Larry Lefever/Grant Heilman Photography; **168,** Herve Donnezan/Photo Researchers; **169,** William James Warren/West Light; **170,** Arthur C. Smith III/Grant Heilman Photography; **171,** Arthur C. Smith III/Grant Heilman Photography.

### Interdisciplinary Exploration
**Page 174t,** Ed Simpson/TSI; **174 inset,** The Granger Collection, NY; **174b,** Werner Forman Archive/Art Resource; **176,** C.M. Dixon; **179,** Isaac Geib/Grant Heilman Photography; **181,** Peter Essick/Aurora.

### Skills Handbook
**Page 182,** Mike Moreland/Photo Network; **183t,** Foodpix; **183m,** Richard Haynes; **183b,** Russ Lappa; **186,** Richard Haynes; **188,** Ron Kimball; **189,** Renee Lynn/Photo Researchers.

### Appendix
**Page 198-199 all,** Russ Lappa.